REALIZING
THE EDUCATIONAL
POTENTIAL OF
RESIDENCE HALLS

Charles C. Schroeder
Phyllis Mable
and Associates

Foreword by Theodore J. Marchese

REALIZING THE EDUCATIONAL POTENTIAL OF RESIDENCE HALLS

Jossey-Bass Publishers • San Francisco

Substantial discounts on bulk quantities of Jossey-Bass books are available to corporations,
professional associations, and other organizations. For details and discount information,
contact the special sales department at Jossey-Bass Inc., Publishers (415) 433-1740;
Fax (800) 605-2665.

For sales outside the United States, please contact your local Simon & Schuster International
Office.

Jossey-Bass Web address: http://www.josseybass.com

 Manufactured in the United States of America on Lyons Falls Turin Book. This paper is
acid-free and 100 percent totally chlorine-free.

Library of Congress Cataloging-in-Publication Data

Schroeder, Charles C.
    Realizing the educational potential of residence halls / Charles C. Schroeder, Phyllis Mable,
and associates. — 1st ed.
        p.   cm. — (The Jossey-Bass higher and adult education series)
    Includes bibliographical references and index.
    ISBN 0-7879-0018-4
    1. Dormitories—United States.   2. College students—United States—Conduct of life.
I. Mable, Phyllis.   II. Title.   III. Series.
LB3227.5.S37   1994
378.1'96'25—dc20   94-25579

FIRST EDITION
HB *Printing*   10 9 8 7 6 5 4 3 2

The Jossey-Bass
Higher and Adult Education Series

Contents

ix

Foreword

"What does America need from her colleges?" That's the provocative question the Johnson Foundation put last year to a distinguished panel of sixteen prominent citizens it convened for a reflective, yearlong study of the matter. The panel's answer came in a widely noticed report—*An American Imperative: Higher Expectations for Higher Education*—and in three parts: greater attention "to the values undergirding American society"; undergraduate reforms that bring "much higher levels of educational achievement"; and ventures that create "high-quality learning opportunities responsive to lifetime needs."

It would be hard to think of a better venue to pursue these goals in than the residence halls of American colleges. The two million or so students living in college housing today represent a special population for us. Among all students, they are the ones on whose lives and time we have greatest call; here, opportunities to influence student learning and growth are highest. The chance to "go away to college" and take up studies in residence has always been a wonderful opportunity for students; today, it's a "best chance" for campus educators.

The need for fresh attention to the quality and effectiveness of the residence hall experience can be seen in data highlighted by the *American Imperative* panel. It cites a 1993 National Adult Literacy Survey (NALS) which shows that a mere half of the college graduates it tested achieve levels four and five on its literacy scales. We could also enter into evidence the fact that student attainment and completion rates in our colleges have been unprepossessing (40 to 60 percent) and flat for decades. One factor behind these modest levels of institutional and student performance shows up in recent data — most of it unpublished, for obvious reasons — revealing that full-time students on several different university campuses devote just eight to ten hours a week to out-of-class study.

Given these findings, Charles Schroeder and Phyllis Mable, quite in the *American Imperative* spirit, have been outspoken advocates within the student affairs world for a sharper focus on issues of student learning and attainment. In this volume, they turn their scrutiny on the opportunities that patterns of residence hall life present to student affairs educators.

What do we know about today's residence halls, and especially about their effects? From the studies synthesized in this volume by Pascarella, Terenzini, and Blimling, we learn that the effects of residence hall living today are mixed, and in one key area disappointing. That is, living on campus (versus commuting) results in discernible gains in student satisfaction, involvement, personal growth, and degree attainment; living in a conventional residence hall, however, leads to no apparent gain in academic achievement.

This last finding, again, is a significant disappointment. How could it be, with all the advantages of student access and professional attention at our disposal, that the academic performance of residents is so unexceptional? Different writers have a go at the question in the chapters that follow: the halls are built and administered wrong (as "dorms"), student culture and peer influences inhibit academic attentions, and (it is said) staff members have a faulty sense of role. Indeed, on the last score, it isn't clear that the parties that build, maintain, and staff these facilities have student learning as their goal in the first place.

To reverse that situation — that is, to use the residence hall experience to enhance student learning — is the goal of this volume. Few aims could be timelier, on two scores. For one, higher education itself, as we've said, is under attack as an underperforming undergraduate function. One can only cheer as Schroeder and Mable urge student affairs professionals to set their sights on student *learning* (not just student development), and as the authors roll out a host of examples on just how to do that. A second dimension of the book's timeliness is this: that even as pressures grow for undergraduate improvement, now also there is a fresh fund of ideas to promote it. The late 80s and 90s have given rise to a host of movements that would transform pedagogies, curricula, organizational structures, and professional roles, on the academic and student affairs "sides" of the house alike. This book itself is testimony to the possibility, filled as it is with insights and examples quite unknown ten years ago.

The time is ripe, then, for what the authors hope for most: a rethinking of residence halls, of student affairs as a profession, indeed of the total campus as a learning organization, inspired by a goal important to us all, a new undergraduate education marked by much higher levels of student learning and attainment. Read on!

July 1994　　　　　　　Theodore J. Marchese
　　　　　　　　　　　Vice president,
　　　　　　　　　　　　American Association for
　　　　　　　　　　　　Higher Education
　　　　　　　　　　　Executive editor, *Change* magazine

This book is dedicated to our mothers, Margaret T. Schroeder and Ethel S. Mable, who have a genuine interest in our vision and dedication to students and their learning in the context of higher education, particularly college residence halls. Both of our mothers have encouraged us to invest our talents in order to do our best and to make a difference; our interests in students and college residence halls stem from enthusiasm inspired by both of them. Our mothers have given us the will and wisdom to be determined and enthusiastic as we devote our professional careers to improving undergraduate education.

Preface

Colleges and universities across the country are being confronted with such major challenges as shifting demographics, increasingly diverse student populations, changing economic agendas, faculty concerns about the widening gap between ideal academic standards and actual student learning, increased demand for greater accountability, and eroding public confidence. During the past thirty years, enrollments have more than quadrupled, yet institutional resources needed to meet increased educational demands have not even kept pace with inflation. To meet the needs of increasingly large and diverse student populations, many institutions have created highly specialized programs and units, which, over time, have become so fragmented and compartmentalized that they operate as "functional silos." Because of these and other challenges, colleges and universities are trying to reaffirm their primary mission — promoting student learning and personal development. As part of this effort, institutions are recognizing that a great deal of learning takes place beyond the classroom. For many campuses, residence halls are an ideal setting for promoting student learning and development.

Realizing the Educational Potential of Residence Halls explains how residence halls can contribute to student learning and personal development by becoming a more integral part of the overall educational experience of college. The book describes ways that residence halls can be structured to provide integration between the instructional environment and various out-of-class experiences of students. We hope the ideas we present will aid the reader in thinking about new ways to utilize the potential of residence halls to achieve important educational outcomes.

This is not a handbook for developing staff skills and competencies, or a treatise on how to manage residential facilities and budgets. It does not describe various theories of student development or discuss staffing patterns and legal and regulatory concerns. Readers interested in these topics will find them addressed in *Student Housing and Residential Life: A Handbook for Professionals Committed to Student Development Goals* (1993) by Winston, Anchors, and Associates.

The primary impetus for this book came from the experiences of the two principal authors. We have been involved in residence hall work for over three decades, and through our experiences, we have become increasingly convinced that residence halls can make unique contributions to achieving the objectives of undergraduate education. We believe, however, that residence halls, as currently conceptualized and managed, are not realizing their full educational potential. Individual chapters suggest ways of making residence halls more intentional and purposeful educational settings. Readers should find the chapters both stimulating and provocative, although not everyone will agree with all the positions advanced.

Over the years, many books have been written about residence halls and residence education. Most have focused on programs implemented within the organizational boundaries of student affairs and residence life. This work takes a different approach by focusing on the need for integrating students' formal academic experiences with their informal out-of-class experiences through collaborative efforts between educators in academic affairs and student affairs. Finally, *Realizing the Educational Potential . . .* is a clarion call for conceptual, educational, and administrative leadership on the part of educators committed to improving the quality of undergraduate education through the untapped potential of residence halls.

Audience

The book was written primarily for three groups. First, it is designed to be useful for professionals who serve as chief student affairs officers and middle managers in student affairs organizations. The various concepts and strategies presented here will help these professionals contribute in new and meaningful ways to achieving the aims of undergraduate education on their campuses.

Second, the ideas we present will be useful to chief academic officers, academic deans, department chairs, and faculty members. Although these individuals are committed to improving undergraduate education, they often overlook the role of residence halls in accomplishing this purpose. We hope we will succeed in stimulating their thinking about the valuable contributions residence halls can make to the broader educational objectives of their institutions.

Finally, this will serve as a textbook for students enrolled in graduate preparation programs in higher education administration and student affairs. We are particularly hopeful that it will stimulate a broader vision on the part of graduate students, helping them to understand ways of connecting residence halls and undergraduate educational objectives.

Overview of the Contents

Realizing the Educational Potential of Residence Halls is organized into three parts. Part One focuses on the role of residence halls in educating students. In Chapter One, Charles C. Schroeder and Phyllis Mable provide a historical overview and context for understanding the relationship between residence halls and institutional educational purposes. In Chapter Two, Ernest T. Pascarella, Patrick T. Terenzini, and Gregory S. Blimling describe the impact of college residence halls on student learning and personal development. Richard Stimpson, in Chapter Three, delineates essential elements that provide a foundation for effective education in residence halls. In Chapter Four, John D. Welty describes a number of innovative ways residence halls can contribute to the achievement of the current objectives of undergraduate education. Arthur Levine reminds us in Chapter Five of the serendipitous nature of student learning and stresses the need for residence halls to become more purposeful and intentional educational settings.

Part Two describes a variety of initiatives for promoting student learning in college residence halls. In Chapter Six, George D. Kuh explores the conditions that foster student learning and personal development and sets forth an agenda for creating a learner-centered climate in campus residences. Elizabeth J. Whitt and Elizabeth M. Nuss, in Chapter Seven, describe innovative programs on four campuses for connecting residence halls to the curriculum; they also identify common characteristics of institutions and programs that have been successful. In Chapter Eight, Charles C. Schroeder discusses the need to develop learning communities and challenges residence hall staff to make the most of the potent impact of peer-group influences on learning and student development. Marvalene Hughes, in Chapter Nine, highlights the need for educating students for diversity through the design of a strategic residence hall curriculum. In Chapter Ten, Susan R. Komives provides an expanded application of student involvement through civic leadership education and illustrates an innovative, empowering paradigm for student leadership development. Part Two concludes with Terry B. Smith's description — in Chapter Eleven — of the role of residential colleges in integrating living and learning experiences.

Part Three describes ways of demonstrating the educational impact of college residence halls. In Chapter Twelve, David H. Kalsbeek discusses six different metaphors for generating insights into alternative approaches to assessing the educational outcomes of residence hall experiences. In the concluding chapter, Chapter Thirteen, Charles C. Schroeder and Phyllis Mable cite five transcendent themes drawn from previous chapters to describe implications and recommendations for realizing the educational potential of college residence halls.

Acknowledgments

Many people contributed to the development of this book. In particular, we want to acknowledge the chapter authors for their creativity, wisdom, and insight. Each has made a tremendous contribution, and we are grateful for their patience and tenacity.

Gale Erlandson and Ann Richardson of Jossey-Bass also deserve our special thanks. They were both instrumental in helping us produce a much more focused and relevant work.

Charles C. Schroeder wishes to acknowledge the constant and unwavering support of his wife, Barbara, and his two children, Jay and Jill. He also owes a tremendous debt to his mentor, W. Harold Grant, who helped him become an educator. Finally, he acknowledges the contributions of his staff at the University of Missouri, Columbia, whose patience and support were absolutely essential to the production of this book.

Phyllis Mable wishes to thank her colleagues at Longwood College for their assistance as the manuscript progressed. She also acknowledges the contributions of Harold Riker in shaping her thinking about the educational role of college residence halls.

July 1994

Charles C. Schroeder
Columbia, Missouri

Phyllis Mable
Farmville, Virginia

The Authors

Charles C. Schroeder currently serves as vice-chancellor for student affairs and as a member of the doctoral faculty in the Higher and Adult Education Department at the University of Missouri, Columbia. He received his B.A. degree (1967) in psychology and history and his M.A. degree (1968) in college student personnel from Austin College in Sherman, Texas. He obtained his Ed.D. degree (1972) in college student personnel administration from Oregon State University.

The focus of Schroeder's teaching and research has been the formation of peer reference groups; the creation of learning communities; and the assessment of learning styles. He is the author of more than forty refereed journal articles and book chapters and is a frequent speaker at local, regional, and national meetings. He is active in various professional associations, having served as president of the American College Personnel Association (ACPA) in 1986–87 and again in 1993–94 and as treasurer and chair of Commission III (Student Residence Programs).

Schroeder previously served as vice president for student services at the Georgia Institute of Technology, vice president for student development at Saint Louis University, and dean of students at Mercer University. He was director of men's housing and assistant to the dean of students at Auburn University and director of the counseling center at Western New England College.

Phyllis Mable is vice president for student affairs at Longwood College. She earned her B.S. degree (1956) in child development and family relationships at Cornell University and her M.Ed. degree (1959) in college student personnel administration at Indiana University, Bloomington.

Mable has served as ACPA president (1979–1980), treasurer (1975–1977), and chair of Commission III (Student Residence Programs) (1970–1972). She acted as co-chair for the joint convention of ACPA and the National Association of Student Personnel Administrators (NASPA) in 1987. She has served on the Council for the Advancement of Standards in Higher Education (CAS) since 1979 and has been CAS president since 1989.

Mable has received extensive professional recognition. She has been a member of the ACPA Senior Scholars Program and has received the following awards: the ACPA Outstanding Professional Service Award (1983), the Elizabeth A. Greenleaf Distinguished Alumnus/a Award from Indiana University (1984), and the Mel Hardee Award for Outstanding Service to Student Personnel Work from the Southern Association for College Student Affairs (1982).

Mable's professional interests include improving undergraduate education, particularly through enhancing student learning and outcomes assessment. Her publications include *Understanding Today's Students* (1981), *Personal Education and Community Development in College Residence Halls* (1980), and *Student Development and Education in College Residence Halls* (1974), all edited with David A. DeCoster.

Mable previously served as dean of student affairs and associate dean of student services at Virginia Commonwealth University and assistant director of housing and senior counselor for the women's residence halls at the University of Florida.

Gregory S. Blimling is vice-chancellor for student development and professor of human development and psychological counseling at Appalachian State University in Boone, North Carolina. He received his B.A. degree (1972) in sociology from Indiana University, his M.Ed. degree (1974) in college student personnel administration from Indiana University, and his Ph.D. degree (1988) in educational policy and leadership in higher education and college student personnel work from Ohio State University. He is the author of *The Resident Assistant: Working with College Students in Residence Halls* (1994), the editor of *The*

Resident Assistant: Case Studies and Exercises (1990), and the author of a number of other books, monographs, and research articles about college students. He was the recipient of the 1989 NASPA Dissertation of the Year Award.

Marvalene Hughes is president of California State University, Stanislaus. Previously, she served as vice president for student affairs and professor of counseling and student personnel psychology at the University of Minnesota, Twin Cities campus. She also served as vice president for the University of Minnesota system, which includes the Crookston, Duluth, and Morris campuses of the University of Minnesota. Previously, she served as vice president for student affairs and professor of counseling at the University of Toledo, associate vice president for student affairs at Arizona State University, and director of counseling services and placement and professor at San Diego State University. Author of numerous book chapters and journal articles, Hughes has brought national and international leadership to the profession of student development, including as president of ACPA. She earned her B.A. degree (1964) in English and history and her M.S. degree (1966) in counseling from Tuskegee University, studied at Columbia University, and earned her Ph.D. degree (1970) in counseling from Florida State University. A community volunteer, she has received several civic and social awards.

David H. Kalsbeek is associate academic vice president at Xavier University in Cincinnati, Ohio, where he is responsible for the Division of Enrollment Services. Formerly he was associate vice president for enrollment management at Saint Louis University. He received his B.A. degree (1978) in philosophy from Muskingum College, his M.A. degree (1980) in education from Ohio State University, and his Ph.D. degree (1992) in public policy studies from Saint Louis University.

Susan R. Komives is associate professor in the Counseling and Personnel Services Department and faculty associate for the Division of Student Affairs at the University of Maryland, College Park. A former president of ACPA, she has been vice president for student affairs at Stephens College and the University of Tampa. She was extensively involved in residence life work at Denison University and the University of Tennessee, Knoxville. She received her B.S. degree (1968) in mathematics from Florida State University, her M.S. degree (1969) in higher education administration from Florida State University, and her Ed.D. degree (1973) in educational administration and supervision from the University of Tennessee.

George D. Kuh is professor of higher education in the Center for Postsecondary Research and Planning at Indiana University. He received his B.A. degree (1968) in English and history from Luther College and his Ph.D. degree (1975) in counselor education and higher education from the University of Iowa. His most recent administrative assignment (1985–1988) was as associate dean for academic affairs in the School of Education at Indiana University. Among his 140 publications is *Involving Colleges: Successful Approaches to Fostering Student Learning and Development Outside the Classroom* (1991, with J. H. Schuh, E. J. Whitt, and Associates). Kuh has received awards from ACPA and NASPA for contributions to the literature.

Arthur Levine is president of Teachers College, Columbia University. Before that, he was a senior faculty member and chair of the Higher Education Program and the Institute for Educational Management at Harvard University. A former president of Bradford College, he is the author of numerous books and articles on higher education and is executive editor of *Change* magazine. He received his B.S. degree (1970) in biology from Brandeis University and his Ph.D. degree (1976) in sociology and higher education from the State University of New York, Buffalo.

Elizabeth M. Nuss is executive director of NASPA. She received her B.A. degree (1967) in Spanish and secondary education from the State University of New York, Albany, her M.Ed. degree (1969) in higher education and student personnel administration from Pennsylvania State University, and her Ph.D. degree (1981) in education policy, planning, and administration from the University of Maryland, College Park. She is the author of ten publications and was the recipient of the NASPA Dissertation of the Year Award (1982).

Ernest T. Pascarella is professor of higher education at the University of Illinois, Chicago. For the past two decades, his research has focused on the impact of college on students. He is coauthor (with Patrick T. Terenzini) of the 1991 book *How College Affects Students: Findings and Insights from Twenty Years of Research,* which received the 1991 Research Achievement Award from the Association for the Study of Higher Education (ASHE). Pascarella has also received research awards from the Association for Institutional Research, Division J of the American Educational Research Association, NASPA, and ACPA.

Terry B. Smith is vice president for academic affairs and professor of political science at Peru State College in Peru, Nebraska. Until 1993 he was dean of the residential colleges at Northeast Missouri State University. He convened the first international residential college conference in 1992 and is editor of the *proceedings* of that conference, editor of *Gateway: Residential Colleges and the Freshman Year Experience,* and of the first and second editions of the *North American Directory of Residential Colleges and Living Learning Centers* (1992, 1993). He received his B.A. degree (1966) from Central Methodist College and his M.A. degree (1968) and Ph.D. degree (1973), all in political science, from Michigan State University. He has also consulted and written extensively on outcomes assessment.

Richard Stimpson is assistant vice president for student affairs and affiliate assistant professor in the College of Education at the University of Maryland, College Park. He earned his B.S. degree (1965) in secondary education from the State University of New York at Geneseo and both his M.A. degree (1968) in guidance and personnel services and his Ph.D. degree (1977) in higher education administration from Michigan State University. He has been actively involved in ACPA and contributed to *Personal Education and Community Development in College Residence Halls* (DeCoster and Mable, 1980) and *The Handbook of Student Affairs Administration* (Barr and Associates, 1993).

Patrick T. Terenzini is professor and senior scientist in the Center for the Study of Higher Education at Pennsylvania State University, where he is also associate director of the National Center on Postsecondary Teaching, Learning, and Assessment. Terenzini is editor-in-chief of *New Directions for Institutional Research,* a consulting editor for *Research in Higher Education,* and an associate editor of *Higher Education: Handbook of Theory and*

Research. He has received the research awards of ACPA, ASHE, and the Association for Institutional Research. He received his A.B. degree (1964) in English from Dartmouth College, his M.A.T. degree (1965) in English/education from Harvard University, and his Ph.D. degree (1972) in higher education from Syracuse University.

John D. Welty is president of California State University, Fresno. He currently chairs the Network Committed to the Elimination of Drug and Alcohol Abuse on College and University Campuses; the California State University Advisory Committee on International Programs; and the Task Force on Student Health Services. His awards include an outstanding service award from ACPA, the Chancellor's Award for Excellence in Administration from the State University of New York, and the Robert H. Shaffer Distinguished Alumnus Award from Indiana University, Bloomington.

Welty has coauthored a book titled *A Changing Cultural Context: A Guide for College Presidents and Governing Boards* (1989, with M. L. Upcraft) and is the author of numerous articles and papers on university students, student affairs programs, and the future of higher education. He received his B.S. degree (1965) in social science from Western Illinois University, Macomb, his M.A. degree (1967) in college student personnel services from Michigan State University, and his Ph.D. degree (1974) in administration of higher education from Indiana University, Bloomington.

Elizabeth J. Whitt is assistant professor of higher education at Iowa State University. She received her B.A. degree (1973) in history from Drake University, her M.A. degree (1977) in college student personnel administration from Michigan State University, and her Ph.D. degree (1988) in higher education and sociology from Indiana University. Whitt served in administrative roles in residence life and general student affairs administration before becoming a faculty member. Her research interests include institutional cultures, student out-of-class learning, experiences of women students in higher education, and qualitative research methodology.

REALIZING
THE EDUCATIONAL
POTENTIAL OF
RESIDENCE HALLS

Part 1

The Role of
Residence Halls in
Educating Students

The role of residence halls in educating students may ultimately be determined by how well the entire campus, not just the classroom, is understood as a student learning community. Research continues to indicate that students learn as much from one another as from the formal curriculum. Residence halls have the potential to challenge and educate students as they connect their learning experiences to their living realities. Furthermore, residence halls can create a curriculum that integrates knowledge, skills, and attitudes and focuses on the applications of learning. Finally, when residence halls are designed as purposeful educational settings, they can promote effective undergraduate education.

Part One challenges us to utilize what is known about student learning and out-of-class experiences and to become *intentional* about ensuring educational success through the residence halls. It emphasizes that the educational potential of residence halls is realized when students are challenged to become more competent and educated human beings, both academically and socially.

In Chapter One, Charles C. Schroeder and Phyllis Mable describe the educational challenge confronting college residence halls — to create environments that support and foster student learning. They provide a historical overview and context

1

for understanding the relationship between residence halls and institutional educational purposes. They argue that if residence halls are to become a locale for student learning and personal development, new partnerships must be forged between educators in academic affairs and student affairs.

During the past forty years, considerable research has demonstrated the impact of college on students. In Chapter Two, Ernest T. Pascarella, Patrick T. Terenzini, and Gregory S. Blimling provide a comprehensive review of the literature and describe the impact of residence halls on students. For residence halls to become educationally purposeful settings, educators must translate knowledge from the literature and utilize it to actively manage the learning process in residence halls.

The educational potential of residence halls cannot be achieved unless a proper setting for success has been established. In Chapter Three, Richard Stimpson presents six elements essential to the successful implementation of effective residential education programs.

In Chapter Four, John D. Welty introduces possibilities for using the residence hall as a vehicle to achieve current objectives for undergraduate education. He describes the residence hall of the future and ways to achieve the future . . . now! From his perspective as a university president, he argues that residence halls should be linked to the classroom experience through new technology, innovative organizational models, and creative teaching strategies.

Educational outcomes in many residence halls occur almost serendipitously, rather than by design. In Chapter Five, Arthur Levine describes the education of two students at Yale three-quarters of a century apart. Stressing the importance of the peer group, he emphasizes that residential education must become more intentional if it is to be effective.

One

Residence Halls and
the College Experience:
Past and Present

Charles C. Schroeder
Phyllis Mable

In recent years, the higher education community has focused increased attention on the quality of undergraduate education. Within the last ten years alone, at least four major reports— *Involvement in Learning* (Study Group on the Conditions of Excellence in American Higher Education, 1984), *To Reclaim a Legacy: A Report on the Humanities in Higher Education* (Bennett, 1984), *Integrity in the College Curriculum: A Report to the Academic Community* (Association of American Colleges, 1985), and *An American Imperative: Higher Expectations for Higher Education* (Wingspread Group on Higher Education, 1993)—have presented clarion calls for reform of higher education. These reports highlight particular concerns regarding the fragmented and specialized curriculum, the lack of clarity about goals and purposes, and the need to integrate out-of-class experiences with the educational mission of the institution. They stress the need to connect undergraduate academic experiences with student services, learning, and development. The most recent of the reports, *An American*

Note: The authors gratefully acknowledge the contributions of Elizabeth J. Whitt and Elizabeth M. Nuss in the preparation of this chapter.

3

Imperative: Higher Expectations for Higher Education (Wingspread Group on Higher Education, 1993, p. 7), states that "given the diversity of American higher education, there can be no single formula for change common to all, but we do believe that there are at least three fundamental issues common to all 3,400 colleges and universities — taking values seriously; putting student learning first; and creating a nation of learners."

Unfortunately, all efforts to reform higher education have overlooked the educational potential of residence halls. What unique contributions, for example, can residence halls make to addressing the issues delineated in *An American Imperative: Higher Expectations for Higher Education*? How can educators use the residence hall environment as a locale for promoting student learning? What are the first steps? Perhaps the initial step is to critically examine a pervasive myth about student learning. Terenzini and Pascarella (1994, p. 31) put to rest one of the most powerful educational myths of this century — the myth that "students' academic and non-academic experiences are separate and unrelated areas of influence on learning." From their study of over 2,600 books, book chapters, monographs, journal articles, technical reports, research reports, and conference papers produced over the past two decades, they concluded that "the greatest impact [on student learning] may stem from the students' *total* level of campus engagement, particularly when academic, interpersonal, and extracurricular involvements are mutually supporting and relevant to a particular educational outcome" (Pascarella and Terenzini, 1991, p. 32).

The recommendations of the reports on the status of higher education, plus those advanced by Terenzini and Pascarella (1994), suggest that residence halls, as the places where students spend most of their out-of-class time, should contribute to improving undergraduate education. Indeed, they should be structured in such a fashion as to provide integration between the instructional environment and various out-of-class experiences of students.

As colleges and universities across the country are being challenged by changing economic agendas, shifting demographics, increasingly diverse student populations, public demand for quality and accountability, and faculty concerns about the widening gap between ideal academic standards and actual student learning, residence halls have an opportunity to shape the transformation of higher education. They have an opportunity to foster student learning through providing well-planned, integrated, and coherent educational experiences.

This chapter provides a historical overview and context for understanding the relationship between residence halls and institutional educational purposes. It also delineates the current challenge for residence halls as well as strategies for addressing the challenge.

Historical Overview and Context

A brief review of the historical development of the relationship between residence halls and institutional educational purposes, as well as of the roles of faculty and student affairs staff, is useful to understand why relationships between residential education and undergraduate education have been difficult to achieve on a consistent and systematic basis.

Residential facilities, originally referred to as dormitories, were rooted in the English universities on which American higher education was modeled. At institutions such as Oxford and Cambridge, residence halls were at the very heart of the educational enterprise, and they "were designed to bring the faculty and students together in a common life which was both intellectual and moral" (Brubacher and Rudy, 1968, p. 42). In the early colonial colleges, dormitories became an essential aspect of what was known as the collegiate way of life, "a notion that a curriculum, a library, a faculty, and students are not enough to make a college" (Rudolph, 1962, p. 87).

Although the early colonial colleges attempted to adopt the British system, many unique circumstances prevented its adoption in toto (Rudolph, 1962). In England, faculty were responsible for instruction, while porters and other officials focused their attention on matters of student supervision and discipline. Free from responsibility for monitoring student conduct, British instructors formed friendships with their students through such activities as tutorials and dining together. The early American colonial colleges did not have the funds to construct an enclosed quadrangle; hence, "a successful commons or dining room, let alone one at which faculty could or would eat, was something that no college achieved in the nineteenth century" (Rudolph, 1962, p. 90). American faculty, unlike their British counterparts, were saddled with the total responsibility of supervising their young charges and enforcing all disciplinary regulations. Such responsibilities spawned the early vestiges of in loco parentis, a student-institutional relationship predicated on paternalistic control of students through rigid enforcement of numerous rules and regulations. Because a primary objective of the early American colleges was to prepare students for civic and religious leadership, faculty were directly involved in all aspects of students' lives, utilizing paternalistic control to foster students' character development (Boyer, 1990; Rudolph, 1962). Distinctions between in-class and out-of-class learning and activities were not apparent, and faculty members viewed themselves as responsible for the total education of the student.

Following the Civil War, young American intellectuals traveled to Germany to study and earn advanced degrees. Teaching and research were the sole purpose of German universities, and little, if any, attention was paid to the "collegiate way of life" embraced by Oxford and Cambridge (Brubacher and Rudy, 1968). When the young scholars returned to America to assume major educational leadership roles, they too saw little need to allocate scarce resources to creating residence hall systems, particularly within the developing research universities, such as the University of Michigan. They regarded residential living as separate from, and unrelated to, the intellectual life of the classroom and the laboratory. Their perspective resulted in a widening gap between the college life of the classroom and the extracurricular life of the campus—a gap that is still apparent in most higher education institutions.

The nineteenth century brought changes in the roles of faculty members. These changes have been attributed to the creation of land-grant colleges, which added the notion of service to the missions of both public and private higher education and the increased expectations of faculty members to create and disseminate new knowledge (Boyer, 1990). As a consequence, faculty increasingly were expected to be involved in service to external publics and in scientific research. Less and less time was available for "the whole student" as faculty spent more time developing expertise in their disciplines. These influences led to distinctions and separation between the in-class and out-of-class aspects of the undergraduate experience. For example, in 1890, President Eliot became so concerned with student relationships outside the classroom that he divided the deanship of Harvard College, with one dean specializing in student relations. This was a significant change within higher education, because this dean not only became the first dean of men — he also became the first college official to be charged with responsibility for student relations as separate and distinct from instruction (Cowley, 1937).

The development of college residence halls was affected by other major higher education trends occurring in the latter half of the nineteenth century and the first fifty years of the twentieth century. This period witnessed the enrollment of women and blacks, the rise of the extracurriculum, and the rapid proliferation of public higher education. These trends contributed to the expansion of residence halls, with the most rapid expansion occurring as a result of the G.I. Bill and Title IV of the Housing Act of 1950, which fueled a massive program of housing construction across the nation. The act's primary focus was to house and feed students through maximizing the number of beds constructed with the funds available. Leadership for this endeavour came primarily from staff in the business and finance areas; hence, little thought was given to opportunities for educational and personal development that was central to the original conceptions of residential life (Frederiksen, 1993).

During the mid-twentieth century, as faculty interests and values changed, student affairs positions were created to attend to the aspects of student life no longer overseen by faculty (Fenske, 1989). At the same time, students of more diverse backgrounds, needs, and interests were entering higher education, and enrollments reached record levels (Appleton, Briggs, and

Rhatigan, 1978). The notion that the faculty was responsible for the students' intellectual development and student affairs staff were responsible for social and personal development came to be taken for granted on many campuses.

The expansion of student affairs prompted the American Council on Education to examine, and identify expectations for, the new field (National Association of Student Personnel Administrators, 1989). The 1937 *Student Personnel Point of View* and the 1949 revision reaffirmed the importance of educating the whole student and underscored additional goals for higher education, including education for democracy, for international understanding, and for the ability to solve social problems. This marked the beginning of the development of distinct faculty and student affairs cultures guided by different values, beliefs, and assumptions (Kuh, Shedd, and Whitt, 1987).

In response to student activism and protest during the 1960s, the role of residence halls and their staff members changed dramatically. Students' demand for freedom from control and supervision resulted in the establishment of coeducational halls, the implementation of visitation or parietal hours, the elimination of curfews and dress codes, and the provision of drinking for students of legal age. On most campuses, housemothers were replaced by residence educators with advanced degrees. Housemothers were usually older women who lived in the residence halls and served as benevolent, parental control agents. They had primary responsibility for enforcing curfews, conducting bed checks, and instructing students in social graces (Frederiksen, 1993). In contrast, residence educators were responsible for coordinating a multitude of organizations, services, and programs, including programming councils, judicial boards, resident assistants, and outreach counselors. Residence educators were also instrumental in implementing a variety of life-style options (such as coed living), unique living-learning centers, and new models for community governance (Schroeder, 1980).

During this period, a new legalistic definition of the student-institution relationship replaced the long-standing doctrine of in loco parentis. This shift in the basic student-institutional relationship was further accelerated by numerous court decisions that clarified students' rights and provided many new student freedoms. The demands of student activists for relevance led to dramatic changes in curricula, student participation in university governance, student evaluation of faculty effectiveness, and a general reexamination of the purposes and goals of higher education. Furthermore, in many states, students "legally" became adults and hence were no longer viewed as children that could be controlled and regulated at the whim of the institution (Schroeder, 1976).

Higher education also experienced other trends during the 1960s and 1970s that had significant impacts on college residence halls. Philosophically, American colleges and universities shifted their focus from elitism to egalitarianism. Federal legislation removed barriers to women, minorities, and the handicapped, thereby creating an access revolution that opened the doors of higher education to the masses. Since 1965, college and university enrollments have more than quadrupled (Levine and Associates, 1989). Substantial increases in the number of students prompted further expansion of campus residence halls and changed the roles and responsibilities of staff. To serve this large and diverse group of residents, highly specialized, professional roles were created within student affairs divisions and housing departments, particularly at relatively large state institutions. Residence hall systems began to provide students with more options, both architecturally and programmatically. As new halls were constructed to accommodate burgeoning enrollments, they included both low- and high-rise structures, usually with long, narrow, double-loaded corridors and community baths. A few institutions, however, designed more innovative structures with suite arrangements, cluster units, and apartment-style accommodations (Winston, Anchors, and Associates, 1993). Programmatic initiatives reflected renewed efforts to focus on the education of the whole student, highlight connections between academic affairs and student affairs, and incorporate human/student development into the work of both faculty and student affairs staff. As a result, living-learning communities in residence halls were developed at institutions such as the University of Nebraska, Michigan State University, Stanford University, and others.

During the late 1960s, another model of the student-institutional relationship began to emerge — the "student development perspective" (Chickering and Reisser, 1993; Miller and Prince, 1976). This perspective was best exemplified by the *Tomorrow's Higher Education (THE) Project,* conceived by the American College Personnel Association in 1968. The project outlined steps to provide learning environments that "maximize the integration of students' cognitive development with the development of the whole personality" (American College Personnel Association, 1975, p. 341). Proponents of the THE model for student development asserted that, if higher education was to have an impact on student learning, changes in academic and student affairs programs were required. They claimed that "an emphasis on student development would integrate out-of-classroom educational experiences into the core educational purposes of the institution" (Kuh, Shedd, and Whitt, 1987, p. 253). Brown (1972), for example, challenged student personnel workers to view themselves as educators in the very broadest sense. He called for student affairs staff to become a part of the academic dimensions of the collegiate experience by undertaking teaching roles and serving as consultants to faculty on student development matters (Brown, 1972).

This new student development perspective had a profound impact on the roles and functions of residence hall staff. Assuming such roles as educators, counselors, and managers, staff members responded to an increasingly diverse student culture, to problems of alcohol and drug abuse, and to behavioral problems associated with the absence of civility. They implemented numerous programs that attempted to address these concerns and facilitate students' personal development. Educational and developmental programs focused on topics like human sexuality, alcohol awareness, personal safety, and assertiveness training, and presentations were organized around psychosocial themes such as freeing interpersonal relationships, developing autonomy, and managing emotions (Chickering and Reisser, 1993). These programs, usually led by resident assistants and residence hall directors, were often scheduled on a monthly basis for one to two hours in various halls during the evening. Staff presenters rarely attempted to determine the impact of these programs on student learning and personal development, and there is "little creditable research evidence published that substantiates . . . that [these] interventions actually affect the level, course, or direction of students' development" (Winston and Anchors, 1993, p. 26). Although many of these programs were certainly well intentioned, some were not unlike the "blue-light specials" of certain retailers, in that "we sell what we have in stock." In other words, the programs often reflected the particular interests and skills of staff, rather than responding to students' expressed educational wants and needs (Schroeder, Nicholls, and Kuh, 1983). They also were not necessarily tied to the primary educational goals and objectives of the institution. The emphasis placed on these various educational and developmental programs, often through a top-down administrative protocol, has been a hallmark of residence education from the 1960s to the present. Their proliferation is reminiscent of Woodrow Wilson's comments on the expansion of the extracurriculum during his tenure as president of Princeton in 1909. He said that "the sideshows are so numerous, so diverting—so important, if you will—that they have swallowed up the circus" (Wilson, 1909, p. 572). Though residence halls attempted to become more educationally and developmentally viable settings, students, parents, faculty, and academic administrators have often viewed their programs and services as removed from the core of undergraduate education and therefore as peripheral to the academic priorities of the institution (Fenske, 1989).

Although student development has guided the work of residence educators during the past two decades, the perspective has not been without its critics. Bloland, Stamatakos, and Rogers (1994) examined and evaluated the student development model from a number of perspectives, including an assessment of student development as (1) a reform movement, (2) a philosophy, (3) a theoretical basis for the profession, (4) a research base, (5) a professional literature, and (6) a foundation for professional practice. Their review showed the student development perspective to be wanting. One of their major concerns was that student affairs educators assumed that student development *was* the educational mission of higher education (Smith, 1982). Bloland, Stamatakos, and Rogers (1994, p. 113) countered this assertion by stating that the educational mission is learning— "learning not only substantive facts but also values, ethics, an informed way of life, an occupational identity, personal and occupational skills—the list goes on, but the focus is on what is learned, not on what is developed." Student development theory and process models undoubtedly contribute to an understanding of college students and how they learn and develop. The theories and models, however, are not ends in themselves, but rather means to a greater end—that end being the enhancement of student learning (Schroeder, 1993).

Recent trends in higher education suggest that a perspective focused primarily on student learning will aid educators in accomplishing the educational missions of their institutions (Stamatakos, 1991; Bloland, Stamatakos, and Rogers, 1994; Schroeder and others, 1994). This renewed emphasis on student learning has emerged as a result of numerous converging forces, including the reports on the status of higher education and the dramatic economic problems that have constrained states' abilities to support public higher education to the fullest. As a result, politicians at both the state and national level have expressed increased concerns about the quality of undergraduate education, focusing particularly on learning outcomes associated with college attendance. Most institutions have responded to these concerns by creating formal outcomes assessment strategies for demonstrating the impact of various *academic* programs. Few, however, have focused attention on learning outcomes associated with broader dimensions of undergraduate education.

The literature on student learning and learning outcomes is replete with references to the importance of peer culture, active student involvement, the seamless nature of student experiences, and the need for new partnerships between academic and student affairs (Astin, 1985; Boyer, 1987; Kuh, Schuh, Whitt, and Associates, 1991; Pascarella and Terenzini, 1991; Terenzini and Pascarella, 1994; Barr and Upcraft, 1990; Mayhew, Ford, and Hubbard, 1990). Residence halls can and should take advantage of this thinking by becoming educationally rich environments, providing students with broad-based learning opportunities that reflect critical objectives of undergraduate education. Residential environments and programs can be structured so as to encourage values inquiry; promote cultural understanding and appreciation; encourage leadership development; and promote self-confidence, perseverance, empathy, and social responsibility — all qualities and outcomes associated with effective undergraduate education. Residence hall learning communities can be designed to focus on what students learn, how they learn it, and what motivates them. To achieve these aims, however, residence hall staff must broaden their emphasis from managing and administering facilities to a central focus on creating environments that support and foster student learning. This is the educational challenge facing college residence halls.

Current Challenge for Residence Halls

If college residence halls are going to significantly contribute to student learning, they must be innovative. Although institutional literature often describes residence halls as educational, they are primarily social settings; they are part of the institution's educational activity, yet not always in a central way. Residence halls have lacked educational planning, strong internal direction, and a set of educational objectives connected to the goals of undergraduate education. They have drifted from their espoused focus on enhancing student learning to simply maintaining the status quo: with policies, procedures, and practices tied primarily to management and administration of facilities and a collection of marginally effective educational and developmental programs that often reflect the staff's need to address the "latest campus life concern." In other words, the management schemes and structures promoted during the last quarter of a century have added up to distractions *from* student learning. Residential life staff have become so tied up in their programs that they have forgotten to consider what students actually learn from them.

That is the bad news, but there is good news! Residence halls have the opportunity, and even the obligation, to transcend the status quo. Administrators do not have to be satisfied with simply providing a comfortable and social living space. They can also exert educational leadership for accomplishing Boyer's (1987, p. 297) vision for undergraduate education: "We more comfortably embrace the notion that the aim of the undergraduate experience is not only to prepare the young for productive careers, but also to enable them to live lives of dignity and purpose; not only to generate new knowledge, but to channel that knowledge to humane ends; not merely to study government, but to help shape a citizenry that can promote the public good." The challenge for residence hall leaders and educators is to form a curriculum to address the tasks of teaching and learning with the preceding concepts in mind. Like the formal academic curriculum, the residence hall curriculum should reflect the broad goals and objectives of undergraduate education and, when appropriate, the specific educational objectives of particular academic departments. Although residence hall objectives must flow naturally from the institution's mission, residence halls committed to student learning would focus on the following:

1. Promoting growth and development of students as whole persons with coherent views of knowledge, life, integrity, and intellectual and social perspectives
2. Constructing a residence hall curriculum that teaches students responsibility, altruism, aspiration, persistence, empathy, ethics, and leadership—along with fluency in answering the questions, "Who am I?" and "What will I be?"
3. Emphasizing skills that challenge a student's ability to use knowledge in work and leisure: critical thinking and interpersonal skills, as well as technical skills; teamwork abilities; flexibility; and creative, cognitive, and caring attitudes
4. Creating environments that celebrate diversity by bringing students together in a community where differences are respected, but where there is a common goal to promote learning

The preceding objectives provide a framework for educating the whole student. The concept of wholeness has been advanced by a number of educational philosophers, but perhaps none so eloquently as Whitehead (1929, pp. 11–12), who, when reflecting on the critical role of wholeness, added that one "may not divide the seamless coat of learning. What education has to impart is an intimate sense of the power of ideas, for the beauty of ideas, and for the structure of ideas, together with a particular body of knowledge which has peculiar reference to the life of the being possessing it." In contrast to Whitehead's "seamless coat of learning," today's collegiate environment is, according to Bloland, Stamatakos, and Rogers (1994, p. 110), "more often than not, more seam than coat." Clearly, most institutional efforts to achieve wholeness are implemented through a variety of fragmented efforts on the part of academic affairs and student affairs. Terenzini and Pascarella (1994, p. 32) underscored this concern when they stated "the academic and student affairs functions of most institutions have been running essentially on parallel but separate tracks; academic affairs tends to students' cognitive development while student affairs ministers to their affective growth." Hence, any attempt to develop a comprehensive, learning-centered residence hall curriculum must not be done in a vacuum — it must be a cooperative and collaborative effort between residence educators, student affairs professionals, students, faculty, and academic administrators. As emphasized by Terenzini and Pascarella (1994, p. 32), "Organizationally and operationally, we've lost sight of the forest. If undergraduate education is to be enhanced, faculty members, joined by academic and student affairs administrators, must devise ways to deliver undergraduate education that are as comprehensive and integrated as the ways students actually learn."

To summarize, the challenge for residence halls is to place a renewed emphasis on promoting student learning through integrating residence hall learning opportunities with the goals and priorities of undergraduate education. To address this challenge, residence educators must overcome the traditional gap that has existed between academic affairs and student affairs. The following section suggests strategies for meeting this challenge.

Strategies for Meeting the Challenge

Senge (1990, p. 1) describes learning organizations as places "where people continually expand their capacity to create the results they truly desire, where new and expansive patterns of thinking are nurtured, where collective aspiration is set free, and where people are continually learning how to learn together." At first glance, it would appear that Senge's definition describes many colleges and universities; however, most do not qualify as learning organizations. Instead, companies such as General Electric, Motorola, and Xerox tend to be exemplars of what Senge and others have described as learning organizations because they, unlike many higher education institutions, have been effective at *creating* or acquiring new knowledge and successful in *applying* that knowledge to their own activities.

Student affairs divisions and residence life departments must become learning organizations if they are to enhance student learning and contribute to the achievement of the goals of undergraduate education. A primary strategy for achieving this objective is to ensure that campus-based practice and inquiry are informed and guided by research on student learning. In Chapter Two, Pascarella, Terenzini, and Blimling provide a comprehensive review of the literature and demonstrate the impact of residence halls on students. In a learning organization, the organization consistently translates knowledge such as this into new ways of behaving. Furthermore, these organizations *actively manage* the learning process to ensure that learning occurs by design rather than by default. If student affairs divisions, and departments of residential life, are to become learning organizations, they not only need to utilize current knowledge on student learning but, equally important, they must *generate* new knowledge to inform and guide their practices.

To promote student learning, residence life professionals must view their roles as educational leaders and forge strong, collaborative partnerships with faculty and other individuals committed to student learning. The efforts of many residence hall professionals are usually confined *within* their organizational boundaries. As a result, these units can be described as "functional silos," isolated principalities that have separate, narrow foci generally disconnected from broader, undergraduate education purposes. A residence life department committed to student learning recognizes that student learning experiences are often seamless and that a variety of environmental conditions promote learning. By fostering collaborative partnerships, residence life staff can stimulate the exchange of ideas by opening up organizational boundaries. Creating cross departmental/division project teams is one way of generating new information and approaches for improving student learning. Numerous additional approaches to developing collaboration between academic affairs and student affairs are described in subsequent chapters.

Finally, residence halls must become purposeful and intentional educational environments. The literature shows that "halls with the strongest impacts on cognitive development and persistence are typically the result of *purposeful, programmatic* efforts to integrate students' intellectual and social lives during college" (Terenzini and Pascarella, 1994, p. 32). Educationally purposeful initiatives must be mission driven, reflecting the values, principles, and objectives of effective undergraduate education. Residence halls can promulgate educationally purposeful activities by developing an explicit curriculum. Such a curriculum would include creating learning communities that directly support the academic mission of the institution, enhancing an appreciation of cultural and racial diversity, developing civic leadership skills, providing opportunities to explore academic, career, and leisure opportunities, and fostering cultural and artistic sensibilities. Components of this curriculum are the subjects of the following chapters, particularly in Part Two. Each chapter provides a comprehensive, in-depth exploration of components of this curriculum and describes purposeful educational objectives.

Conclusion

This chapter began with a brief discussion of recent reports on the status of higher education. Although these reports have called for the transformation of higher education, few of the reform efforts have focused on the educational potential of residence halls. The remainder of this book attempts to answer the central question posed at the outset of this chapter: "How can educators use the residence hall environment as a locale for promoting student learning?" Although subsequent chapters will address this question in unique and interesting ways, it is essential that educators in academic affairs and student affairs forge collaborative partnerships and exert educational leadership if the full educational potential of residence halls is to be achieved.

References

American College Personnel Association. "A Student Development Model for Student Affairs in Tomorrow's Higher Education." *Journal of College Student Personnel,* 1975, *16,* 334–341.

Appleton, J., Briggs, C., and Rhatigan, J. *Pieces of Eight.* Portland, Ore.: National Association of Student Personnel Administrators, 1978.

Association of American Colleges. *Integrity in the College Curriculum: A Report to the Academic Community.* Washington, D.C.: Association of American Colleges, 1985.

Astin, A. W. *Achieving Educational Excellence: A Critical Assessment of Priorities and Practices in Higher Education.* San Francisco: Jossey-Bass, 1985.

Barr, M. J., Upcraft, M. L., and Associates. *New Futures for Student Affairs: Building a Vision for Professional Leadership and Practice.* San Francisco: Jossey-Bass, 1990.

Bennett, W. J. *To Reclaim a Legacy: A Report on the Humanities in Higher Education.* Washington, D.C.: National Endowment for the Humanities, 1984.

Bloland, P. A., Stamatakos, L. C., and Rogers, R. R. *Reform in Student Affairs: A Critique of Student Development.* Greensboro, N.C.: ERIC/CASS Publications, 1994.

Boyer, E. L. *College: The Undergraduate Experience in America.* New York: HarperCollins, 1987.

Boyer, E. L. *Scholarship Reconsidered: Priorities of the Professoriate.* Princeton, N.J.: Carnegie Foundation for the Advancement of Teaching, 1990.

Brown, R. D. *Student Development in Tomorrow's Higher Education: A Return to the Academy.* Student Personnel Series, no. 16. Washington, D.C.: American College Personnel Association, 1972.

Brubacher, J. S., and Rudy, W. *Higher Education in Transition: An American History: 1636–1956.* New York: HarperCollins, 1968.

Chickering, A. W., and Reisser, L. *Education and Identity.* (2nd ed.) San Francisco: Jossey-Bass, 1993.

Cowley, W. H. "The Disappearing Dean of Men." Paper presented at the 19th annual conference of the National Association of Deans and Advisors of Men, Austin, Tex., Mar. 1937.

Fenske, R. H. "Historical Foundations of Student Services." In U. Delworth, G. R. Hanson, and Associates, *Student Services: A Handbook for the Profession.* (2nd ed.) San Francisco: Jossey-Bass, 1989.

Frederiksen, C. F. "A Brief History of Collegiate Housing." In R. B. Winston, Jr., S. Anchors, and Associates, *Student Housing and Residential Life: A Handbook for Professionals Committed to Student Development Goals.* San Francisco: Jossey-Bass, 1993.

Kuh, G. D., Schuh, J. H., Whitt, E. J., and Associates. *Involving Colleges: Successful Approaches to Fostering Student Learning and Development Outside the Classroom.* San Francisco: Jossey-Bass, 1991.

Kuh, G. D., Shedd, J. D., and Whitt, E. J. "Student Affairs and Liberal Education: Unrecognized (and Unappreciated) Common Law Partners." *Journal of College Student Personnel,* 1987, *28*(3), 252–260.

Levine, A., and Associates. *Shaping Higher Education's Future: Demographic Realities and Opportunities, 1990–2000.* San Francisco: Jossey-Bass, 1989.

Mayhew, L. B., Ford, P. J., and Hubbard, D. L. *The Quest for Quality: The Challenge for Undergraduate Education in the 1990s.* San Francisco: Jossey-Bass, 1990.

Miller, T. K., and Prince, J. S. *The Future of Student Affairs: A Guide to Student Development for Tomorrow's Higher Education.* San Francisco: Jossey-Bass, 1976.

National Association of Student Personnel Administrators. *Points of View.* Washington, D.C.: National Association of Student Personnel Administrators, 1989.

Pascarella, E. T., and Terenzini, P. T. *How College Affects Students: Findings and Insights from Twenty Years of Research.* San Francisco: Jossey-Bass, 1991.

Rudolph, F. *The American College and University: A History.* New York: Knopf, 1962.

Schroeder, C. C. "A Bicentennial Perspective on the Origins of College Student Personnel Work." *Alabama Personnel and Guidance Journal,* 1976, *3*(1), 17–28.

Schroeder, C. C. "Territoriality: An Imperative for Personal Development and Residence Education." In D. A. DeCoster and P. Mable (eds.), *Personal Education and Community Development in College Residence Halls.* Cincinnati, Ohio: American College Personnel Association, 1980.

Schroeder, C. C. "Presidential Address." Paper presented at the annual conference of the American College Personnel Association, Kansas City, Mo., Mar. 1993.

Schroeder, C. C., Nicholls, G. E., and Kuh, G. D. "Exploring the Rain Forest: Testing Assumptions and Taking Risks." In G. D. Kuh (ed.), *Understanding Student Affairs Organizations.* New Directions for Student Services, no. 23. San Francisco: Jossey-Bass, 1983.

Schroeder, C. C., and others. "ACPA's Student Learning Project: A Clarion Call for Educational Leadership!" Paper presented at the annual conference of the American College Personnel Association, Indianapolis, Ind., Mar. 1994.

Senge, P. *The Fifth Discipline.* New York: Doubleday, 1990.

Smith, D. G. "The Next Step Beyond Student Development — Becoming Partners Within Our Institutions." *NASPA Journal,* 1982, *19*(4), 33–62.

Stamatakos, L. C. "The Great Expectations of Student Affairs and Lessons from Reality: A Contextual Examination." Paper presented at the Virginia Association of Student Personnel Administrators/Virginia Association of College and University Housing Officers fall conference, Wintergreen Resort, Va., Oct. 1991.

Study Group on the Conditions of Excellence in American Higher Education. *Involvement In Learning.* Washington, D.C.: U.S. Department of Education, 1984.

Terenzini, P. T., and Pascarella, E. T. "Living with Myths: Undergraduate Education in America." *Change,* 1994, *25*(6), 28–32.

Whitehead, A. N. *The Aims of Education and Other Essays.* New York: Free Press, 1929.

Wilson, W. "What Is a College for?" *Scribner's Magazine,* Nov. 1909, pp. 572–575.

Wingspread Group on Higher Education. *An American Imperative: Higher Expectations for Higher Education.* Racine, Wis.: Johnson Foundation, 1993.

Winston, R. B., Jr., and Anchors, S. "Student Development in the Residential Environment." In R. B. Winston, S. Anchors, and Associates, *Student Housing and Residential Life: A Handbook for Professionals Committed to Student Development Goals.* San Francisco: Jossey-Bass, 1993.

Winston, R. B., Jr., Anchors, S., and Associates. *Student Housing and Residential Life: A Handbook for Professionals Committed to Student Development Goals.* San Francisco: Jossey-Bass, 1993.

Two

The Impact of Residential Life on Students

Ernest T. Pascarella
Patrick T. Terenzini
Gregory S. Blimling

An extremely large body of research has addressed the educational impact of a student's place of residence during college. In this chapter, we summarize and draw conclusions from this body of evidence, focusing on answers to the following questions:

1. How do we determine the educational impact of students' place of residence during college?
2. What is the educational impact of living on campus versus commuting to college?
3. What is the educational impact of different institutionally sponsored on-campus living arrangements?
4. What are important directions for future research?

This chapter draws heavily on two existing research syntheses. The first, by Pascarella and Terenzini (1991), reviews the impact of place of residence within the larger context of the overall influence of college on students. The second (Blimling, 1993) is a more focused review of the impact of college residence halls on a wide range of student outcomes. While the

22

present summary attempts to selectively highlight many of the major findings from these two research syntheses, readers wishing greater detail and a more comprehensive analysis are urged to peruse these two sources.

Impact of Students' Place of Residence

Attempts to determine the unique impact of college residence halls on various educational outcomes have typically taken one of two basic forms. The first form is the randomized or true experiment design, and the second is the quasi-experiment/correlational study. In the randomized, true experiment, individual students are typically assigned randomly to two or more different residential arrangements. For example, students might be assigned to two different roommate arrangements, one in which they are matched with roommates by personality type or aptitude and one in which they are assigned with no special attempt to match on those traits. What random assignment of individuals accomplishes, of course, is to distribute individual student traits across the different roommate arrangements in a nonsystematic or unbiased manner. Consequently, a subsequent comparison between the two roommate arrangements on some outcome — say, first-year grades — would provide an estimate of the effect of roommate arrangement on academic achievement that is largely unconfounded by the characteristics of the students in the study. Through the powerful mechanism of random assignment, randomized, true experiments give us our most unambiguous estimate of the *net effects* of different residence arrangements. *Net effect* is the term used in the remainder of this chapter to indicate the effect or impact that is uniquely attributed to place of residence and not to other extraneous causes.

Although randomized, true experiments maximize our ability to obtain unambiguous estimates of net residential effects, they are not without their problems. Perhaps the most relevant for our discussion in this chapter is that in the vast majority of situations, random assignment is impossible. Rather, students most often self-select into different residential arrangements during college, and when self-selection occurs, separating the influence of the student aptitudes and traits that lead to different residential options from the actual environmental impact of the different residential options themselves is a nontrivial task. Consider, for example, the complex cluster of individual student aptitudes and background traits that shape the decision to live in a college residence hall or to live at home and commute to college. If the choice is to live on campus, one must decide among living in a conventional residence hall, living in an experimental living-learning center, or joining and living in a fraternity or sorority. Without taking such differences in student aptitudes and traits into account, it is easy to mistakenly conclude that different residential arrangements are causing different student outcomes, when the different student outcomes observed may simply reflect the fact that substantially different kinds of students select, or are recruited to, different residential arrangements to begin with.

This major methodological problem has given rise to the second and, by far, the predominant approach to estimating the net effects of different residential arrangements—the use of quasi-experimental or correlational designs with statistical controls for salient confounding variables. For example, consider the challenge of estimating the net effect on first-year grades of living on campus versus living at home and commuting to college. In a typical nonrandomized, quasi-experimental or correlational investigation, the net effect of living on campus versus commuting to college is represented by the differences (or variance) in first-year grades explained by place of residence above and beyond the variance explained by important confounding variables such as academic aptitude, high school grades, academic motivation, aspirations, and so on. Estimating the net variance in grades uniquely attributable to place of residence is usually accomplished by any of a related set of procedures (such as residual scores, partial correlation, multiple regression, or analysis of covariance) that statistically remove the unwanted influence of confounding variables.

It should be noted that quasi-experimental or correlational designs, even when combined with the power of statistical controls for important confounding influences, do not permit causal inference with the same level of certitude as do randomized experiments (for example, Light, Singer, and Willett, 1990; Pascarella and Terenzini, 1991). But they remain an important procedure by which to estimate the plausibility of causal relationships and, perhaps more important, guard against mistaking specious associations for causal ones (Linn and Werts, 1969). In our review of the existing evidence on the educational impact of place of residence during college, we place the greatest interpretative credibility on findings that come from the types of designs discussed above, namely, randomized experiments and quasi-experimental/correlational investigations that employ appropriate statistical procedures to control for the influence of salient confounding effects. Studies based on designs that fail to control for students' precollege characteristics and other confounding variables are given less credence.

Educational Impact of Living on Campus Versus Commuting to College

As pointed out in previous reviews (Blimling, 1993) the vast preponderance of research on the influence of living on campus versus living at home and commuting to college takes a social-ecological approach. These studies assume that educational environments influence or "cause" students to behave in certain ways and to develop certain cognitive and noncognitive skills or perspectives. In the case of college residences, the premise is that residential living creates a social-psychological environment for students that is qualitatively different from that experienced by those who live at home or elsewhere off campus and commute to college. Simply put, this perspective hypothesizes that living on campus will maximize opportunities for social, cultural, and extracurricular involvement, and this increased involvement will account for residential living's impact on various indices of student development. The weight of evidence clearly supports this set of interrelated propositions.

Involvement and Satisfaction

Residential living during college is consistently one of the most important determinants of a student's level of involvement or integration into the various cultural, social, and extracurricular systems of an institution. Compared to their counterparts who live at home and commute to college, resident students have significantly more social interaction with peers and faculty and are significantly more likely to be involved in extracurricular activities and to use campus facilities (for example, Billson and Terry, 1982; Chickering, 1974; Everett, 1979; Foster, Sedlacek, and Hardwick, 1977; Nelson, 1982; Pascarella, 1984; Stockham, 1974; Welty, 1976). Moreover, this influence appears to persist even when controls are made for differences in students' precollege characteristics, such as aptitude, socioeconomic status, and secondary school extracurricular involvement, as well as the size, private/public affiliation, and student body selectivity of the institution attended (Pascarella, 1985b).

Given resident students' greater social and extracurricular involvement, it is not surprising that residents, as compared to their commuter counterparts, have different perceptions of the social climate of their institution and express different levels of satisfaction with college. While some exceptions exist (for instance, Dollar, 1966; Ryan, 1970), the clear weight of evidence, particularly from national, multi-institution samples, indicates that residents are significantly more satisfied with college and are more positive about the social/interpersonal environment of their campus than are their commuter counterparts (for example, Berdie, 1966; Goetz, 1983; Lundgren and Schwab, 1979; Pascarella, 1985a; Welty, 1974).

Persistence and Graduation

A large body of evidence underscores the importance of social integration during college as a significant determinant of persistence and graduation (for instance, Tinto, 1987). Consequently, as one might expect, a substantial body of research has also focused on the influence of residence status on these same outcomes. The weight of evidence from this inquiry is clear, if not unequivocal. Even when controls are applied for differences in past academic performance, aptitude, socioeconomic status, and other factors associated with educational attainment, students who live in residence halls consistently persist and graduate at significantly higher rates than students who have not had this experience (for example, Anderson, 1981; Astin, 1975, 1977, 1982; Herndon, 1984; Howell, Perkins, and Young, 1979; Levin and Clowes, 1982; Pascarella and Chapman, 1983; Velez, 1985).

Residential living appears to influence persistence and graduation by accentuating the initial advantages of those who live on campus. Irrespective of college type, students who live on campus (compared to those who commute) enter college with traits that make them more likely to persist and graduate to begin with (Astin, 1985; Chickering, 1974; Pascarella, 1984; Ryan, 1970). Such precollege traits include higher levels of academic aptitude, family socioeconomic status, high school extracurricular involvement, educational aspirations, and precollege commitment to the institution attended (Pascarella and Terenzini, 1991). Residential living seems to provide an additional advantage for students who begin college with individual attributes that make them more likely to exploit and benefit from this advantage. The actual magnitude of the net advantage in persistence and degree attainment attributable to living on campus is not entirely clear, largely because much of the research does not provide adequate statistical data. However, Astin (1977), in his analysis of a large national data base, provides a reasonable estimate that living in a residence hall adds about a 12 percent net advantage to students' chance of persisting in college and graduating.

Personal Growth and Development

The evidence shows that living in college residence halls (versus commuting to college) has its strongest and most consistent positive influence in the areas of social/extracurricular involvement, satisfaction with college, persistence in college, and degree attainment. The effects of living on campus on the dimensions of student personal growth and development are less clear and consistent. Nevertheless, we can have reasonable confidence in several conclusions.

First, although the evidence is not unequivocal, students living in traditional residence halls tend to make significantly greater positive gains in a number of areas of psychosocial development than their counterparts who reside off campus and commute to college. These greater gains are in autonomy and inner-directedness (Kuder, 1970; Lundgren and Schwab, 1979; Sullivan and Sullivan, 1980), intellectual orientation (Chickering and Kuper, 1971; Welty, 1976), and academic and social self-concepts (Baird, 1969; Chickering, 1974; Pascarella, 1984, 1985a). Such differences in gains tend to persist even after controlling for gender and academic ability when the outcomes are autonomy and inner-directedness, and for gender, ability, and precollege levels of the respective trait when the outcomes are intellectual orientation and self-concept. Evidence also exists that, compared to their commuter counterparts, students living in residence halls show higher levels of self-esteem over time (Lemoal, 1980; Lundgren and Schwab, 1979; Marron and Kayson, 1984), greater growth in ego development (Goetz, 1983), and greater reductions in authoritarianism (Chickering and Kuper, 1971; Matteson, 1974). However, issues of uncontrolled confounding influences and/or lack of independent replication make conclusions from this evidence somewhat tentative and, perhaps, premature.

The residence effect on changes in self-concept is particularly interesting, because it may indicate the nature of the major causal mechanisms at work. In an analysis of a large national sample, Pascarella (1984, 1985a) found that living on campus (versus commuting) did not have a significant direct influence on development of student self-concept. Rather, the significant influence of living on campus was indirect. Living in college residences positively influenced the amount of social interaction students had with both faculty and peers. In turn, amount of social interaction with faculty and peers was a major positive determinant of self-concept. Thus, place of residence exerted its major educational impact by shaping the nature of the student's social/interpersonal environment. We suspect that much of the developmental influence of place of residence during college reflects this general causal mechanism.

A second interesting trend in the data is that studies of freshman samples tend to produce net effects of living on campus (versus off campus) that are smaller in magnitude than studies of sophomore or mixed-class (for example, freshmen, sophomores, juniors) samples. While it is risky to make causal inferences from such an observation, the evidence does suggest that the net effects of residence hall living tend to be cumulative, and thus may increase in magnitude during the student's college career.

Values, Attitudes, and Moral Judgment

One might expect that the challenges presented to students in adjusting to the heterogeneous social environments of residence halls would influence their values and attitudes as well as their personal growth and development. Once again, the evidence is far from unequivocal, but it does suggest that students living on campus may experience somewhat greater value changes than their counterparts who live off campus and commute to college. The strongest evidence is in the areas of aesthetic, cultural, and intellectual values, social and political liberalism, and secularism. In all three areas, students living in college residence halls tend to make significantly larger gains than their commuter counterparts, even when controls are made for such confounding influences as gender, race, socioeconomic status, aptitude, and precollege values (Astin, 1972, 1977; Chickering, 1974; Chickering, McDowell, and Campagna, 1969; Chickering and Kuper, 1971; Katz and Associates, 1968; Welty, 1976).

The evidence in the area of principled moral judgment is less consistent. Hawkins (1980) used the Defining Issues Test to compare the moral development stages of students living in residence halls with those of students in private, off-campus housing and found no significant differences between the two groups. On the other hand, Rest and Deemer (1986)—also using the Defining Issues Test—found that living on campus versus commuting to college was part of an academic orientation or involvement dimension positively linked to gains in the use of principled moral judgment. This effect remained significant even after statistical controls were introduced for precollege levels of moral judgment. To our knowledge, however, this finding has not been replicated.

Academic Performance

A large body of inquiry has addressed the question of whether students who live in residence halls perform better academically (that is, earn higher grades) than those who live at home and commute to college. The existing evidence on this question is mixed, with some studies indicating that residents earn higher grades (such as Burtner and Tincher, 1979; May, 1974; Nowack and Hanson, 1985; Simono, Wachowiak, and Furr, 1984), while another group of studies finds either no group differences or that students living off campus performed better (for example, Call, 1974; Hountras and Brandt, 1970; Hunter, 1977; Mussano, 1976; Taylor and Hanson, 1971). In an attempt to bring some resolution to this issue, Blimling (1989) conducted a meta-analysis of the influence of college residence halls on academic performance. He found that, after controlling for differences in past academic performance, living in a college residence hall provided neither an advantage nor a disadvantage in academic performance compared to living at home and commuting to college. Thus, we are led to conclude that living in a conventional residence hall, compared with commuting to college, is not likely to have an appreciable influence one way or the other on a student's academic achievement. This conclusion is reinforced by the evidence suggesting that living in college residence halls does not appear to enhance study habits over living at home (for example, Dollar, 1966; Hawkins, 1980; Kuder, 1970; Stockham, 1974). Indeed, although the evidence is far from conclusive, it may be that the normative social milieu of residence halls can at times provide greater opportunities for socializing than for studying. Such opportunities may be less likely when a student lives at home or in an apartment.

General Cognitive Growth

While it is reasonably clear that living in college residence halls has no appreciable influence on the grades one earns in college, it is not entirely clear that a one-to-one correspondence exists between grades and more general measures of cognitive growth. (See Pascarella and Terenzini, 1991, page 63, for studies addressing the reliability, validity, and comparability of college grades). Since interpersonal interaction appears to play a nontrivial role in many dimensions of cognitive growth (for example, Baxter Magolda, 1987; Kitchener and King, 1981; Perry, 1970), and since living on campus enhances interpersonal interaction with a diversity of peers and faculty, one might hypothesize that residential living fosters greater general cognitive growth than living at home and commuting to college. This proposition has received only limited attention from researchers. In a study at a large urban university, Pascarella and others (1993) compared the freshman-year gains in standardized measures of critical thinking, reading comprehension, and mathematics reasoning between students living in campus residence facilities and students living at home. With statistical controls for precollege level of cognitive development on each scale, precollege academic motivation, age, work responsibilities, and freshman-year credit hours taken, the resident students had significantly larger gains in critical thinking and larger gains in reading comprehension that were marginally significant. No significant group differences were noted in the mathematics reasoning gains.

While these findings await replication, they suggest that college residence halls may have a nontrivial role in students' general cognitive growth. This may be particularly the case in areas such as critical thinking, which, unlike mathematics reasoning, are not necessarily tied to coursework experiences.

Educational Impact of Different On-Campus Living Arrangements

If we know anything from the vast literature on the impact of college on students, it is that an institution does not provide a single campus environment. Rather, institutions tend to consist of multiple subenvironments or subcultures that have more proximal, and often more powerful, consequences for student change and development. The residential environment of a campus is typically not monolithic, either. Different types of on-campus living arrangements can produce different kinds of interpersonal climates and normative peer cultures, which, in turn, have potentially important implications for how students change during college (Kuh, Schuh, Whitt, and Associates, 1991; Pascarella and Terenzini, 1991). In this section, we review the accumulated evidence on the impact of some of the major different institutionally sponsored residential arrangements on college campuses.

Living-Learning Centers

A fairly large body of evidence focuses on the impact of living-learning centers (LLCs) on student growth during college. While the concept of the LLC is broadly interpreted in terms of organizational and structural components on different campuses, the central theme appears to be one of bringing about a closer integration of the student's living environment with his or her academic or learning environment. Typical features of LLCs include: classes taught in the residence hall, increased student-faculty contact, cultural events and faculty lectures in the residence halls, and LLC students taking a common course together. Most LLCs also include some form of coeducational living arrangement. Usually some form of application and selection to the LLC is required, which of course means that LLCs often attract students with characteristics significantly different from their counterparts in more conventional residence halls. However, a number of the studies addressing the educational impact of LLCs take such student recruitment factors into account.

On most educational outcomes considered, the evidence suggests that residing in an LLC is more educationally beneficial to students than living in a conventional residence hall. For example, with the exception of Centra (1968), most research has found that students in LLCs have significantly more informal interaction with faculty and perceive a significantly stronger intellectual dimension to their living environment than do students in conventional residence halls (Clark and others, 1988; Magnarella, 1976; Pascarella and Terenzini, 1980, 1981). Similarly, with the exception of a study by Nosow (1975), the weight of evidence suggests that students in LLCs tend to report a much more rewarding or personally satisfying social climate in their living arrangements than do students in conventional residences (Barnes, 1977; Centra, 1968; Goebel, 1977; Vander Wall, 1972; Viehe, 1977). LLC students also tend to perform better academically than their counterparts in conventional residence halls, and this effect persists even after controls have been made for such influences as academic aptitude and past academic achievement (Barnes, 1977; Felver, 1983; Pascarella and Terenzini, 1980, 1981; Vander Wall, 1972). Only Pemberton (1969) found no academic achievement advantage for LLC students, although he did find that LLC students made an easier transition and adjustment to college than their counterparts in conventional residence halls.

Given the advantages in academic achievement and the more favorable social and intellectual climate found in LLCs than in conventional residences, it is not surprising that the weight of evidence suggests that students living in LLCs are also more likely to persist in college and to graduate from college than their counterparts in conventional college residences (Felver, 1983; Pascarella and Terenzini, 1980, 1981). The only exception to this conclusion is Vander Wall (1972). The generally higher persistence rate of students in LLCs remains statistically significant even after controls are introduced for such important determinants of persistence in college as prior academic achievement and family socioeconomic status (Pascarella and Terenzini, 1980, 1981).

Evidence pertaining to the direct impact of LLCs on more general forms of intellectual and personal development during college is mixed. In quasi-experimental studies of two independent samples, Pascarella and Terenzini (1980, 1981) found that, compared to their counterparts in conventional residences, LLC freshmen reported significantly higher levels of freshman-year gains in both cognitive and personal development. These advantages accruing to the LLC students persisted even when statistical controls were made for such salient confounding influence as academic aptitude, family socioeconomic status, secondary school academic and social achievement, and expectations of college. Studies by Nosow (1975) and Pemberton (1969), however, fail to support these findings, at least with respect to personal growth and development.

Similarly, the evidence pertaining to the influence of LLCs on dimensions of student growth other than general measures of cognitive and personal growth is also mixed. Newcomb and others (1970, 1971) investigated differences in the intellectual orientation and the aesthetic and cultural interests of LLC students and students in conventional residence halls. Although the LLC students made greater gains on all three constructs than their counterparts in conventional residences, only the group differences in intellectual orientation gains remained significant when precollege levels of each construct were taken into account. Similarly, both Lacy (1978) and Suczek (1972) found that, even when controlling for initial differences in authoritarianism, LLC students tended to show greater reductions in authoritarianism than control groups of students in conventional residences. This finding, however, was not replicated in a similar comparison of LLC and conventional residence hall students by Cade (1979).

Perhaps one explanation for these mixed findings is that LLCs exert most of their influence on student personal and intellectual development indirectly. In their analyses of the educational effects of LLCs, both Lacy (1978) and Pascarella and Terenzini (1980) found that, when they added variables reflecting students' interpersonal relationships with faculty and peers to their multiple-regression or path models, the direct effects of LLCs on various dimensions of student growth and development were substantially reduced in magnitude—often to the point of statistical nonsignificance. These findings indicate that the impact of structural residence arrangements such as LLCs are indirect, being mediated by the peer and faculty interactions they foster and that, in turn, exert strong, direct influences on various dimensions of student growth and development during college. Such a conclusion is supported by a growing body of research suggesting that the educational impacts of many of the structural and organizational aspects of colleges and universities are mediated by the nature of the cultural, social, and interpersonal subenvironments they shape (Astin, 1992; Pascarella and Terenzini, 1991).

Homogeneous Assignment of Students by Academic Ability

One of the questions frequently asked about purposeful residence hall programs and policies is whether the normative peer culture of a residence hall can be structured in such a way as to enhance students' academic performance. Studies on the impacts of homogeneous assignment of high-ability and honors students suggest that it can. A substantial body of research indicates that, even when individuals are equated on past academic performance, high-ability students assigned to room with other high-ability students perform better academically than high-ability students assigned randomly (DeCoster, 1966, 1968; Duncan and Stoner, 1976; Scholz, 1970; Stewart, 1980; Streeter, 1972; Taylor and Hanson, 1971). Blimling (1993) attempts to explain the better academic performance of homogeneously assigned high-ability students in residence halls in terms of the potential socializing power of the values and attitudes held by the normative peer culture. He suggests that "the social organization of students with superior academic skills establishes a peer-supported standard of academic achievement, manifest through increased competition for grades among students, peer recognition and status for academic performance, and the establishment of study group networks supporting informal tutoring in common areas of academic inquiry" (p. 268). In short, the residence grouping of high-ability students creates a peer culture in which initial aptitudes and motivation are accentuated and converted into academic accomplishments that are even higher than expected.

It may also be possible to purposefully structure the study environment of residences so that benefits of homogeneous grouping of high-ability students can be approximated with students of average academic ability. Blimling and Hample (1979), for example, conducted a quasi-experiment in which students who chose to live on "study floors" with established and enforced study hours were contrasted with students on conventional residence hall floors for a two-year period. After controlling for differences in gender, academic aptitude, and prior achievement, students on study floors had an advantage of about .20 of a grade (on a 4-point scale) over their conventional residence hall floor counterparts. The magnitude of this advantage is consistent with evidence reported by DeCoster (1966, 1968), who found that high-ability students assigned to live together earned a grade-point average between .10 and .20 of a grade higher (on a 4-point scale) than similar high-ability students assigned at random.

Homogeneous Assignment by Academic Major

Another popular type of homogeneous grouping in residence halls has been by academic major. A small body of inquiry has addressed the impact of grouping by academic major on such outcomes as satisfaction with the residence unit social climate, scholarly orientation, academic achievement, and persistence in college. The findings are somewhat mixed with respect to effects on academic performance. Both Schroeder and Belmonte (1979) and Schroeder and Griffin (1977) found that students homogeneously assigned to residence halls by major performed better academically than students in the same academic majors assigned at random. However, these findings were not confirmed in similar studies by Elton and Bate (1966) and McKelfresh (1980). Morishima (1966) found that, after two years, students homogeneously assigned to residence hall floors by academic major showed greater gains in scholarly orientation but did not perform academically better than students assigned randomly.

Though sparse, the evidence is more consistent with respect to the effects of grouping by major on satisfaction and social climate and on persistence in a particular field of study. Investigations by Madson, Kuder, Hartanov, and McKelfresh (1976) and McKelfresh (1980) suggest that students homogeneously grouped by academic major are significantly more satisfied with their living arrangements than students with the same major randomly assigned. Similarly, even though only trivial differences turned up on most group comparisons, Schroeder and Belmonte (1979) report that women students who lived on a homogeneously assigned floor for pharmacy students engaged in more supportive and affiliative types of behavior than a control group not grouped by major.

Although it is not totally consistent, a modicum of evidence suggests that homogeneous grouping in residence halls by major can have positive implications for persistence, both in that major and in college. With the exception of Taylor and Hanson (1971), the modest weight of evidence would suggest that engineers are more likely to remain in engineering, and science majors are more likely to remain in college, when they are homogeneously assigned to live with students in the same respective majors than when they are assigned at random (Chapple, 1984; Schroeder and Griffin, 1977). One possible explanation for this finding is that homogeneous grouping by major creates a peer culture particularly supportive of the individual, because all members must learn to cope with similar academic challenges and course content. A related explanation may involve the formation of mutually supportive informal study groups on homogeneously assigned floors. Light (1990), for example, found that science students who studied science as part of a study group were significantly more likely to persist in a science curriculum than science students who studied alone. He points out, however, that this effect may be situationally specific to science majors. Study groups may not have the same impact in the humanities and social sciences, where a greater premium is often placed on independent learning and writing.

Freshman Residence Halls

The influence of assigning freshman students to all-freshman residences versus residences with both freshmen and upperclass students has been the focus of a small body of research. Generally the evidence from this research tends to be mixed. For example, Ballou (1984, 1986), Cheslin (1967), and Hebert (1966) found that freshmen assigned to an all-freshman residence hall received significantly higher grades than freshmen assigned to live with upperclass students. However, Schoemer and McConnell (1970) found just the opposite — that freshmen assigned to live with upperclass students did better — and Beal and Williams (1968), Moen (1989), and Washington (1969) report nonsignificant group differences. If anything, the evidence suggests that only a slight advantage in academic performance may be gained from assigning freshmen to all-freshmen residence halls. Such a conclusion, however, should be regarded as tentative.

Coeducational Residence Halls

Not surprisingly, given the controversy surrounding their inception in the 1960s, a substantial body of research has focused on the impact of coeducational versus single-sex residence arrangements. While a detailed review of this literature is beyond the scope of this chapter, Blimling (1993) has synthesized this evidence and offers the following general conclusions. First, living in coeducational residences does not appear to have an appreciable impact on academic achievement (for example, Croake, Hansen, and Kirkland, 1980; Frichette, 1976; Moos and Otto, 1975) or on participation in extracurricular activities (Dailey and Stafford, 1975; Jacokes, 1976; Stockham, 1974). Some evidence suggests that students living in coeducational residence halls have more informal and friendship-type social involvement with members of the other gender than students living in single-sex residence halls, and this has potential for reducing stereotypical gender-role perceptions (Blimling, 1993). However, the evidence is unclear whether coeducational residences actually socialize men and women in the direction of greater interaction and a reduction in stereotypical gender roles. An alternative explanation is that coeducational residence halls may simply attract or recruit students with these more progressive orientations to begin with.

Important Directions for Future Research

In this section, we first summarize the research findings, then make recommendations for future research.

Summary

In synthesizing over 2,600 studies on the impact of college on students, Pascarella and Terenzini (1991, p. 611) concluded that living in college residence halls versus commuting to college is perhaps the "single most consistent within-college determinant of impact." Our rereading of the research, combined with the additional perspective of Blimling's (1993) synthesis, leads us to essentially the same conclusion. Residential living can be a powerful force in shaping both the essential character and the developmental impact of an individual's college experience.

Compared to their counterparts who live at home and commute to college, students living in college residence halls

1. Participate in a greater number of extracurricular, social, and cultural events on campus
2. Interact more frequently with faculty and peers in informal settings
3. Are significantly more satisfied with college and are more positive about the social and interpersonal environment of their campus
4. Are more likely to persist and graduate from college
5. Show significantly greater positive gains in such areas of psychosocial development as autonomy and inner-directedness, intellectual orientation, and self-concept
6. Demonstrate significantly greater increases in aesthetic, cultural, and intellectual values, social and political liberalism, and secularism

Clearly, campus residence halls recruit or attract students with substantially different characteristics from those who live at home and commute. But the effects of living in college residences (versus commuting to college) do not just reflect the tendency for students living on campus to be more open to the developmental influences of college to begin with. Rather, the net effects of college residence halls persist even when controls are introduced for salient differences in students' background traits and aptitudes.

We found no compelling evidence to suggest that living in college residence halls, as compared to commuting to college, provides any appreciable positive advantage in either student study habits or academic performance. Since the major areas where residence halls typically shape a student's experience of college are in social and interpersonal domains, rather than the formal academic program, this is not particularly surprising. However, we did find evidence, as yet unreplicated, to suggest that residential living may foster general cognitive growth in areas not necessarily linked closely to the student's formal academic experience (for example, critical thinking). Such evidence is consistent with a growing body of inquiry suggesting that students' cognitive, psychosocial, and attitudinal changes are not independent of one another (Pascarella and Terenzini, 1991).

The residential environment on a campus is not monolithic. The evidence suggests that it may be possible to structure and organize residences in ways that enhance their developmental impact. Compared to students who live in conventional residence halls, and controlling for differences in precollege traits, students in LLCs

1. Report a higher-quality social climate, engage in more informal contact with faculty, and report a more intellectual atmosphere in their residence arrangement
2. Perform better academically
3. Are more likely to persist in college

LLCs also appear to have significant positive indirect effects on student academic and personal growth and development, mediated by the distinctive social, interpersonal, and cultural living environments that they shape.

High-ability students homogeneously assigned to live together in residence halls perform better academically than high-ability students assigned at random to residence halls. The impacts of other purposeful attempts to structure residence environments (for example, homogeneous grouping by academic major, freshman versus mixed-class residence halls, or coeducational versus single-sex residence halls) tend to be mixed, thus making firm conclusions problematic.

In addition to underscoring the developmental impacts of college residence halls, the evidence we reviewed permits us to offer two general observations about the *nature* of residence halls' developmental impact on students. First, it is reasonably clear that, whether the issue is living on campus versus commuting to college or differences among college residence structures, the developmental impacts exerted on students tend to be indirect. They are transmitted largely by distinctive peer environments and increased opportunities for interpersonal and cultural involvement. Second, college residence halls (as compared to living at home and commuting to college) and LLCs (as compared to conventional residence halls) tend to attract students who are, by initial inclination, somewhat more open to the influences those particular residential arrangements are likely to exert. Consequently, although it does not totally account for their net impacts, a tendency exists for different residential arrangements to accentuate the traits of students who are attracted or recruited to them.

This second general observation about the nature of residential effects has a corollary — that purposeful interventions that homogeneously assign students to residence halls will tend to increase or accentuate the trait on which students are assigned. For example, the homogeneous assignment of academically gifted students tends to create a normative peer culture that rewards the values and behaviors in which those students are already accomplished — exceptional academic performance. From one perspective, such homogeneous grouping interventions in residence halls can be seen as a potentially powerful vehicle for advancing the educational mission. But there may also be a price to be paid in terms of a student's experience of diversity during college.

Whenever students are assigned to residence halls so as to advance a particular institutional goal, they lose something of the experience of diversity gained from others in less specialized living environments. When high-ability students are assigned to live together, this special assignment procedure helps gifted students achieve academically but deprives students living in conventional residence halls of exposure to these students as role models. When establishing special assignment programs, one probably needs to weigh the advantages of such programs against the goal of achieving a well-rounded education for all students (Blimling, 1993, p. 65).

Recommendations

The evidence suggests a number of fruitful directions for future research on the educational impact of college residences. First, because the impact of college residences is apparently complex and indirect, the most revealing future studies will employ research designs and analytical approaches that mirror this complexity. Particularly useful will be conceptually generated causal models that permit the investigator to assess the indirect as well as the direct impacts of different residence arrangements while controlling for salient student precollege traits. Lacy (1978) and Pascarella and Terenzini (1980, 1981) provide examples of the assessment of indirect residence effects using causal models. We suspect the failure to consider and assess such indirect effects can produce misleading estimates of both the character and magnitude of many residence impacts.

Similarly, with few exceptions, research on the educational impact of college residence halls has been concerned with general effects. In focusing on general effects, one implicitly assumes that all students benefit to the same extent from the same residential experience. But the psychology of individual differences reminds us that this assumption may not always reflect reality. Conditional effects, as an application of the psychology of individual differences, anticipate the possibility that different kinds of students may benefit differently from the diversity of residential experiences. Indeed, we strongly suspect that students' individual characteristics may frequently determine the magnitude of the educational impact of college residences. Given the growing diversity of the American postsecondary student body, the examination of these conditional effects takes on added importance. If certain residential experiences are shown to be beneficial for particular kinds of students, more developmentally specific and influential residential structures and programs can be crafted.

The existing research has focused almost exclusively on the effects of residence arrangement on academic achievement; it has virtually ignored residential impacts on more general dimensions of cognitive or intellectual growth. Given the social/interpersonal base for much cognitive development, we suspect that the residential experience can play a significant role for a substantial number of students. At least one study suggests that this is the case, and the mapping and estimation of the cognitive impacts of college residence halls is a third important area for future research.

Finally, most research on the impact of college residences has relied on quantitative, positivistic approaches. An important direction for future research will be a greater dependence on qualitative and naturalistic methodologies (for example, Lincoln and Guba, 1985; Moffatt, 1989). Such approaches may be particularly sensitive to the individual social and interpersonal realities that exist for diverse students in residence halls. They may also provide a powerful vehicle for understanding the impact of different roommate relationships and friendship patterns that develop in different residences.

Conclusion

The evidence is clear that college and university residence halls, through the intellectual and interpersonal climate they foster, play a substantial role in the growth and development of students who live in them. The challenge that researchers and student affairs professionals face is threefold: (1) to better understand the dynamics of the residential impact, (2) to find ways to bring the full power of this influence to bear on student learning and cognitive development, and (3) to develop policies and programs that bring the educational equivalent of the residence experience more within the reach of commuting students.

References

Anderson, K. "Post-High School Experiences and College Attrition." *Sociology of Education,* 1981, *54,* 20.

Astin, A. "The Measured Effects of Higher Education." *Annals of the American Academy of Political and Social Science,* 1972, *404,* 1–20.

Astin, A. *Preventing Students from Dropping Out: A Longitudinal, Multi Institutional Study of College Dropouts.* San Francisco: Jossey-Bass, 1975.

Astin, A. *Four Critical Years: Effects of College on Beliefs, Attitudes, and Knowledge.* San Francisco: Jossey-Bass, 1977.

Astin, A. *Minorities in American Higher Education: Recent Trends, Current Prospects, and Recommendations.* San Francisco: Jossey-Bass, 1982.

Astin, A. *Achieving Educational Excellence: A Critical Assessment of Priorities and Practices in Higher Education.* San Francisco: Jossey-Bass, 1985.

Astin, A. *What Matters in College? Four Critical Years Revisited.* San Francisco: Jossey-Bass, 1992.

Baird, L. "The Effects of College Residence Groups on Students' Self-Concepts, Goals, and Achievements." *Personnel and Guidance Journal,* 1969, *47,* 1015–1021.

Ballou, R. "An Analysis of Freshman Students' Perceptions of the Living Environment: Behavior and Academic Achievement in the Residence Systems of Twelve Colleges and Universities." Unpublished doctoral dissertation, Department of Guidance and Counseling, Purdue University, 1984. *Dissertation Abstracts International,* 1985, *45,* 1989A.

Ballou, R. "Freshmen in College Residence Halls: A Study of Freshman Perceptions of Residence Hall Social Climates at Ten Colleges and Universities." *Journal of College and University Student Housing,* 1986, *16,* 7–12.

Barnes, S. "An Evaluation of the 1971–72 Live and Learn Program and Its Effect on Residence Hall Social Ecology, Academic Achievement, Interpersonal Growth, and Study and Communication Skills Development of University of Oregon Freshmen." Unpublished doctoral dissertation, Department of Higher Education, University of Oregon, 1977. *Dissertation Abstracts International,* 1977, *38*(3), 1242A.

Baxter Magolda, M. "Comparing Open-Ended Interviews and Standardized Measures of Intellectual Development." *Journal of College Student Personnel,* 1987, *28,* 443–448.

Beal, P., and Williams, D. *An Experiment with Mixed-Class Housing Assignments at the University of Oregon.* Eugene, Oreg.: Student Housing Research, Research and Information Committee, Association of College and University Housing Officers, 1968.

Berdie, R. "College Expectations, Experiences, and Perceptions." *Journal of College Student Personnel,* 1966, *7,* 335–344.

Billson, J., and Terry, M. "In Search of the Silken Purse: Factors in Attrition Among First-Generation Students." *College and University,* 1982, *58,* 57–75.

Blimling, G. "A Meta-Analysis of the Influence of College Residence Halls in Academic Performance." *Journal of College Student Development,* 1989, *30,* 298–308.

Blimling, G. "The Influence of College Residence Halls on Students." In J. Smart (ed.), *Higher Education: Handbook of Theory and Research.* New York: Agathon Press, 1993.

Blimling, G., and Hample, D. "Structuring the Peer Environment in Residence Halls to Increase Academic Performance in Average-Ability Students." *Journal of College Student Personnel,* 1979, *20,* 310–316.

Burtner, R., and Tincher, W. "A Study of Resident and Nonresident Students at Auburn University." Unpublished manuscript, Auburn University, 1979. (ED 172 664)

Cade, S. "A Comparison of the Developmental Impact of Homogeneous and Heterogeneous Housing Conditions on Freshmen." *Journal of College and University Student Housing,* 1979, *9,* 18–21.

Call, R. "A Comparison of Resident Students' Quality Point Averages with Those of Commuting Students." Unpublished manuscript, 1974. (ED 094 809)

Centra, J. "Student Perceptions of Residence Hall Environments: Living Learning vs. Conventional Units." *Journal of College Student Personnel,* 1968, *9,* 266–272.

Chapple, J. "Freshmen Housing Assignments: A Road to Student Retention." *Journal of College Admissions,* 1984, *102,* 27–28.

Cheslin, S. "The Differential Effects of Housing on College Freshmen." Unpublished doctoral dissertation, Department of Education, Michigan State University, 1967. *Dissertation Abstracts International,* 1967, *28,* 1675A.

Chickering, A. *Commuting Versus Resident Students.* San Francisco: Jossey-Bass, 1974.

Chickering, A., and Kuper, E. "Educational Outcomes for Commuters and Residents." *Educational Record,* 1971, *52,* 255–261.

Chickering, A., McDowell, J., and Campagna, D. "Institutional Differences and Student Development." *Journal of Educational Psychology,* 1969, *60,* 315–326.

Clark, J., and others. "Freshman Residential Programs: Effects of Living-Learning Structure, Faculty Involvement, and Thematic Focus." *Journal of College and University Student Housing,* 1988, *18,* 7–13.

Croake, J., Hansen, L., and Kirkland, K. "Personality and Campus Residential Selection." *Journal of College and University Student Housing,* 1980, *10,* 25–29.

Dailey, D., and Stafford, T. "Coed and Single Sex Living Environments: A Study of Changes at NCSUI." Unpublished manuscript, North Carolina State University, 1975. (ED 169 845)

DeCoster, D. "Housing Assignments for High Ability Students." *Journal of College Student Personnel,* 1966, *7,* 19–22.

DeCoster, D. "Effects of Homogeneous Housing Assignments for High Ability Students." *Journal of College Student Personnel,* 1968, *2,* 75–78.

Dollar, R. "Student Characteristics and Choice of Housing." *Journal of College Student Personnel,* 1966, *7,* 147–150.

Duncan, C., and Stoner, K. "The Academic Achievement of Residents Living in a Scholar Residence Hall." *Journal of College and University Student Housing,* 1976, *6,* 7–9.

Elton, C., and Bate, W. "The Effect of Housing Policy on Grade-Point Average." *Journal of College Student Personnel,* 1966, *7,* 73–77.

Everett, C. *An Analysis of Student Attrition at Penn State.* University Park: Office of Planning and Budget, Pennsylvania State University, 1979.

Felver, J. "A Longitudinal Study of the Effects of Living/Learning Programs." Unpublished doctoral dissertation, Northern Illinois University, 1983. *Dissertation Abstracts International,* 1983, *44*(12), 3607A.

Foster, M., Sedlacek, M., and Hardwick, M. "Student Recreation: A Comparison of Commuter and Resident Students." Unpublished manuscript, University of Maryland, 1977. (ED 165 531)

Frichette, S. "Factors Associated with the Social Climate of Single-Sex and Coeducational Residence Halls, Cooperatives, Fraternities, and Sororities on the Oregon State University Campus." Unpublished doctoral dissertation, Department of

Education, Oregon State University, 1976. *Dissertation Abstracts International*, 1976, *31*(1), 146A.

Goebel, J. "Alienation in Dormitory Life." Unpublished doctoral dissertation, Department of Social Psychology, Texas Christian University, 1977. *Dissertation Abstracts International*, 1977, *38*(1), 415B.

Goetz, S. "Authoritarianism and Ego Development in Four-Year and Two-Year College Students: A One-Year Impact Study." Unpublished doctoral dissertation, Department of Educational Psychology, University of Washington, 1983. *Dissertation Abstracts International*, 1983, *44*(8), 2414A.

Hawkins, L. "A Comparative Analysis of Selected Academic and Nonacademic Characteristics of Undergraduate Students at Purdue University by Type of Housing." Unpublished doctoral dissertation, Department of Guidance and Counseling, Purdue University, 1980. *Dissertation Abstracts International*, 1980, *41*(6-A), 2451. (University Microfilms No. 8027, 284.)

Hebert, D. "The Relationship Between the Percentage of Freshmen on a Residence Hall Corridor and the Grade Point Averages of the Occupants." *College and University*, 1966, *41*, 348–352.

Herndon, S. "Recent Findings Concerning the Relative Importance of Housing to Student Retention." *Journal of College and University Student Housing*, 1984, *14*, 27–31.

Hountras, P., and Brandt, K. "Relation of Student Residence to Academic Performance in College." *Journal of Educational Research*, 1970, *63*, 351–354.

Howell, L., Perkins, M., and Young, S. "Characteristics of Student Persisters and Non-Persisters at Old Dominion University." Unpublished manuscript, Old Dominion University, 1979. (ED 180 366)

Hunter, J. "A Comparison of the Academic Achievement of Sophomores Living in University Residence Halls with That of Sophomores Living Off-Campus in Selected State Universities in North Carolina." Unpublished doctoral dissertation, Department of Higher Education, Duke University, 1977. *Dissertation Abstracts International*, 1977, *38*(8), 4604A.

Jacokes, L. "Coeducational and Single Sex Residence Halls: An

Experimental Comparison." Unpublished doctoral dissertation, Department of Social Psychology, Michigan State University, 1976. *Dissertation Abstracts International,* 1976, *36*(9), 4755B.

Katz, J., and Associates. *No Time for Youth: Growth and Constraint in College Students.* San Francisco: Jossey-Bass, 1968.

Kitchener, K., and King, P. "Reflective Judgment: Concepts of Justification and Their Relationship to Age and Education." *Journal of Applied Developmental Psychology,* 1981, *2,* 89–116.

Kuder, J. "A Comparative Study of Selected Characteristics of Junior and Senior Male University Students Residing in Fraternities and Residence Halls at Oregon State University." Unpublished doctoral dissertation, Department of Education, Oregon State University, 1970. *Dissertation Abstracts International,* 1970, *30*(10), 4244A.

Kuh, G., Schuh, J., Whitt, E., and Associates. *Involving Colleges: Successful Approaches to Fostering Student Learning and Development Outside the Classroom.* San Francisco: Jossey-Bass, 1991.

Lacy, W. "Interpersonal Relationships as Mediators of Structural Effects: College Student Socialization in a Traditional and an Experimental University Environment." *Sociology of Education,* 1978, *51,* 201–211.

Lemoal, M. "Residents and Commuters: A Study of Change in Attitudes, Values, and Personality Factors." Unpublished doctoral dissertation, Department of Higher Education, Columbia University Teachers College, 1980. *Dissertation Abstracts International,* 1980, *41*(4), 1429A.

Levin, B., and Clowes, D. "The Effect of Residence Hall Living at College on Attainment of the Baccalaureate Degree." *Journal of College Student Personnel,* 1982, *23,* 99–104.

Light, R. *The Harvard Assessment Seminars: First Report.* Cambridge, Mass.: Graduate School of Education, Harvard University, 1990.

Light, R., Singer, J., and Willett, J. *By Design: Planning Research on Higher Education.* Cambridge, Mass.: Harvard University Press, 1990.

Lincoln, Y., and Guba, E. *Naturalistic Inquiry.* Newbury Park, Calif.: Sage, 1985.

Linn, R. and Werts, C. "Assumptions in Making Causal Inferences from Part Correlations, Partial Correlations, and

Partial Regression Coefficients." *Psychological Bulletin,* 1969, *72,* 307–310.

Lundgren, D., and Schwab, M. "The Impact of College on Students: Residential Context, Relations with Parents and Peers, and Self-Esteem." *Youth and Society,* 1979, *10,* 227–236.

McKelfresh, D. "The Effect of Living Environments on Engineering Students." *Journal of College and University Student Housing,* 1980, *10,* 16–18.

Madson, D., Kuder, J., Hartanov, T., and McKelfresh, D. "Residential Academic Groupings — A Program Evaluation." *Journal of College and University Student Housing,* 1976, *6,* 16–20.

Magnarella, P. "The University of Vermont's Living-Learning Center: A First-Year Appraisal." *Journal of College Student Personnel,* 1976, *16,* 300–305.

Marron, J., and Kayson, W. "Effects of Living Status, Gender, and Year in College on College Students." *Psychological Reports,* 1984, *55,* 811–814.

Matteson, D. "Changes in Attitudes Toward Authority Figures with the Move to College: Three Experiments." *Developmental Psychology,* 1974, *10,* 340–347.

May, E. "Type of Housing and Achievement of Disadvantaged University Students." *College Student Journal,* 1974, *8,* 48–51.

Moen, J. "Academic Classification: A Factor in Assignment of Residence Halls Roommates." *Journal of College and University Student Housing,* 1989, *19,* 24–28.

Moffatt, M. *Coming of Age in New Jersey.* New Brunswick, N.J.: Rutgers University Press, 1989.

Moos, R., and Otto, J. "The Impact of Coed Living on Males and Females." *Journal of College Student Personnel,* 1975, *16,* 459–467.

Morishima, J. "Effects on Student Achievement of Residence Hall Groupings Based on Academic Majors." In C. Bagley (ed.), *Research on Academic Input: Proceedings of the Sixth Annual Forum of the Association for Institutional Research.* Cortland: State University of New York, 1966.

Mussano, F. "The Effects of a Compulsory On-Campus Residency Policy upon Academic Achievement for Freshmen." Unpublished manuscript, Nova University, 1976. (ED 129 378)

Nelson, J. "Institutional Assessment of a Private University by

Commuter and Resident Students." Unpublished doctoral dissertation, Department of Higher Education, University of Pittsburgh, 1981. *Dissertation Abstracts International,* 1982, *43,* 90A–91A.

Newcomb, T., and others. "Self-Selection and Change." In J. Gaff (ed.), *The Cluster College.* San Francisco: Jossey-Bass, 1970.

Newcomb, T., and others. "The University of Michigan's Residential College." In P. Dressel (ed.), *The New Colleges: Toward an Appraisal.* Iowa City, Iowa: American College Testing Program and American Association for Higher Education, 1971.

Nosow, S. "An Attitudinal Comparison of Residential College Seniors with Other Seniors." *Journal of College Student Personnel,* 1975, *16,* 17–23.

Nowack, K., and Hanson, A. "Academic Achievement of Freshmen as a Function of Residence Hall Housing." *NASPA Journal,* 1985, *22,* 22–28.

Pascarella, E. "Reassessing the Effects of Living on Campus Versus Commuting to College: A Causal Modeling Approach." *Review of Higher Education,* 1984, *7,* 247–260.

Pascarella, E. "The Influence of On-Campus Living Versus Commuting to College on Intellectual and Interpersonal Self-Concept." *Journal of College Student Personnel,* 1985a, *26,* 292–299.

Pascarella, E. "Students' Affective Development Within the College Environment." *Journal of Higher Education,* 1985b, *56,* 640–663.

Pascarella, E., and Chapman, D. "Validation of a Theoretical Model of College Withdrawal: Interaction Effects in a Multi-Institutional Sample." *Research in Higher Education,* 1983, *19,* 25–48.

Pascarella, E., and Terenzini, P. "Student-Faculty and Student-Peer Relationships as Mediators of the Structural Effects of Undergraduate Residence Arrangement." *Journal of Educational Research,* 1980, *73,* 344–353.

Pascarella, E., and Terenzini, P. "Residence Arrangement, Student/Faculty Relationships, and Freshman-Year Educational Outcomes." *Journal of College Student Personnel,* 1981, *22,* 147–156.

Pascarella, E., and Terenzini, P. *How College Affects Students: Findings and Insights from Twenty Years of Research.* San Francisco: Jossey-Bass, 1991.

Pascarella, E., and others. "Cognitive Impacts of Living on Campus Versus Commuting to College." *Journal of College Student Development*, 1993, *34*, 216–220.

Pemberton, C. "An Evaluation of a Living-Learning Residence Hall Program." Unpublished manuscript, 1969. (ED 077 399)

Perry, W. *Forms of Intellectual and Ethical Development in the College Years.* Troy, Mo.: Holt, Rinehart & Winston, 1970.

Rest, J., and Deemer, D. "Life Experiences and Developmental Pathways." In J. Rest (ed.), *Moral Development: Advances in Research and Theory.* New York: Praeger, 1986.

Ryan, J. "College Freshman and Living Arrangements." *NASPA Journal*, 1970, *8*, 127–130.

Schoemer, J., and McConnell, W. "Is There a Case for the Freshman Women's Residence Hall?" *Personnel and Guidance Journal*, 1970, *49*, 35–40.

Scholz, N. "Attitudes of Women Students Toward Residence Hall Experiences at the University of Georgia: A Comparison of an Honor Hall and Conventional Halls." Unpublished doctoral dissertation, Department of Higher Education, University of Georgia, 1970. *Dissertation Abstracts International*, 1970, *11*, 5780A.

Schroeder, C., and Belmonte, A. "The Influence of Residential Environment on Pre-pharmacy Student Achievement." *American Journal of Pharmaceutical Education*, 1979, *43*, 16–18.

Schroeder, C., and Griffin, C. "A Novel Living-Learning Environment for Freshman Engineering Students." *Engineering Education*, 1977, *67*, 159–161.

Simono, R., Wachowiak, D., and Furr, S. "Student Living Environments and Their Perceived Impact on Academic Performance: A Brief Follow-up." *Journal of College and University Student Housing*, 1984, *14*, 22–24.

Stewart, G. "How Honors Students' Academic Achievement Relates to Housing." *Journal of College and University Student Housing*, 1980, *10*, 26–28.

Stockham, D. "A Comparison of Attitudes Between Students Living in Coeducational and Non-Coeducational Housing and a Pre and Post Assessment of Academic Performance of Coed Residents." Unpublished doctoral dissertation, Department of Higher Education, University of Kentucky, 1974. (University Microfilms No. 75-05, 857.)

Streeter, R. "Relationship of Social Interaction and Housing Facility Types to Academic Achievement Among Selected High-Ability Male College Freshmen." Unpublished doctoral dissertation, Department of Higher Education, University of Miami, 1972. *Dissertation Abstracts International,* 1972, *33,* 2741A.

Suczek, R. *The Best Laid Plans.* San Francisco: Jossey-Bass, 1972.

Sullivan, K., and Sullivan, A. "Adolescent-Parent Separation." *Developmental Psychology,* 1980, *16,* 93–98.

Taylor, R., and Hanson, G. "Environmental Impact on Achievement and Study Habits." *Journal of College Student Personnel,* 1971, *12,* 445–454.

Tinto, V. *Leaving College: Rethinking the Causes and Cures of Student Attrition.* Chicago: University of Chicago Press, 1987.

Vander Wall, W. "A Comparison of College Environmental Perceptions, Academic Achievement, and Attrition of Student Participants and Non-Participants in a Special University Living-Learning Residence Hall Program." Unpublished doctoral dissertation, Department of Higher Education, North Carolina State University at Raleigh, 1972. *Dissertation Abstracts International,* 1972, *33,* 4134A.

Velez, W. "Finishing College: The Effects of College Type." *Sociology of Education,* 1985, *58,* 191–200.

Viehe, J. "A Study of Selected Determinants and an Outcome of the Student Subculture Within University Residence Halls." Unpublished doctoral dissertation, Department of Agricultural Education, North Carolina State University at Raleigh, 1978. *Dissertation Abstracts International,* 1977, *38*(10), 5852A.

Washington, C. "All-Freshman Residence Halls: Do They Make a Difference?" Unpublished manuscript, 1969. (ED 123 524)

Welty, J. "The Impact of the Residence Hall, Off-Campus, and Commuter Living Situations on College Freshmen." Unpublished doctoral dissertation, Department of Higher Education, Indiana University, 1974. *Dissertation Abstracts International,* 1974, *35*(9), 5879A.

Welty, J. "Resident and Commuter Students: Is It Only the Living Situation?" *Journal of College Student Personnel,* 1976, *17,* 465–468.

Three

Creating a
Context for
Educational Success

Richard Stimpson

Residence hall environments and programs significantly enhance the educational experience of college students. As emphasized in Chapter Two,

- Not all learning occurs in the classroom or as a result of formal structured academic experiences. Learning also occurs as students go about the business of daily living; much of it takes place in a residence hall or as a result of interaction with fellow residents.
- The quality of out-of-class educational experiences is enhanced when residence hall environments are carefully developed and programs available in residence halls are thoughtfully implemented. And these experiences are most successful when students, faculty, and residence hall staff deliberately join together to formulate educational initiatives.

This book shows how residence hall experiences can be enhanced and how students, faculty, and staff can collaborate to improve the quality of the educational environment within these facilities. But a constructive educational program will not emerge and cannot be maintained unless a proper setting for success has been established. Valuable insights into the characteristics of well-organized residence hall programs are provided by the *CAS Housing and Residential Life Programs Self Assessment Guide* developed by the Council for the Advancement of Standards (Miller, Thomas, Looney, and Yerian, 1988) and the *Standards for College and University Student Housing* developed by the Association of College and University Housing Officers–International (1991). Additional useful information is presented in DeCoster and Mable (1980) and Winston, Anchors, and Associates (1993).

While many factors contribute to the proper management of an undergraduate residential environment, some are more critical than others. This chapter presents six elements essential to the successful implementation of an educational program in residence halls. These elements are (1) fulfilling basic residence hall functions, (2) establishing appropriate educational initiatives, (3) participating in institutional management and governance forums, (4) maintaining enough support to ensure program success, (5) articulating expectations clearly, and (6) implementing an assessment and evaluation plan.

Fulfilling Basic Residence Hall Functions

Residence hall staff and their campus colleagues interested in promoting residentially based educational programs must recognize that they will receive little support from the larger campus community and, in particular, from residents, parents, and administrators if essential "housing" services are not effectively provided. Students begin their residence hall experience with a basic expectation that living environments

- Are reasonably well maintained, with equipment in proper operating order and furnishings in place.
- Are kept clean; repairs should be accomplished in a timely manner.
- Include the equipment, programs, and services necessary to provide reasonable levels of safety, security, and public health.
- Include opportunities to meet fellow students, establish positive roommate relationships, and become a responsible community member.

Residence hall supervisors and campus administrators share these expectations and further assume that

- Disciplinary processes, which include clearly stated and communicated rules as well as an effective hearing process, are maintained.
- Facilities renewal and long-term facilities development plans are in place.
- The relationships, duty systems, and training programs necessary to provide effective response to emergencies and crises exist.
- Procedures exist to ensure that necessary information can be communicated to residents in a timely manner.
- Staff are properly selected, trained, and evaluated.

These lists could be expanded. The exact content is not as important as the basic point that clear expectations should exist for residence hall staff performance. These expectations must be met before the educational environment in residence halls can be enhanced. Most faculty, students, and parents assume that staff have been hired to meet basic expectations such as those noted above, not to contribute directly to the educational mission of the university or college.

As noted in Chapter One, the predecessors of current residence hall staff were appointed to relieve faculty living in dormitories of the oversight and disciplinary responsibilities they had assumed during much of higher education's history, not to play a role in achieving the instructional or academic mission of the institution. Some faculty colleagues and campus administrators have grasped the educational potential of college residence halls and have helped the residence halls realize that potential. At the same time, however, they have insisted that the residence halls carry out their basic responsibilities — and do so as a first priority.

Over twenty years ago, Riker and DeCoster (1971, p. 6) outlined the range of functions or "levels" one might expect to see as objectives for a college housing program. They included:

Level One	Provision of a satisfactory physical environment through new construction and renovation	
Level Two	Adequate care and maintenance of the physical facilities	Management Functions
Level Three	Establishment of guidelines that provide structure for compatible and cooperative community living	
Level Four	Development of an interpersonal environment that reflects responsible citizenship and a concern for others, as well as an atmosphere conducive to learning	Educational Functions
Level Five	Opportunities for individual growth and development	

Source: Riker and DeCoster, 1971, p. 6. Used by permission.

While these authors stress that all the functions are essential to the success of the residence hall program and that they are "interrelated and interdependent," each level represents a somewhat distinct set of student needs. Success at any one level will depend to a large degree on how well student needs are fulfilled at lower levels. We are unlikely to engender much interest in educational or cultural programs (Level 4), for example, if students are pre-occupied with excessive noise in their residential unit (Level 3), or if they perceive their physical environment as grossly inadequate (Level 1) (p. 5).

Campus colleagues, as well as students and parents, will be much more willing to support efforts to promote the educational potential of college residence halls if the residence hall staff have established a reputation for carrying out their basic responsibilities effectively. Sophisticated residence hall staff realize that as they handle these responsibilities, there are opportunities to establish working relationships with faculty and academic services staff. These contacts will help set the stage for future involvement in more complex educational initiatives. Residence hall staff should take advantage of opportunities to demonstrate how they and academic personnel can work together to promote the achievement of the institution's educational mission. For example:

• As residence hall staff develop handbooks and posters or organize floor meetings to encourage campus involvement, they should be sure to include information on academic clubs, internships, service organizations, and so on. Faculty committed to the success of these activities within their academic discipline will appreciate the support. Further, when students ask about involvement, resident assistants can inquire about the student's major and encourage participation in relevant activities and programs sponsored by the student's college or academic department.

• As faculty or academic departments develop plans for the visit of a noteworthy scholar, specific opportunities for the guest's informal involvement with a group of students within the residence hall community should be included. This experience could be arranged by a faculty member and hall staff member, with the staff member responsible for completing a space reservation and handling setup tasks and the faculty member providing introductions and group discussion leadership.

Cooperative undertakings such as these illustrate to residents that their education is important to staff and faculty alike and that activities within the residence hall environment can contribute to their educational experience. Such involvement can be accomplished without neglecting basic responsibilities assigned to hall staff or faculty. Most important, they help create effective working relationships between faculty and staff. These relationships will prove helpful as faculty and staff attempt to develop and implement the more complex and integrative educational experiences discussed throughout this book.

Establishing Appropriate Educational Initiatives

Staff, faculty, and students involved in developing or enhancing programs in residence halls should make sure that their goals are consistent with the academic/educational mission of the institution. In his provocative article "College Residence Halls: In Search of Educational Leadership," Stamatakos (1984, p. 81) notes that "we know that to bring about maximum positive growth and development in young people, it is necessary that formal and informal instruction, life-styles, opportunities for change, and the entire spirit of the environment be reasonably if not highly congruent with a pervasive, persuasive, and sensitively communicated institutional purpose." In short, the educational mission for residence halls should be compatible with the institution's undergraduate agenda and not peripheral to its educational priorities.

Each institution has a particular educational character — the academic emphasis it wishes to pursue and the experiences it wishes to provide to its students. In some instances, the institution's educational mission is not explicitly defined or overtly articulated. However, public statements by campus leaders, periodic reports to governing boards, published information in recruitment materials or student handbooks, a review of the institution's founding and history, and visits with senior faculty will reveal implicitly, if not explicitly, what the institution and its leadership seek to achieve. To be most successful, both in terms of impact on residents and from the standpoint of securing support within the institution, residence hall educational programs should reflect appropriate elements of the institution's mission.

Many residence hall programs are in place because they are the types of activities students express interest in, because staff feel they are important to the growth and welfare of students, and/or because they help meet an expectation that individual staff members (for example, resident assistants) offer a certain number of programs each year. While such programs are valuable for student or residential community development, they should not be promoted as being a part of the educational enterprise unless they are clearly related to the overall mission of the institution and have the understanding and support of the academic community. For instance, although programs devoted to responsible drinking or the issue of date rape may help promote mature and responsible resident behavior, neither of these activities should be viewed as directly contributing to the institution's academic mission. In contrast, a session involving residents and a campus art professor designed to examine student perceptions of an exhibit at a local gallery helps meet the institution's mission to advance students' education in the liberal arts.

Striving to ensure that residentially based educational programs are extensions of the overall mission of the institution does not diminish the importance of more traditional residence hall programs. In fact, members of the academic community should be encouraged to recognize that these undertakings contribute to the achievement of the institution's educational efforts. For example, residence hall staff should try to help faculty and institutional leaders understand that residence hall programs as basic and seemingly nonacademic as safety and security programs are a fundamental part of achieving the educational mission. Students will be hesitant to make full use of libraries and computer facilities or attend lectures and cultural events sponsored by academic departments if they do not believe they can do so safely. Residence hall–based programs often help residents develop the knowledge necesary to feel comfortable on campus. Similarly, programs designed to establish and maintain civil living environments, promote respect for individual differences, and encourage students to feel socially included within their peer environment contribute to the comfort level of residents and, in turn, to student retention.

Participating in Institutional
Management and Governance Forums

Staff, faculty, and administrators who wish to promote the quality of the educational environment within residence halls must actively participate in the management and governance processes of the institution. Such involvement will help ensure that the stated educational purpose of the institution reflects an understanding of how residence halls contribute to students' academic success and enrich their educational experience. The involvement of staff, faculty, and administrators in the institution's management process will also make it easier to implement successful educational programs in the residence hall setting.

There are many opportunities to become involved and to help promote the educational mission of the institution. For example:

- Institutions formulate and periodically review their long-range strategic plans and related goals and objectives. There are frequently opportunities for committee membership and usually opportunities to review and comment on drafts of planning documents.
- Each institution has a governance structure (campus senate or faculty council) that provides input to senior administrators and helps shape campus issues or agendas. As a part of that structure, standing committees and issue-specific work groups are often formed. In most instances, opportunities for membership in such groups exist.
- Various departments and units throughout the institution form committees or task groups to assist in the implementation of activities or programs necessary to achieve educational goals. For example, admissions staff seek help with recruitment, orientation requires coordination by many agencies, welcoming convocations need to be planned and implemented, and staff responsible for major speaker series often need input and support.

The list of such opportunities could be expanded, since, as Garland (1985, p. 66) argues, "Now more than ever, conditions argue for a greater integration of academic and student life. Concern for academic quality, attention to the needs of diverse student groups, and efforts to manage enrollments all argue for coordinated responses. Furthermore, growing concern for the quality of the academic experience argues for coordinated responses. The coordination of all campus professionals to address these concerns and conditions provides significant motivation for greater campus integration."

Specific opportunities will vary from campus to campus. But it is important to identify these opportunities and actively participate. Although the agenda may not be related specifically to the residence hall mission or goals, being included will ultimately prove valuable. Interacting with faculty and academic administrators will present opportunities to discuss residence hall programs and priorities, to provide information and answer questions about residents and their community, and to explore ideas or suggestions that residence hall staff or others may have for the development of expanded educational initiatives within the residential environment. Such undertakings can contribute to enrollment management, support retention initiatives, and improve the quality of faculty-student interaction outside the classroom.

By working within the campus community and helping its members understand the educational contributions of residence halls, residence hall staff can win support from key campus leaders and encourage them to invest additional resources in support of these contributions. In addition, chief student affairs officers and key department or unit heads are frequently in situations where they can influence institutional decision making. Keeping these individuals informed so they can be effective advocates for residence hall goals and initiatives helps focus interest and promote support. As they participate in campus forums, these individuals, as well as residence hall staff, should look for opportunities to directly involve the administrative and governance processes of the institution in the development of the residence hall program.

One such undertaking occurred at the University of Maryland, College Park, in the late 1980s when President William E. Kirwan accepted a proposal submitted by the Division of Student Affairs to appoint a campus committee charged with improving the academic environment in residence halls. Referred to as the Academic Environment in Campus Residence Halls Committee, this high-profile group was co-chaired by an assistant vice president from student affairs and the dean for undergraduate studies. Committee members included respected senior faculty members, residence hall student representatives, and selected residence hall staff members, including the director of residence life.

A significant outcome of the committee's deliberations was a statement designed to provide focus to the development of educational programs in residence halls. Recognizing the mix of personal, social, and educational activities important to residents, the statement explained that

> while programs to improve the academic climate must consider both student social agendas and the effects of a crowded physical environment, the institution should generate — should insist upon — a strong commitment to expectations and mutual obligations supporting the primacy of the life of mind.
>
> Students must know about the special nature of outstanding universities, and this university in particular. They must be persuaded that the task of collecting, preserving, expanding, transforming, and disseminating information is precious work — and that life in the residence halls is important to that work. Programs that reward contemplation, that invite faculty contact with students, that complement curricular demands, that stimulate intellectual discourse must be integrated within the mainstream of any social compact we make with those who would reside there. . . . We suggest a three-pronged strategic approach. The first (Community Formation) would fashion a community characterized by behavior and norms that value and contribute to academic achievement. The second (Curricular Support) would aid student efforts in completing their curricular requirements. And the third (Educational Enhancement) would create (and maintain) a residential setting in which students can improve their understanding of the contingent natures of their studies, increase their appreciation of individual dif-

ferences, improve their ability to function fully and effectively as citizens, hone their appreciation for the arts, and generally inspire their imaginations. . . . Initiatives aimed at improving the academic environment will not achieve their full potential if they do not take the social environment, which is a natural feature of residence halls, into consideration. In addition, such initiatives must be the result of a partnership among students, Resident Life staff, faculty, and University administrators if they are to be successful [Academic Environment in Campus Residence Halls Committee, 1990, pp. 5–8].

The committee recommended various initiatives to create the effective educational environment it envisioned. Steps taken have included developing a student desk calendar with suggestions for "academic success," establishing a "residential scholars" hall where faculty are involved in academically related activities within the residence hall environment, designating budgetary support for resident- or faculty-initiated programs that have an educationally related set of goals, and encouraging the "living-learning" programs (such as the Honors Living/Learning Center, Language House, and International House) described in Chapter Seven.

While the goals and programs will vary from institution to institution, the important point is that when the governance processes of the institution are invested in the development of residence hall environments and encourage initiatives for action, residence hall programs will be more clearly recognized as key contributors to the institution's educational mission. Hall staff will gain credibility and, because they are broadly embraced by the community at large, will be more likely to receive resources and other support for specific educational endeavors.

Maintaining Enough Support
to Ensure Program Success

Residence hall staff should make sure that the resources needed to accomplish educational initiatives are available. Such support is critical; program implementation should not be pursued unless the necessary resources are at hand. Without such support, programs will not meet expectations, staff will be frustrated, students will be disappointed and skeptical, and faculty will lose interest. Being willing to delay implementation until support is in place is particularly challenging for residence hall staff because they tend to be idealistic, often blessed with youthful enthusiasm, and more often than not willing to "make do." However, rather than behaving as if resource support is not important or risking failure due to inadequate support, staff should formulate a set of goals and priorities, implement programs that can be done well, and use those initial successes as a basis for obtaining support for more ambitious programs. Strategic planning and implementation are needed, not wishful thinking that available resources will somehow be sufficient.

The degree and type of support necessary will vary depending on the characteristics of the program. It is beyond the purpose of this chapter to examine the specific types of support needed for every type of program. However, the following points deserve consideration.

• Clearly articulated support from campus leaders is necessary to encourage the involvement of faculty and to obtain funds. Leaders who should make their support clear to the campus community include the president, provost, vice presidents, deans, senior faculty leaders (including those who are involved in campus governance or who have previously participated in educational programs), student leaders, and residence hall administrators.

• Adequate facilities are essential. Meeting rooms, faculty offices, study rooms, computer networks, audiovisual equipment, room furnishings, and so on must be provided. Many residence halls were built only to provide housing for students. They do not include the space and technology necessary to support a broad-based educational program. For some initiatives to succeed, investments in residence hall space modifications and major renovation will be necessary.

• There need to be sufficient staff resources to meet program goals. The credentials, training, and supervision of residence hall staff must be formulated to support the educational programs selected for implementation. Job descriptions need to clarify expectations related to educational programming. Staff should have opportunities to develop the skills and knowledge necessary to design and implement programs. These include skills in organizing, publicizing, and evaluating as well as knowledge about campus resources and personnel available for use in program implementation. Faculty and staff from supporting agencies must be available and have the time and commitment necessary for success.

• Operating budgets must be adequate to provide the supplies, materials, honoraria, and audiovisual support needed for program success. Sufficient funds may be necessary to pay for incentives (such as food or the cost of transportation to a local museum or theater) that encourage participation. This is particularly desirable when programs are new or occur early in the academic year, when new residents have to be encouraged to participate. Resources should also be available to properly recognize faculty, hall staff, and student leaders responsible for the success of these endeavors. When budgets are in a steady state or declining, priorities need to be established and the timing of the implementation of various objectives adjusted. If budgets are reduced, specific initiatives can be removed from the program and be reintroduced when funding is restored or other resources become available.

• A less tangible but equally important factor is the deliberate structuring of program continuity as involved faculty, staff, and students pursue other priorities, leave campus employment, or graduate. The transfer of responsibilities, training and orientation of new team members, and proper recognition of those departing are all essential aspects of a well-developed management plan that accommodates change in personnel.

Articulating Expectations Clearly

Educators have long known that student participation and learning occur most effectively when expectations are clearly articulated (Study Group on the Conditions of Excellence in American Higher Education, 1984). The same holds true for educational programs provided within the residential setting. Clarifying expectations is a key element of program success. Beginning with early communication with prospective residents and continuing through opening-day check-in, a well-crafted marketing effort should be in place. Such an undertaking should present an overview of what the residence hall program offers and explain what will be expected of residents as well as what they will need to do to take full advantage of the educational program in residence halls.

Those involved in shaping and implementing the educational program should explain the characteristics of the various residential environments (for example, international or foreign language halls, quiet hours floors, honors or academic scholars units) and how each is designed to contribute to a student's educational success. Opportunities for interaction with faculty and other campus educational or cultural offerings should be discussed. Residents should be encouraged to recognize how involvement in various experiences will contribute to their overall academic and social success. As emphasized in Chapter Nine, the diverse nature of the residence population and the value of such diversity to the learning experience should also be articulated.

Students need to understand that they are members of an educational community and that their actions influence how much they and others will benefit from the residence hall experience (Chickering and Reisser, 1993). They should know that residence hall staff believe that each resident's active involvement in programs and activities will enrich the experience for others as well as the participating individual. Residents need to recognize that their exercise of personal freedom must occur within reasonable limits so that the ability of others to study, rest, and participate is not inappropriately disrupted or compromised. They should be encouraged to reflect on and accept Boyer's (1987, p. 206) point that "in a community of learning, as in any community, we need a sense of order to protect the requirements of all, while still respecting the dignity and rights of individuals." Students should also be encouraged to exercise their responsibilities as community citizens (for example, by participating in governance opportunities or offering suggestions and feedback regarding services), much the way they might be expected to in society at large.

Implementing an Assessment and Evaluation Plan

To ensure that residentially based educational initiatives meet desired outcomes, the thoughtful assessment and evaluation of implementation strategies and program components must occur. The systematic collection and use of data will greatly contribute to the success of the initiatives. Therefore, as programs are being designed, assessment procedures for generating relevant information should be an integral component.

Assessment should measure resident satisfaction with the residence hall experience in general and how it contributes to overall educational success. Reactions to specific residence hall–based educational programming efforts are also valuable. Residents should be encouraged to suggest areas for improvement as well as new educational initiatives that they believe should be undertaken. As Garland (1985, p. 69) notes, when it is time to allocate limited resources, "those activities that succeed in fulfilling students' expressed needs and are consonant with institutional goals (such as retention) will be attractive to institutional leaders. Programs designed to meet students' expressed needs will be more justifiable to decision makers than programs designed to meet needs that are not self-reported."

As described in Chapters Two and Twelve, assessment efforts include multiple approaches such as standardized instruments, surveys, focus groups, telephone interviews, and so on. Specific assessment strategies should be developed cooperatively with hall staff, faculty, staff from other campus agencies (for example, counseling center, institutional research office), and student leaders. Including questions that reflect each group's interests or concerns will help ensure data credibility and the usefulness of results in shaping improvements or expanding programs.

Beyond the assessment of resident satisfaction and program effectiveness, evaluation efforts should examine how the involvement of residents in residence hall–based educational initiatives influences their view of the institution's overall educational program. As noted earlier, residence hall programs should be an outgrowth of the institution's mission. Residents involved in these programs should recognize relationships to their academic endeavors and have a more positive view of the quality of their academic experience as a result of such participation. Furthermore, evaluation data should demonstrate a positive impact on the academic success of residents who take part in residence hall–based initiatives. Comparative data should also demonstrate improved retention and graduation rates.

Conclusion

This chapter has described six key elements necessary for the success of residence hall–based educational endeavors. These elements form a foundation for specific educational programs developed and implemented on individual campuses and described in subsequent chapters of this book. While these programs will be tailored to the mission of each institution, their success and longevity are predicated on the degree to which the key elements discussed in this chapter are in place.

These elements can be summed up as follows: (1) primary residence hall functions must be successfully accomplished, (2) educational initiatives implemented within residence halls must be consistent with the institution's academic mission, (3) staff must be actively involved in and influence institutional management and governance processes on behalf of the educational agenda for residence halls, (4) sufficient support must be in place to ensure success, (5) residents must know what is expected of them and what they can expect, and (6) assessment and evaluation must occur to determine if goals are being met and to provide data to help support the achievement of the educational agenda. Without these elements in place, a foundation for success will not exist and the success of the residentially based educational opportunities discussed in this book will be difficult, if not impossible, to achieve.

References

Academic Environment in Campus Residence Halls Committee. *Report on Enhancement of the Academic Environment in Residence Halls.* College Park: University of Maryland, 1990.

Association of College and University Housing Officers–International. *Standards for College and University Student Housing.* (rev. ed.) Columbus, Ohio: Association of College and University Housing Officers–International, 1991.

Boyer, E. L. *College: The Undergraduate Experience in America.* New York: HarperCollins, 1987.

Chickering, A. W., and Reisser, L. *Education and Identity.* (2nd ed.) San Francisco: Jossey-Bass, 1993.

DeCoster, D. A., and Mable, P. (eds.). *Personal Education and Community Development in College Residence Halls.* Washington, D.C.: American College Personnel Association, 1980.

Garland, P. H. *Serving More Than Students: A Critical Need for College Student Personnel Services.* ASHE-ERIC Higher Education Report No. 7. Washington, D.C.: Association for the Study of Higher Education, 1985.

Miller, T. K., Thomas, W. L., Looney, S. C., and Yerian, J. M. (eds.). *CAS Housing and Residential Life Programs Self Assessment Guide.* Iowa City, Iowa: Council for the Advancement of Standards for Student Services/Development Programs, 1988.

Riker, H. C., and DeCoster, D. A. "The Educational Role in College Student Housing." *Journal of College and University Student Housing,* 1971, *1,* 3–7.

Stamatakos, L. C. "College Residence Halls: In Search of Educational Leadership." *Journal of College and University Student Housing,* 1984, *14,* 10–17.

Study Group on the Conditions of Excellence in American Higher Education. *Involvement in Learning.* Washington, D.C.: U.S. Department of Education, 1984.

Winston, R. B., Jr., Anchors, S., and Associates. *Student Housing and Residential Life: A Handbook for Professionals Committed to Student Development Goals.* San Francisco: Jossey-Bass, 1993.

Four

Achieving Curricular Objectives Through Residence Halls

John D. Welty

Higher education in America was established in the colonial period to prepare men for leadership positions as well as for the ministry. The Founding Fathers believed that the purposeful training of the leaders of the New World was crucial to the success of this new society. They assumed that there were certain basic tenets that every person in leadership should know. The American debate concerning what an individual must know to be an educated person got underway in this period and has continued with varying degrees of intensity ever since.

Provost William Smith at the College of Philadelphia let it be known that "thinking, writing, and acting well . . . is the grand aim of the liberal education" (Cheyney, 1940, p. 83). The early colonial colleges were founded on the conviction that the curriculum should not provide a narrow vocational education, but rather should promote a broad liberal arts education that enabled students to become fully educated men.

Over the years, the debate about the purposes and objectives of undergraduate education has continued. Significant events have caused administrators and faculty to frequently ponder the purpose of higher education and how that purpose should be achieved. This chapter examines these debates — with particular emphasis on the past fifteen years — and discusses ways residence halls can help meet current objectives for undergraduate education.

Evolution of Undergraduate Education

Higher education in the early 1800s was impacted by the War of 1812, declining enrollments, significant instability in knowledge, and rapid social and economic changes. These factors led to renewed thinking about the curriculum. The debate focused on the belief that colleges must become more utilitarian while maintaining an intellectual focus. Experimentation began to take place. The primary reformers who attempted to bring about these changes were Philip Lindsley of the University of Nashville, George Tickman of Harvard, James Marshall of the University of Vermont, and Jacob Abbott of Amherst. The influence of the German university system on these individuals led to the introduction of the sciences into the curriculum. In addition, courses with a utilitarian focus were added. Students could not be required to take all of these new courses in addition to the existing courses, so the system of elective courses began.

However, at the same time, the Yale Report of 1828 became a "classic statement in defense of the old order" (Rudolph, 1962, p. 130). Princeton joined Yale in combating the new movement toward elective subjects. During this period, the debate about what constituted an educated person again raged throughout higher education. The impact of the Yale Report was to ensure that real change in the college curriculum would not occur until after the Civil War. In the last decades of the nineteenth century, earlier proposals of Thomas Jefferson at the University of Virginia and others gained significant attention. The new emphasis on applied areas of study and the introduction of the sciences helped stimulate the Industrial Revolution.

The next significant period of change in undergraduate education was the unsettling period of the 1920s and 1930s. During this time, John Dewey's insistence that education and experience were the same thing won support. His concern over the mismatch between education and society also gained acceptance in higher education circles (Rudolph, 1962, p. 468). This so-called Progressive Movement brought disciplines together in new ways and gave rise to other methods of linking education and society.

Although it did not directly attack the Progressives, the report of the Harvard Committee on General Education and a Free Society, published in 1945, responded to the Progressives by again seeking to address the question of what an educated person ought to know (Rudolph, 1962, p. 474). The Progressive Movement spawned other responses, such as the Great Books approach to education, and intensified the debate about what an educated person should know and whether higher education should serve vocational ends.

The next significant period of debate concerning undergraduate education occurred in the aftermath of the Sputnik era, during the 1950s. Sputnik led to renewed attention to federal spending for research. The dramatic shift in favor of research rather than teaching in the sciences negatively impacted undergraduate teaching, leading to the formation of many irrelevant courses taught by poorly prepared teachers. This phenomenon, combined with the social unrest of the 1960s, contributed to a general disarray of undergraduate education in colleges and universities (Gaff, 1983).

The importance of general education in the undergraduate curriculum continued to decline in the 1970s as a result of several factors. First, a growing emphasis was placed on careerism and the need for students to pursue coursework that led to a specific, tangible career or job on completion of a degree. Second, colleges and universities admitted large numbers of students who, by earlier standards, were unprepared for higher education. Many institutions tended to stress job preparation or training — rather than a traditional liberal arts education — for these students. Finally, fiscal strains began to emerge that undermined efforts to focus more broadly on curriculum enhancements and reform.

However, with the advent of the 1980s, interest in general education began to blossom again. Some cynics suggested that this trend reflected "a way for faculty to hold on to jobs [or a] desire to return to an imagined golden age when a limited body of knowledge was shared by all educated persons" (Gaff, 1983, pp. 187–188). Nevertheless, there were real factors influencing the need to attend to general education. The concern for the declining number of students, the emphasis on improving quality, the need to deal with rapidly expanding amounts of knowledge, and the need to reduce the proliferation of courses in the curriculum were all factors spurring the renewed interest in general education. In addition, as noted in Chapter One, the attention focused on outcomes assessment and accountability at both the state and national levels brought increased attention to general education. This decade produced additional investigations of general education, which in turn resulted in several major reports.

The first major report — *To Reclaim a Legacy* (1984), by William J. Bennett, former chair of the National Endowment for the Humanities — sounded the alarm by indicating that "the humanities have been siphoned off, diluted, or so adulterated that students graduate knowing little of their heritage" (p. 1). The report further stressed that the humanities and Western civilization are no longer central to an undergraduate curriculum. It also stated that "a student can obtain a bachelor's degree in 75 percent of all American colleges and universities without having studied European History, from 72 percent without having studied American Literature or History, and from 86 percent without having studied the Civilization of Classical Greece and Rome" (p. 1). The report concluded that leaders of modern colleges and universities must develop a clear vision of the educated person. As before, the issue of what constitutes an educated person was at the center of the debate.

A second major report, *Involvement in Learning* (Study Group on the Conditions of Excellence in American Higher Education, 1984) stated that the university experience and general education were now characterized by "fragmented and limited knowledge" and that the bachelor's degree has "lost its potential to foster the shared values and knowledge that bind us together as a society" (p. 10). The report asserted that this is a new era in which excellence must be expected of all students and that educational effectiveness can be achieved by applying "existing knowledge about three critical conditions of excellence—(1) student involvement, (2) high expectations, [and] (3) assessment and feedback" (p. 17). This report identified several additional conditions that should be met to improve the undergraduate experience, and in particular general education. These conditions will be discussed later in this chapter.

The third major study of general education, conducted by the Carnegie Commission (Boyer, 1987), found that "general education is the neglected stepchild of the undergraduate experience" (p. 83). Interestingly, the study found among students themselves a desire to obtain a "more coherent view of knowledge," and students spoke enthusiastically about courses where "great teachers link learning to contemporary issues" (p. 85). In this study, Boyer concluded that "general education should seek to become the integrated core" of the curriculum (p. 91)—a core that would introduce students to essential knowledge and connections across disciplines. A unique feature of Boyer's plan is that it tries to identify universal experiences common to all and to relate these experiences to the student's individual life experience. Such a core would eliminate many of the boundaries developed by departmental arrangements and encourage disciplines to begin to interact with each other. Boyer further proposed the following academic architecture for general education:

> Language: the crucial connection
> Art: the aesthetic experience
> Heritage: the living past
> Institutions: the social web
> Nature: ecology of the planet
> Work: the value of vocation
> Identity: the search for meaning [p. 92]

Thus, the 1980s were characterized by the ongoing debate over the general education core and its purpose on hundreds of college and university campuses. Throughout this period, dramatic changes were made in general education, and many of the changes led to a more coherent curriculum. In addition, there was experimentation designed to improve the effectiveness of the general education core and to involve students through internships, research, field trips, and cooperative learning. The question of what an educated person is was frequently discussed and debated in the 1980s. This question will be addressed again in coming decades, but the 1980s had a profound impact on the shape of general education and the method of delivery at colleges and universities across the country.

As the 1990s began, there was growing concern about a "disturbing and dangerous mismatch" between the needs of the society and what higher education is providing. The Wingspread Group on Higher Education cited this mismatch in its report *An American Imperative: Higher Expectations for Higher Education* (1993). This report highlighted the belief that the knowledge-based economy of the future will require educators to prepare highly skilled and competent people. This means that higher education should change its function from "weeding out" to "cultivating" (p. 1). The report concluded that colleges and universities must address three fundamental issues: "taking values seriously; putting student learning first; creating a nation of learners" (p. 7). Clearly, both academic and student affairs educators must focus increased attention on undergraduate education and its delivery.

Future of Undergraduate Education

As a new century commences, the issue of the objectives and purposes of undergraduate general education arises once again. The current period is characterized by dramatic growth in knowledge, the emergence of an interconnected global village, increased diversity of the population, and signs of deterioration in our major cities. Individuals must now learn how to manipulate and manage large amounts of information. An undergraduate general education must prepare people to function in the world of the future.

This world of the future will be connected electronically, with a super information highway making instant communication possible and allowing for interactive instructional media. New trade arrangements will actualize the often-discussed world economy. The advances of medical technology will require the resolution of some of the most complicated moral and ethical issues human society has ever faced. To adapt to this future, undergraduate education must become even more effective.

Looking back over the debate concerning undergraduate general education, a common set of objectives seems to emerge. General education should contribute toward helping students understand "(1) interrelationships among areas of knowledge and how to think more critically; (2) major methods of intellectual inquiry; (3) history and the evolution of civilization; (4) forms of government in society; and (5) the world in which they live" (Gaff, 1983, pp. 84–97).

There is an emerging consensus among educators that general education should also help students develop self-esteem and self-confidence, understand their social responsibility, gain an understanding of and tolerance for different cultures (Boyer, 1987, p. 98), and develop values to guide their behavior (Wingspread Group on Higher Education, 1993, p. 9). These objectives have evolved over time, and many have been emphasized in other time periods. But the world in which we live is changing, so the ways we seek to fulfill these objectives must change as well.

If we accept the preceding objectives for undergraduate general education, we need to identify the conditions under which they can be achieved. These conditions, in combination with the effective use of residence hall environments, can make the difference for the future.

Necessary Conditions

Educators' opinions have varied about the conditions that have to be met for undergraduate educational objectives to be achieved. In its publication *Seven Principles of Good Practice in Undergraduate Education* (1987), the Johnson Foundation argues convincingly that seven conditions are especially important. The critical conditions include student-faculty contact, cooperation among students, active learning, prompt feedback, time on task, high expectations, and diverse ways of learning.

Student-Faculty Contact

Research has consistently documented the importance of student-faculty interaction in promoting the successful undergraduate experience. Pascarella and Terenzini (1991) completed an extensive review of research and concluded that "a large part of the impact of college is determined by the extent and content of one's interactions with major agents of socialization on campus, namely, faculty members and student peers" (p. 620). They emphasize that outcomes related to strong student-faculty interaction include learning and cognitive growth, occupational values, sociopolitical attitudes and values, academic and social self-concepts, intellectual orientation, moral development, maturity and personal development, educational aspirations, and persistence and attainment (pp. 621–622).

Cooperation Among Students

Only recently have educators begun to understand the relationship of the next condition—cooperation among students—to learning. Our educational system in the past was highly competitive, which led to such practices as grading on the curve. These activities were designed to instill a sense of individualism and competition among learners. Seymour (1992) points out that a dramatic outcome of the recent total quality management revolution, spearheaded by Edward Deming and others, has been a better understanding of the need for people to work together in teams rather than to constantly compete against one another. The undergraduate experience of the future must encourage students to work together and help each other solve problems. Learning to collaborate and achieve consensus should be a high priority. The residence hall provides a perfect setting for peers to collaborate on a project. Collaboration is a relatively new concept except in some of America's best classrooms; however, it must be developed as we work toward the previously mentioned objectives, especially in relating fields of study, developing self-esteem, and encouraging social responsibility and tolerance.

Active Learning

The third condition is that of emphasizing active learning. This condition requires that students take responsibility for their education and that they be given a chance to do so. They could, for example, be given opportunities to engage in team research projects, internships, small discussion groups, simulations, independent study, group living experiments, and related activities. Residence halls can provide the perfect setting for these activities, because they offer multiple opportunities for student involvement. As emphasized in *Involvement in Learning* (Study Group on the Conditions of Excellence in American Higher Education, 1984), research has demonstrated that "the more time and effort students invest in the learning process and the more intensely they engage in their own education, the greater will be their growth and achievement, their satisfaction with their educational experience, and their persistence in college, and the more likely they are to continue their learning" (p. 17). Active learning will also help students understand the major methods of inquiry, acquire a better understanding of government, gain a greater understanding of the world in which they live, and increase self-confidence.

Prompt Feedback

The fourth condition is prompt feedback. The importance of timely feedback in the undergraduate experience cannot be overestimated. This means that faculty should utilize frequent quizzes and should provide other forms of feedback about students' performance on a regular basis. In addition, students could keep logs or records of their progress and should offer constructive feedback to their peers. Because of intense and ongoing peer interaction, the residence hall setting does provide students with frequent feedback that enhances learning and personal development. This can be facilitated by technology, since current technology makes it possible to receive almost instantaneous feedback. The emergence of "intimate computing" characterized by smaller units with enormous power has brought with it other advantages. This condition will enhance active learning and increase students' general ability to achieve educational objectives.

Time on Task

Fifth, time on task is critical to success. To begin with, students must be encouraged to devote more of their time to reading and studying. Student success results from both the quantity and quality of time devoted to the accomplishment of academic tasks. In addition, it is important to find a time for them to interact with faculty and others and to dialogue about academic matters. The opportunity for students to "test out" new ideas and explore these ideas is essential. Cocurricular experiences in the living areas that complement academic coursework can play a major role in students' development.

High Expectations

The sixth condition is to create high expectations for student achievement. If students are challenged intellectually and socially, they will view their experience as a more positive one. The learning environment should be characterized by an expectation that students must work hard and that when they do work hard, the rewards will be worth it. But these high expectations must be tempered with mechanisms that give students a sense that they are making progress. When appropriately implemented, this approach can increase students' self-confidence and self-esteem.

Diverse Ways of Learning

Finally, educators must recognize that students learn in diverse ways, based on their background, experiences, and culture. This means that students should have a wide variety of opportunities to engage in learning. If one examines the objectives for general education and the conditions necessary for a high-quality educational experience, it is clear that a major opportunity exists to integrate the classroom experience directly with students' cocurricular life.

The residence hall is one of the major vehicles for achieving this integration because it can provide a place to improve student-faculty contact, foster cooperation among students, promote active learning, allow for prompt feedback, increase time on task, create high expectations, and provide a variety of alternative ways in which students may learn. This focus on discovering creative teaching methods can be especially useful in increasing students' understanding of and tolerance for other cultures and worldviews.

The Residence Hall of the Future

The future provides an unparalleled opportunity to more effectively achieve the objectives of the undergraduate experience through new linkages with residence halls. Before examining ways that undergraduate education and the residence hall can be linked, imagine a possible environment of the college or university of the future. Students entering our hypothetical "Twenty-First-Century University" will choose their residence hall based on their interest in a particular learning theme that will be addressed during their first-year experience. The themes — which are carefully identified by the faculty and groups of students who are now seniors — may include such things as food and the agritech revolution, the uses of the arts to understand one's feelings, electronics and the healthy body, the study of the homeless, the lives of the elderly, the development of the new multiethnic community, and the integration of robots into society.

After students choose their living area, they arrive on campus carrying their personal computer, which is automatically connected to a wide array of university resources and worldwide data bases. All students at the Twenty-First-Century University are expected to acquire a new hand-held, intimate computer that makes current versions look like high-quality slide rules. After connecting their personal computer, students immediately complete registration for courses as well as take care of the necessary administrative steps for checking into their residence hall — all in a matter of fifteen minutes! The personal computer unit is the same unit students use to place a phone call home to regularly report on their activities, schedule return trips home for vacation, order books from the bookstore, and even order their preferred weekly meals in the residence dining hall.

They also conduct financial transactions such as paying tuition and other expenses by computer.

On the evening of that first day, students gather with their undergraduate learning assistant, the residence educator, and the faculty member who will lead their special theme study. In addition to the courses they have chosen as part of their required field of study, there will be the theme experience, which is designed to apply and integrate the learning that will occur in the first-year courses. The credit-bearing theme experience requires students to identify a problem and eventually outline solutions. Materials that have been made available to them include not only a bibliography on the theme but a wide array of video materials that can be accessed directly through their personal computer unit, which contains a television screen and provides immediate access to data as well as video. On the first evening, the students receive the results of their Myers-Briggs Type Indicator (MBTI) (Myers, 1980), which is designed to help them understand different learning styles and methods of approaching the investigation. During the first two weeks, project teams are formed and work begins in identifying the problem they will seek to solve. The problem is focused within their immediate community, and the team includes resource members, such as a professional from the community. For example, the homeless theme project includes a social worker, homeless person, faculty member, undergraduate learning assistant, and residence educator.

The first step in the learning process is for the team to engage in an in-depth analysis of the problem. The team members are also assigned duties and responsibilities, and they routinely share their results at a weekly team meeting with various resource people. After the first three weeks, the team identifies the problem and begins work to cooperatively solve it. To facilitate collaborative learning, this effort includes as many people as possible. During this period, the students have access to their faculty member through the use of electronic mail, and the faculty member queries them on a weekly basis to assess how the team is functioning. The residence educator focuses on the interpersonal effectiveness of the team and is available to advise on process. In the meantime, faculty from whom the students are taking other classes are aware that they are engaged in a particular project. Faculty make every effort to make reading and writing assignments relevant to the themes of the projects, thereby bringing integration and coherence to the subject matter. To further enhance team learning, each residence hall lounge is equipped to allow students to access video lectures offered on the various themes from time to time. Finally, teams are visited on a biweekly basis by the president, vice president, dean, and other university administrators. At the study break, the students are asked about their experience and give and receive feedback.

By the end of the first semester, the students will have carefully researched the issue they have chosen to focus on and will have completed the plan to address the problem. The second semester is devoted to attempting to solve the problem by addressing it through a team-centered approach and by analyzing the results obtained. Throughout this process, the resource learning team, which includes faculty, professionals from the field, and others, will be available to meet with the project team on a weekly basis. It will also maintain regular contact through the personal computer with a video screen and on its new interpretive computing unit, which provides for periodic assessment of progress. Focus groups are conducted at least twice a semester to receive feedback and make changes in approach if necessary.

The preceding scenario from the Twenty-First-Century University describes what is possible if we begin to consider new ways of linking undergraduate education and residential life. By utilizing modern technology, much of which is readily available, the prior example incorporates the principles of continuous quality improvement in the learning environment and links the classroom experience with the living situation.

Ways to Achieve the Future . . . Now!

The time has come to reexamine the role that residence halls can play in achieving the objectives of the undergraduate general education experience. What is required is a fundamental decision. Will colleges and universities try to take advantage of residential living to help realize educational objectives? If a conscious decision is made to integrate the living situation with the undergraduate experience, unlimited positive outcomes are possible. On the other hand, if colleges and universities decide that it is too complicated and unwieldy to link residential living with the undergraduate experience, the residence halls will probably end up merely being places for students to live and revenue centers that must balance their budget.

Linking undergraduate education with the living area requires the development of new organizational patterns. New approaches to teaching and learning must also be created that consciously and continuously seek to link knowledge and cognitive development to the living experience.

Creating a New Organizational Model

New organizational approaches must be employed to make the residence hall of the future a current reality. Residence halls have developed cumbersome bureaucracies that limit their ability to respond directly and effectively to the students they serve. To link the undergraduate education experience with the living experience requires a new model of organization in which people perform very different functions from the ones they now carry out.

As suggested in Chapter One, this new organizational model should try to adopt the characteristics of the learning organization identified by Senge (1991). Senge suggests that the learning organization is characterized by a sharper vision, the merging of thinking and acting at all levels, systematic thinking, empowerment of committed people, and learning processes designed to help make good decisions (p. 5). The organization should constantly be seeking to learn from its experience.

In the new organizational model, the residence hall staff will consist of an undergraduate learning assistant, the residence educator, and the faculty member responsible for the design of the theme experience that the student has chosen. The undergraduate learning assistant is conceived of as a junior or senior student who has engaged in a theme experience and has an academic background related to the theme. The undergraduate learning assistant will also participate in some of the traditional training given to resident assistants. In addition, he or she will have participated in seminars involving faculty from the area in which the theme is offered.

The residence educator will have completed graduate work to learn the basic knowledge base for student development, learned assessment tools — such as the Myers-Briggs — that can be utilized to assess learning styles, and learned to use the technology available in the living unit to maximize the learning experience. The residence educator will hold an adjunct appointment in one of the academic departments and may assist faculty in the department in traditional courses. The residence educator may also be involved in a graduate program in the discipline from which the theme comes. Many of the traditional duties of former residence directors, which involved high-level paper shuffling and bookkeeping, will be eliminated or made easier through the use of technology. Traditional forms of residence hall government, which were previously the job of the residence educators, will be eliminated, and team learning experiences that enhance the theme experience may be used instead. The residence educator will recruit members of the community to come to the residence area to increase learning opportunities for students. The focus will be on how to combine intellectual knowledge with the learning experience.

The faculty member who leads the team will participate in the university's new instructional development center. This center will place heavy emphasis on using continuous quality improvement principles in the teaching process. In addition, the faculty member will have benefited from similar experiences on the part of other faculty who have actually engaged in planning the theme projects. Faculty who participate in these team experiences will earn credit toward an earlier sabbatical, and their work will be given special recognition for tenure and promotion purposes. (Costs of the earlier sabbatical will be absorbed by the residence hall budget.) These forms of recognition clearly demonstrate the emphasis the university places on the unique learning-living experience.

The learning team, consisting of the undergraduate learning assistant, residence educator, and faculty member, will meet on a weekly basis to assess the progress of the teams they coordinate. They will be in constant communication via videophone. The performance evaluation for the residence educator and faculty member focus on the overall success of the team and the change in learning that occurs among students. A significant amount of time will be spent in examining the process the team is utilizing in its learning and in providing adequate resources for the team to function effectively.

As we begin to implement new teaching and learning models and strategies within the living areas, we should not overlook the need for student input. This can be accomplished through the use of periodic focus groups, questionnaire surveys, and other forms of data gathering. It then becomes possible to not only assess what is happening to students as a result of their learning experiences, but also to examine how improvements can be made. Students must become full partners in the educational process that is guided by the learning team.

The above organizational relationship is an example of what might be developed to better link the undergraduate experience with residence halls. This organization might look very different at some universities. However, the key is that there would be an integration of individuals who have responsibility for students' learning with individuals who have responsibility for students' personal development. This integration would occur in a meaningful way that requires staff to work together as a team. Performance evaluations would be based on the ability of the team to enhance students' learning. Other learning opportunities may be created, depending on the goals and objectives of the university. However, the key principles are as follows:

1. There should be a direct link between staff responsible for the classroom experience and those responsible for the student development experience.
2. The role of residence directors in the future should be changed dramatically from functioning in a bureaucratic organization to functioning in a learning organization.

3. The residence hall must be equipped with some of the modern technology, so that technology can be utilized to enhance students' living and learning experience.
4. The current hierarchical organizational relationships must be eliminated.

This new organizational model will enable the linkage of undergraduate learning with the residence halls. But a new organizational structure is not enough; creative approaches to teaching and learning must also be developed.

Encouraging Creative Teaching and Learning

The most significant opportunity to improve undergraduate education through the use of residence halls lies in creative approaches to teaching and learning. In this area, we can go beyond linking the living experience with the learning experience; we can begin to meet the conditions necessary for achieving undergraduate educational objectives. As we look to the future, a major paradigm shift in the way we approach teaching and learning in the university must occur. The boundaries should be removed from the traditional classroom, and we should look at ways to use the entire campus environment, especially residence halls, to promote learning. With increasing emphasis on assessment of undergraduate outcomes, the university that is able to add value to the undergraduate experience through the use of residence halls and other settings will be more successful in the coming years. Meeting the seven conditions necessary to achieve the undergraduate educational objectives mentioned earlier can be particularly helpful.

Research has documented the importance of student-faculty contact (Pascarella and Terenzini, 1991). The technology of the future that provides the computer link to video over the phone line can make access to faculty members even more significant. Emphasis should be placed on developing communication links that give students video access to their faculty member. In addition, consideration should be given to the continued use of residence halls in which faculty become members of student living communities. The videophone will provide faculty with direct access to residence hall rooms and removes the psychological barriers that inhibit faculty from physically going to residence halls. Once these barriers are reduced, it is possible to look at other ways that faculty can be encouraged to join the living community.

The residence hall environment also provides an ideal place in which to use cooperative learning strategies. The continuous quality improvement movement has shown how important it is for people to work as teams to be successful. Examples of cooperative learning strategies were mentioned earlier when describing the residence hall of the Twenty-First-Century University. Many other strategies could be followed utilizing cooperative learning principles. For example, campuses could create special communities such as a women's engineering learning community or a multicultural community. Students who voluntarily live together could achieve more support and engage in cooperative learning activities around a particular problem. Upper-class women engineering students could come together and focus on the issue of women in engineering and how they can become more effective within the engineering community. Obviously, for this approach to be successful, faculty trained in cooperative learning techniques would be needed. If colleges and universities are serious about improving their commitment to teaching, they must change the reward structure so that faculty will be encouraged to learn more about these methodologies. A university willing to place a high priority on using a variety of instructional methodologies as a condition of tenure or promotion will make it possible for faculty to focus on these approaches. Incentives could be provided in the form of additional resources and instructional materials to encourage faculty to utilize these new strategies. Students would benefit from learning in a cooperative manner. Increasingly, business and industry are indicating that students capable of learning this way will make more desirable employees. Thus, the university capable of adopting this strategy will have graduates who are much more marketable in the future. The ability to identify problems and have students participate in a cooperative learning methodology is unlimited.

There is no question that active learning increases students' ability to learn. Role playing, case studies, interactive multimedia, modeling simulations, videocassette recordings of recent historical events, tapes, and other methods are available to engage students in their learning. Residence halls can provide access to many of these learning tools. With the use of technology, students can access videos through the library and can also obtain other helpful learning materials. In addition, residence educators and faculty should be prepared to utilize critical incidents as learning tools. This is where the approach of a learning team consisting of the faculty member and residence educator can be invaluable in designing learning experiences. These experiences can be brought to students who are grouped according to particular issues and opinions, or if a campus has not chosen to adopt this approach, the experiences can be utilized through a variety of programming and other activities. The use of active learning strategies can be particularly valuable in teaching critical thinking, problem solving, and communication skills. Once again, for these techniques to be effective, faculty and staff must be well acquainted with them.

A residence hall that utilizes new technology to link itself to the entire campus will enable students to receive timely feedback on their learning tasks. A computer link with faculty allows faculty to provide prompt feedback, regardless of whether an individual student is involved with a writing task or a group of students are working on a common problem and need advice on how to proceed. The ability to get feedback on learning tasks becomes extremely important in motivating students to continue their involvement in the project. In addition, the computerization of many learning tasks will allow students to get feedback without even interacting directly with the faculty member.

Obviously, the linking of the residence hall with the undergraduate experience will make it possible for students to spend more time on the task in which they are engaged. Previously, we have tended to separate campus units into little fiefdoms that have rarely talked with each other. The ability to link communication now ensures that some common approaches can be taken to themes we wish students to learn about. As a result, they will spend more time focusing on particular issues and expectations. This is one important way to more closely relate students' coursework to their own lives, while at the same time meeting the condition for increased time on task.

A campus that is able to integrate its academic and cocurricular systems to develop a common undergraduate experience can set high expectations for students. Students will immediately sense that the campus has integrated its entire experience, and if the expectations are uniformly high, students will respond appropriately. One of the tragedies of the democratization of higher education is the belief that increased access to higher education must result in reduced expectations. To the contrary, if we focus on helping students learn, we can stretch their abilities by establishing high expectations. The key is that we must be able to relate to all students who are participating in the university experience and set expectations that allow them to continue to grow and learn.

Finally, the university that links its undergraduate education with residence halls can benefit significantly from the recognition that students learn in diverse ways (Schroeder, 1993). As Rosen (1988, p. 9) points out, "While print literacy continues to determine who succeeds and who does not in old-wave higher education settings, new-wave learners require differentiated alternatives for acquiring course information." Rosen notes that the opportunity to learn from printed text as well as to utilize computer-assisted approaches, computer searches, video materials, and so on is important to the diverse learners now coming to higher education. Residence hall communities — which are diverse by their very nature — provide excellent opportunities to demonstrate how students from varying backgrounds can learn using different approaches. Again, living areas can be grouped into communities that focus on multicultural themes, or communities can be developed around subject themes such as women in engineering, men in nursing, or other related areas. In addition, we could look at how students with certain learning styles can be linked more effectively with faculty who use particular methodologies supportive of those learning styles.

If we can begin to apply some of the recent research and link learning styles with teachers, we can approach the undergraduate experience more effectively. If we can link the way students learn with what we feel needs to be learned from the college curriculum utilizing the residence hall community, we can have an extraordinarily positive impact on students. With the increasing emphasis on the outcomes of undergraduate education, new and creative approaches to teaching and learning are absolutely necessary. Much has been written about the need to place new emphasis on teaching at the undergraduate level (Wingspread Group on Higher Education, 1993). The opportunity is before us. It is essential that we adopt some new strategies and apply what we know about undergraduate learning utilizing the residence hall experience as a primary delivery system.

If we are successful in applying creative teaching and learning strategies to our residence hall communities, we can create an environment that is exciting, stimulating, and extremely attractive to students. Students' ability to see the connections between what is happening in the classroom and what is happening in their residential communities is important, and the theme experience makes this possible. The dilemma we face in higher education is how to break through the barriers we have created in the form of departments, offices of residence life, student development, and other such units.

Conclusion

This chapter has described how residence halls can be used as vehicles for achieving the objectives of undergraduate education. We began by looking at the debates on the objectives of undergraduate education. Once we determined some common objectives, we then looked at the conditions necessary to meet these objectives. Finally, we examined how residence halls could be linked to the classroom experience through new organizational models and creative teaching strategies. Attempts have been made many times to utilize residence halls more effectively. However, in the recent reexamination of the undergraduate experience and, in particular, of general education, we have not focused clearly enough on the use of residence halls as important vehicles in improving the effectiveness of undergraduate education. This issue can be approached in many ways. I hope this chapter has helped to stimulate some thinking about possible strategies.

From a president's perspective, to remain effective and competitive in the coming years, universities will have to be able to maximize all their resources and focus them on achieving the objectives of undergraduate education. Steps must be taken to break down the organizational barriers that have compartmentalized and fragmented knowledge and students in such a way as to create bureaucracies that do not work effectively. It is time to begin experimenting with new approaches and to learn ways in which we can be more effective in achieving the basic objectives of undergraduate education. We must be willing to reexamine every aspect of the student experience, including residence halls, to determine the best way to meet the challenges of the future. The key to survival for universities becomes our willingness to find and use innovative methods to meet the circumstances of the present and future.

References

Bennett, W. J. *To Reclaim a Legacy.* Washington, D.C.: National Endowment for the Humanities, 1984.

Boyer, E. L. *College: The Undergraduate Experience in America.* New York: HarperCollins, 1987.

Cheyney, E. P. *History of the University of Pennsylvania, 1740–1940.* Philadelphia: University of Pennsylvania Press, 1940.

Gaff, J. G. *General Education Today: A Critical Analysis of Controversies, Practices, and Reforms.* San Francisco: Jossey-Bass, 1983.

Johnson Foundation. *Seven Principles of Good Practice in Undergraduate Education.* Racine, Wis.: Johnson Foundation, 1987.

Myers, I. *Introduction to Type.* Palo Alto, Calif.: Consulting Psychologists Press, 1980.

Pascarella, E. T., and Terenzini, P. T. *How College Affects Students: Findings and Insights from Twenty Years of Research.* San Francisco: Jossey-Bass, 1991.

Rosen, C. L. "New Wave College Instruction: Some Thoughts and Approaches." Paper presented at the annual meeting of the International Reading Association, Toronto, May 1988.

Rudolph, F. *The American College and University.* New York: Knopf, 1962.

Schroeder, C. C. "New Students — New Learning Styles." *Change,* 1993, *25*(4), 21–27.

Senge, P. M. "Transforming the Practice of Management." Paper presented at the Systems Thinking in Action Conference, Boston, Nov. 1991.

Seymour, D. T. *Causing Quality in Higher Education.* New York: American Council on Education/Macmillan, 1992.

Study Group on the Conditions of Excellence in American Higher Education. *Involvement in Learning.* Washington, D.C.: U.S. Department of Education, 1984.

Wingspread Group on Higher Education. *An American Imperative: Higher Expectations for Higher Education.* Racine, Wis.: Johnson Foundation, 1993.

Five

Guerrilla Education in Residential Life

Arthur Levine

Students get an education in residence halls. Study after study has shown that undergraduates living on campus learn all sorts of things that commuters do not. They develop stronger academic skills in areas such as writing, public speaking, the arts, and leadership. They feel better about themselves — becoming more autonomous, having higher levels of self-esteem, and being more self-confident. They acquire greater social skills with peers, adults, faculty, and others. They develop a more liberal political orientation, less sectarian religious views, an increased sense of altruism, higher levels of moral development, and a greater intellectual orientation. On top of all this, they are more involved in cocurricular activities, have lower attrition rates, and achieve higher graduation rates (Pascarella and Terenzini, 1991).

This is an amazing set of outcomes, if only for their breadth. But what the list always reminds me of is a visit to my dentist. Not only do I get my teeth cleaned when I see him, but I also learn about the pressing international issues. The reason is that my dentist is invariably twenty minutes behind schedule. I, therefore, have the choice of sitting in the waiting room and reading an armful of dental journals or *Foreign Affairs* quarterlies. For me there is no choice. I always choose *Foreign Affairs*. In this sense, my global education is not something the dentist intended, nor something I actively sought. To be quite candid,

93

when I selected my dentist I did not realize this was an option or even a matter to consider in choosing him. It was just serendipity.

The educational outcomes of residential life are a bit like that, too. They seem to occur almost incidentally on many campuses, rather than by design. They can even occur when undesired. For example, a Christian college recently discovered that the students living in its residence halls were becoming less sectarian than commuters. This was not the college's goal. In fact, administrators were appalled. They wanted the opposite result.

The typical full-time residential undergraduate spends approximately 15 hours per week in a classroom. The remaining 153 hours of the week in one form or another constitute residential life (and undergraduates do not sleep a lot). This chapter examines how that enormous block of time has been used to educate students and how that education can be made more intentional in the future.

The More Things Change . . .

One of the best sources about what and how students learn in residence halls is the books they write about college life. There is a long tradition of such volumes in higher education. They include works such as *Plastic Age* (Marks, 1924) (about the 1920s), *This Side of Paradise* (Fitzgerald, [1920] 1970) (1920s), *Revolt on the Campus* (Wechsler, [1935] 1973) (1930s), *The Group* (McCarthy, 1963) (1930s), *The Final Club* (Wolff, 1990) (1950s), *The Strawberry Statement* (Kunen, 1969) (1960s), and *The Secret History* (Tartt, 1992) (1980s), among others.

Two volumes were written about student life at Yale three-quarters of a century apart. They are worth focusing on. The first, by Owen Johnson and titled *Stover at Yale,* was published in 1912. It is the story of the college education of John Humperdink Stover — "Dink" to his friends. He is handsome, seemingly confident, and a natural leader who came to Yale from the elite Laurenceville Academy, where he was a "BMOC" football hero. Dink has been a winner all his life and wants to be a winner at Yale.

Soon after arriving at the college, he is taken aside by one of the leaders of the sophomore class, an Andover graduate who had played football against Dink at prep school. He explains quite accurately how one goes about succeeding at Yale.

> This college is made up of all sorts of elements. . . . And it is not easy to run it. Now in every class there are just a small number who are able to do it and will do it. They form the real crowd. All the rest don't count [p. 26].

> You may think the world begins outside of college. It doesn't; it begins right here. You want to make the friends that will help you along, here and outside. Don't lose sight of your opportunities, and be careful how you choose [p. 25].

> Don't ticket yourself for drinking [p. 28].

> Or get known for gambling [p. 28].

> And another thing: no fooling around with women [p. 29].

> Now you've got to do a certain amount of studying here. Better do it the first year and get in with the faculty [p. 29].

> You're going to be judged by your friends and it is just as easy to know the right crowd as the wrong . . . the crowd you will want to know all through your life [pp. 26–27].

The mark of success at Yale, Stover is told, is to be selected for one of the senior societies. The selections are made by the graduating class. However, the path to a society is narrow and starts early. It is built on leadership in campus organizations and selection into the sophomore and junior societies.

Dink's sophomore mentor leaves him with these words, "I don't want you to make any mistakes. Remember you're going to be watched from now on" (p. 28).

Stover heeds this advice. He makes the right friends. He distinguishes himself by beating a sophomore at a wrestling match. He is an outstanding member of the varsity football team, likely to become its captain in the future. He is selected for one of the sophomore societies and rated the leading prospect in his class for a senior society.

All goes awry during the second year at Yale. Dink becomes friends with the "wrong people" — students who have come to Yale for an education, who oppose the society system, and who think the university is moving in the wrong direction — serving purely and simply as a business college. These students are concerned with issues of the day.

Stover undergoes an epiphany. He concludes that his notions of success are wrong: "We shut ourselves up, withdraw from the big life of the college, know only our own kind, that kind we will know all our life; surrender our imagination. We represent only a social idea, a good time, good friends. . . . But we miss the big chance to go out and mingle with everyone, to educate ourselves by knowing opposite lives" (p. 265).

Dink's old friends resent his infidelity and question both his judgment and his character. He is told by a group of upper-class leaders that he is jeopardizing or "queering" his chances for success at Yale. Stover blows up and tells them "you and the whole university can go to hell" (p. 270).

The moment of self-righteousness is followed by a bout of drinking and gambling. A gentlemanly act to assist a young woman becomes, unfairly, a cause for scandal for Dink. He withdraws from the competition for captain of the football team because he is too controversial.

But Yale is changing. Student opposition to the sophomore societies for being undemocratic is mounting. The university president asks the second-year societies to plan reforms. When they are unable to do so, he abolishes them. In this climate, Dink is a leader in creating a university debating society that appeals to a broad cross section of the student body.

In the end, Dink is rewarded for his independence. The young woman he loves, who earlier criticized him for his conformity, agrees to marry him, and he is selected for Skull and Bones, the most eminent of the senior societies.

The second book tells of undergraduate life at Yale seventy-five years later from the point of view of an outsider. Authored by a member of the Yale class of 1987, Hugh Kennedy, *Everything Looks Impressive* (1993) is the story of Alex MacDonald from Maine.

Like Dink Stover, Alex comes to New Haven seeking success in life and personal distinction. He breaks off his relationship with his hometown girlfriend and reduces contact with his family.

Arriving at Yale, he cuts the final sessions of freshmen orientation to play squash with a popular and well-to-do sophomore. Alex wants to make sure he does not get left out of college life.

One of his roommates is a fourth-generation Yalie with a father who is a newspaper editor in the Hamptons and a mother who is an interior decorator in Manhattan. The other roommate is from a well-to-do Connecticut industrial family. The father is a doctor. His sister lives in Switzerland. In contrast, Alex's father is unemployed, and his mother treks three miles to pick up the family's food stamps.

Both roommates are far more sophisticated than Alex about academic life. One is in an honors program and the other points out gut courses such as "Postmodernism and Cultural Codes." They know about social life, too. They introduce Alex to the best bars and the rituals of Yale drinking games. They help him locate the right parties to attend. They know about sports and other activities and their importance at Yale. As with Dink Stover, crew and publications are thought good investments of time.

Drinking is more prominent at Alex MacDonald's Yale than Dink Stover's. Students go to bars and parties in groups. They drink to get drunk. Alex is pleased to get out one evening thinking it "beat another night sitting in our common room killing a case of beer" (p. 41). Fake I.D.'s are standard equipment.

Sex is more casual seventy-five years later, too. It is often tied to drinking. A friend goes to bed drunk with a woman one night and wakes up the next morning unable to remember whether they had had sex.

But the greatest difference in the two books is diversity. The student segregation based on family background and academic class has diminished at Alex's Yale. Discrimination was a fact of life at Dink's college. Students spoke of "dagos," "niggers," "coons," and "coloreds" and complimented a classmate by describing him as a "real white." At Yale in the 1980s, this is not acceptable, at least overtly. Alex tells three friends that a woman he knows is gay. The revelation produces the following comment.

Male: She's a dyke?

Female: I'd appreciate it if you didn't use that word.

Other male: Yeah . . . that's pretty insulting [p. 68].

A key element of *Everything Looks Impressive* is the clash between gay rights and homophobia. In his first days at Yale, Alex meets an intelligent, attractive, cultivated, and very appealing senior named Jill Lanigan. She and Alex become friends of a sort. She is a lesbian and an activist in the women's center. Their relationship is partly a friendship, partly a physical attraction, and partly antagonistic, since she opposes the Yale Alex is seeking to cultivate — sports, old boys and girls, and unthinking and uncaring politics. Jill and a group of gay students crash an off-campus party. A fight breaks out. Jill is beaten up. Alex's roommate is said to be involved in the beating. The *Yale Daily News* prints several articles on the attack, including one entitled "Misogynistic Violence or Gay Rights?" The articles are placed by activist women on the doors of thirty students, disproportionately athletes, thought to be gay bashers. There is a rally by the victims of the attack. Jill ultimately dies as a consequence of the beating.

After her death, the divisions grow even greater at Yale. There are more rallies. A memorial service takes place. The university is forced to launch an inquiry into how Jill died. Alex gives a list of names of those involved, which he has heard from Jill and others, to the dean. Among the names is his roommate's.

In this sense, like Stover, Alex gives up the notion of success he came to Yale to achieve. He turns in his roommate, who represents the old Yale, for Jill, the antagonist of that Yale. He reestablishes ties with his old girlfriend, Katharine. They attend a plush party at a nightclub in New York rented for the birthday party of a Yale friend. Both Alex and Katharine leave the party early. Katharine says of Alex's roommates, "They obviously care about you." He replies, "As long as I behave" (p. 231).

On returning from Christmas break, at the book's conclusion, Alex says he never felt as real in his life as at Yale. He has made peace with his past — family and Katharine — and has given up the questionable values he brought to Yale in September.

. . . The More They Remain the Same

What stands out is the similarity between the two novels. This is true despite the fact that Yale is virtually unrecognizable between the two books. The differences range from growth in institutional size and the introduction of coeducation to the dramatic shift in student behaviors and real diversity in their values. Nonetheless, there are enduring commonalities in the accounts of residential life with regard to what students learn and how they learn it.

The most basic commonality is that life inside the classroom is dwarfed by life outside. In both books, only passing reference is made to classes. In *Stover at Yale*, the general attitude is "don't let your classes get in the way of your education." We are told that Stover sleeps through an occasional recitation and that his mind wanders while instructors teach esoterica. In *Everything Seems Impressive*, the classes are certainly more important, but they remain somewhat peripheral to many students' lives, except to the extent that they require all-nighters. The inescapable reality in both books is that residential undergraduates live their lives through the cocurriculum.

A second commonality between the books is that the primary educators of students are students rather than faculty or administrators. Administrators rarely touch students' lives in either book. In *Stover at Yale,* the only references to administrators are to the president — who seeks to remake the sophomore societies — and to the dean, who punishes student hijinks. Three-quarters of a century later, the situation seems largely unchanged. The president is given credit for a series of high-tone dinners around campus designed to improve morale, and the provost's office conducts a hearing into Jill's death.

Interestingly, faculty as a group are painted as even more remote from student life. There is not one meaningful interaction between professors and students at Stover's Yale. In Alex MacDonald's university, individual relationships exist between some students and faculty. For example, Jill has a close relationship with her faculty adviser, who is active in the women's center and is guiding Jill through her senior thesis. However, none of Alex's other friends have such a relationship. In 1987, Yale seems reminiscent of Golding's *Lord of the Flies* (1962). There are no adults after 5:00 P.M., particularly faculty.

Both books are principally about student-to-student relationships. This is the way undergraduates are shown to spend their time; this is the relationship they clearly prize above others. They educate one another formally and informally by word and by deed.

A third commonality is that students have continued to educate one another in the same areas. They set standards for dressing. Stover seeks to be a trendsetter but fears being labeled an odd duck. They teach a generational language. In Stover's day, it includes expressions such as "galoot," "daisy bunch," "dudes," and "my aunt's cat's pants." Seventy-five years later, they are "chilling," "negging," "dudes," and "no way." Students teach each other which life goals should be given priority; they define the meaning of success. Undergraduates help one another to know the place that academics should have in their lives. They decide which cocurricular activities should be given status. In Stover's day, eight activities or leadership groups stand out in the eyes of most students. In the era of Alex MacDonald, greater heterogeneity exists in the Yale community, but there is agreement within subgroups about which activities were prized. It is football for the athletes and service for Jill and her friends. In the same way, students establish unwritten codes of conduct for one another. These cover activities such as sexuality, alcohol use, and smoking. For Stover and his friends, offering tobacco is the way to be a good host. It is consumed often in cigars, cigarettes, and pipes. Smoke-filled rooms are a regular feature of college life. In contrast, sexually active women are seen as whores. By 1987, the tables had been turned. Sexual activity was common among men and women and heavy smoking was not.

A final commonality with regard to education is that student-initiated activities are widely preferred over university-sponsored events. Sports seem to be the only exception. Stover misses chapel and MacDonald cuts out of orientation. But no one rejects a senior society bid or fails to attend the right parties.

In sum, the two novels tell us a lot about how students have been educated in residential life throughout this century. They offer us four realities that must be addressed if colleges and universities are to be more intentional about educating students in the future.

1. Education outside the classroom may be the most potent form of education on any residential campus.
2. The principal teachers of students are students.
3. In many areas of campus life, ranging from definitions of success and the importance of learning to what constitutes acceptable conduct and prized activities, students determine the standards and teach them to one another.
4. Student-initiated activities are preferred over institutionally sponsored activities by undergraduates.

Toward More Intentional Residential Education

The implications of these realities are daunting. They indicate that adults in general, and student affairs professionals in particular, have limited access to students and less opportunity to educate them intentionally than might be desired. As a result, several approaches seem to offer more promise than others.

Early intervention stands out. The rationale is that it is easier for an institution to educate or influence its students before a common group identity forms and upperclass students pass down norms and values to freshmen. This makes freshmen orientation — a time in which new students are more likely to listen because they are frightened — a special time for education. Orientation should emphasize critical issues an institution is eager to educate students about rather than providing a general introduction to every office on campus. But as Alex MacDonald makes clear, this does not work for all students.

Another critical juncture for educating students is how the environment is structured. If students are going to instruct students and impart values and beliefs to one another, one of the most powerful ways colleges and universities can influence that teaching before students ever arrive on campus is in the way they design residential life. The use of physical space, in both new and existing residence halls, determines who interacts with whom. The mix of public space and personal space, of shared facilities (computer rooms, courses, study rooms) and private facilities, shapes education too. The kinds of students — in terms of numbers, background, interests, ethnicity, gender, age, and all other characteristics — who live together in a residential unit can have a profound impact on the education that takes place. The use of theme-oriented residence halls (for example, French-speaking, environmentally concerned, students involved in service) versus general undifferentiated dormitories offers the potential for diverse outcomes. So too do living-learning arrangements in which classes occur in residence halls and faculty live with students — in contrast to the more traditional practice, which separates faculty from students as well as living from learning.

A related area of unrealized potential is extending residential education to students who do not traditionally live on campus. Minority students and students in need of compensatory education tend to be overrepresented in commuter populations. These groups are far more likely to be first-generation college students and tend to spend less time on campus than other groups. They are never exposed to the powerful peer education residential students receive. Their education would benefit from the 153 additional hours of enrichment residential life offers each week. Several actions might be taken to ensure this. The first is the construction of a small number of residence units at commuter institutions to be used to provide short-term residential experiences for most students. A second need is a greater effort on the part of residential schools to recruit these students full time. A third initiative is for schools with commuter and residential populations to consider making residential facilities available to commuter populations during calendar breaks. For example, one-week or one-month summer residences might be appealing to older students.

As for the students already living on campus, another vehicle for making education more intentional is leadership training. Some colleges and universities now do a great deal of this. However, the focus is usually on official student leaders — resident assistants, student government types, Greek heads, and club presidents. It might be useful to extend these programs to the unofficial opinion leaders on campus who hold no rank in organized activities, but who may already be the most influential teachers in residential life. Similarly, the curriculum in many leadership programs is diffuse, focusing primarily on skill development. If a college has a particular set of concerns it wishes students to learn about, the curriculum should reflect these concerns as well.

Another possibility is that colleges and universities are sometimes handed opportunities to teach by events on campus or in the larger world. For example, the Rodney King affair offered higher education a chance to educate students about race relations. The Gulf War produced a similar opportunity at the global level. On campus, well-publicized events such as drinking accidents, graffiti incidents, Greek violence, and sexual misconduct provide what is commonly called the teachable moment. These are times in which campus life seems to stop and students are especially open to education.

Building on this approach is the idea of developing educational programs for residential students based on their evolving interests. For instance, throughout the century colleges and universities have been eager to teach their students about altruism and responsibility. Many schools are finding that an excellent way of doing this teaching is by capitalizing on students' booming participation rates in community service programs. Nearly two out of three of all traditionally aged undergraduates were involved in service programs during their high school years and are now continuing in college (Levine, 1993). The rising concern with environmentalism among students is providing another useful venue for education. In this sense, institutions of higher education seem increasingly to be extending the notion of the teachable moment into the teachable trend. They are finding that going with the flow is a lot easier than going against it.

Awards and honors are another way that colleges and universities can educate their students. Every award or honor highlights a particular set of values. These values should reflect what an institution wishes to teach. By attaching values to awards, such as a service requirement to scholarship aid, institutions of higher education educate their students. By publicizing honors, colleges and universities also engage in instruction.

Finally, because students are not greatly influenced by administratively sponsored activities and publications, alternative means need to be found for conveying the values that institutions wish to teach. This requires redundancy. The message should be conveyed again and again and again through mission statements, publications, speeches, events, administrative policies and practices, and all the activities in which a college is involved. It should saturate the campus. Eventually students will run into it somewhere. Institutions have been effective in figuring out how to amplify their messages. They have frequently combined them with food and/or music, both of which have a magnetic power over students. They also have brought in popular speakers to spread the message—people who students admire and might even be willing to come and see. Athletes, media stars, entertainers, and best-selling authors top the list.

Conclusion

Colleges and universities have the capacity to make residential education more intentional (or, in plain English, more effective), but it is not at all easy—which is no surprise, or more colleges would already be doing it.

The principal challenge to institutions is that residential education is dominated by students. For the most part, they design, teach, and evaluate the out-of-class curriculum. University administrators and faculty play a subsidiary role in cocurricular life.

The techniques or approaches that seem most likely to increase the intentionality of residential education are the following.

- Taking advantage of design opportunities for residential space, old and new, and the populations that will inhabit them
- Intermixing student residences with faculty and administrative offices
- Extending residential education to the nontraditional students who are least likely to receive it
- Providing leadership training that includes opinion leaders without formal roles in student organizations
- Taking advantage of teachable moments
- Tying teaching to evolving student interests
- Recognizing exemplary behavior and publicizing it via honors and awards
- Amplifying and regularly repeating the teaching message through institutional publications, activities, and speeches

What all of this adds up to is a guerrilla approach to residential education. The name is a bit unconventional and even troubling. But who knows, it might just work.

References

Fitzgerald, F. *This Side of Paradise.* New York: Charles Scribner's Sons, 1970. (Originally published 1920.)

Golding, W. *Lord of the Flies.* New York: Coward-McCann, 1962.

Johnson, O. *Stover at Yale.* New York: Stikes, 1912.

Kennedy, H. *Everything Looks Impressive*. New York: Doubleday, 1993.

Kunen, J. *The Strawberry Statement*. New York: Random House, 1969.

Levine, A. *1993 Survey of Undergraduates*. Unpublished paper, Harvard University, 1993.

McCarthy, M. *The Group*. Orlando, Fla.: Harcourt Brace Jovanovich, 1963.

Marks, P. *Plastic Age*. New York: Century, 1924.

Pascarella, E. T., and Terenzini, P. T. *How College Affects Students: Findings and Insights from Twenty Years of Research*. San Francisco: Jossey-Bass, 1991.

Tartt, D. *The Secret History*. New York: Knopf, 1992.

Wechsler, J. *Revolt on the Campus*. Seattle: University of Washington Press, 1973. (Originally published 1935.)

Wolff, G. *The Final Club*. New York: Knopf, 1990.

Part 2

Promoting Student Learning in Residence Halls

To realize their educational potential, residence halls must become purposeful and intentional educational environments. Educationally purposeful initiatives must be mission driven, reflecting the values, principles, and objectives of effective undergraduate education. Residence halls can promulgate educationally purposeful activities by developing an explicit curriculum. Components of this curriculum are the subject of the chapters included in Part Two.

In Chapter Six, George D. Kuh summarizes what is known about the conditions that foster student learning and personal development and discusses how to create these conditions in residential settings. He makes six recommendations for creating a learner-centered climate in campus residences and challenges educators in academic and student affairs to work collaboratively to create them.

Elizabeth J. Whitt and Elizabeth M. Nuss explain in Chapter Seven the need to make explicit connections between residence halls and curricula. They define *connections* as systematic and sustained efforts to achieve institutional academic purposes and implement curricular goals through residence hall programs and activities. Drawing on examples from Earlham, Stanford, Michigan State, and the University of Maryland, they demonstrate how well-designed and focused learning experiences can achieve the institution's educational goals.

In Chapter Eight, Charles C. Schroeder demonstrates the importance of developing learning communities that maximize peer-group influences. He delineates four essential principles for the development of such communities and illustrates new perspectives and roles for staff interested in designing different kinds of learning communities in residence halls.

In Chapter Nine, Marvalene Hughes describes challenges associated with an increasingly diverse student population. She suggests avenues for building a diverse residential community using knowledge from the literature and the insights from a study conducted with residence hall students at the University of Minnesota. She presents an innovative residence hall curriculum on diversity and a pedagogical process for implementing it.

Susan R. Komives, in Chapter Ten, challenges prevailing staff assumptions about leadership education and suggests strategies to promote empowering civic leadership among students and staff. She presents a new, empowering paradigm that encourages students to realize their obligation to be involved in creating a shared vision for the greater good of their community.

In Chapter Eleven, Terry B. Smith explores the nature and history of residential colleges and the benefits of the residential college experience to faculty, staff, and students. He compares and contrasts programs at two different universities — Yale and Northeast Missouri State — and suggests that residential colleges embody a commitment to academics by providing an educational environment that values students and their holistic development.

By implementing initiatives such as the ones described in Part Two, educators can play a critical role in realizing the educational potential of college residence halls and make a profound contribution to student learning on their campuses. But initiatives such as these are not stopgap measures or "quick fixes"; they are systematic, intentional, and ongoing commitments to improve student learning through residence hall education.

Six

Creating Campus Climates That Foster Learning

George D. Kuh

The college outcomes literature yields two unequivocal conclusions (Astin, 1977, 1992; Bowen, 1977; Chickering and Reisser, 1993; Feldman and Newcomb, 1969; Pascarella and Terenzini, 1991). First, many of the institutional conditions that encourage students to take advantage of learning opportunities are known, particularly for white, traditional-age students enrolled full time who live on campus. Second, no single policy, program, or practice significantly influences student learning and personal development. Rather, the greatest educational effects result from complementary academic and student life policies and practices. As Heath (1968, pp. 242–243) puts it, "A college community . . . has, in effect, expectations for what its members are to become. Such ideals or expectations may be more silent than vocal; they may work their effects out of awareness. . . . When such expectations are consistently expressed in all structures and activities of the institution, then different communal experiences may mutually reinforce one another. It is rare that a specific type of educational experience is very significant. . . . Rather, it is the coherence, the consistency, the 'atmosphere' . . . that makes its impact on development."

Robert H. Shaffer, first president of the American Guidance and Personnel Association and dean of students at Indiana

University from 1955 to 1969, described the important role of community in shaping behavior: "I grew up in a little Hoosier town called Pittsburg, a village of 300 to 400 people; I knew everybody in town, everybody in town knew me. . . . In a community, everyone knows, or at least thinks they are known by, everyone else; therefore, there is considerable pressure to always be on one's best behavior . . . out of class as well as in class" (Kuh and Coomes, 1986, p. 618).

The observations of Heath and Shaffer are captured in an African proverb: "It takes a whole village to raise a child." That is, every aspect of an institution contributes to the educational impact of college on students. Nevertheless, certain kinds of experiences are more congruent with the aims of higher education than others. For example, learning how to resolve personal differences with a roommate contributes to attaining the practical competence goal of general education (Bowen, 1977); playing euchre several nights a week in the hall study lounge probably does not. To the extent that the former kinds of experiences characterize student behavior, a residential environment can be said to be educationally purposeful.

This chapter summarizes what is known about the conditions that foster student learning and personal development and discusses how to create these conditions in residential settings. The presentation is divided into two parts. In the first part, nine institutional characteristics are described that encourage students to take advantage of learning and personal development opportunities. In the second part, six strategies are offered for creating an educationally purposeful climate in campus residences.

Conditions That Foster Student Learning

None of the conditions described in this section, standing alone, is sufficient to promote student learning and personal development. Taken together, however, they constitute what many scholars agree is a desirable learning environment for most undergraduates.

1. *Clear, coherent, and complementary educational purposes, policies, and practices:* The single most important factor in channel-

ing student effort toward educationally purposeful activities is a clear, coherent institutional mission (Chickering and Reisser, 1993; Kuh, Schuh, Whitt, and Associates, 1991). Clarity and coherence of educational purpose do not just happen. Nor once obtained do clarity and coherence persist without attention. These qualities must be assiduously cultivated over time by every generation of institutional agents — faculty, academic administrators, and student affairs administrators, including residence life staff.

Achieving clarity of mission in large, state-assisted institutions is difficult. However, it is possible to attain clarity and coherence in residence life, if not across a large residential system, within a specific residence or cluster of residences. For example, a particular residence hall, or floors of a hall, can be organized around students' interests, such as major field or preferred vocation, or other themes consistent with the educational purposes of the institution.

2. *An institutional philosophy that emphasizes a holistic view of talent development:* Developmental processes are epigenetic, cumulative, and complicated (Sanford, 1962). Thus, it is not surprising that many of the positive changes that occur during college result from interrelated, mutually supporting experiences sustained over an extended period of time (Light, 1992; Pascarella and Terenzini, 1991). For example, as students become more cognitively advanced and exhibit a greater capacity for critical, abstract, and symbolic thinking, changes also are taking place in their attitudes, values, and psychosocial behavior. That is, student development is a cumulative, general phenomenon, not a series of discrete, catalytic responses to specific episodes (Terenzini, 1992), such as a dynamic lecture, a difficult lab experiment, or a moving poetry reading. In short, students change as whole, integrated persons as a result of participating in a variety of intellectual and social experiences (Pascarella and Terenzini, 1991).

No wonder, then, that studies of student learning and development show that life beyond the classroom is important, particularly for students who live in campus residences (Astin, 1977, 1992; Chickering, 1974). For example, Moffatt (1989) concluded that for the vast majority (90 percent) of undergraduates at Rutgers, what took place outside the classroom was at least as influential to their learning as what happened in the classroom. Students who participate in extracurricular activities and engage with faculty after class get better grades, are more satisfied, and are more likely to graduate (Astin, 1977, 1992; Pascarella and Terenzini, 1991). They also exhibit gains in such areas as social competence, autonomy, confidence, and self-awareness (Kuh, 1993d). And participation in extracurricular activities typically is a more accurate predictor of workplace competence than grades (Cappelli, 1992). Thus, student learning is fostered when institutional agents acknowledge that thoughts and feelings are inextricably intertwined (Webster, Freedman, and Heist, 1962) and attempt to blur boundaries between classroom and out-of-class experiences (Kuh, Schuh, Whitt, and Associates, 1991).

3. *High expectations for student performance:* According to Wilson (1992), president of Radcliffe College, the most pressing need facing higher education is the education of our aspirations. Indeed, at every level of education, establishing high expectations for student performance is considered essential for fostering learning (Angelo and Cross, 1993; Doyle and Pimental, 1993; Sizer, 1992; Study Group on the Conditions of Excellence in American Higher Education, 1984). Although high expectations cannot ensure student success, low expectations are almost always deleterious. Changing expectations, then—those that students have for themselves and those that the faculty and staff have for students—is a continuing challenge for student affairs professionals. Students most likely to have low aspirations include those who have previously been excluded from higher education, such as students of color, and those whose experiences have been undervalued, such as women.

4. *Ample opportunities for student involvement:* The more time and energy students devote to educationally purposeful activities, the more they benefit (Astin, 1977, 1984, 1992; Chickering and Reisser, 1993; Kuh, 1981; Pace, 1990; Pascarella and Terenzini, 1991). Highly motivated students typically direct their energy to pursuits that help them develop their talents. However, on many campuses, such students represent a small frac-

tion of undergraduates. The largest group of students may be less inclined or able to find ways of using the institution's resources to educational advantage. Thus, a college must intentionally create opportunities so that many students can actively participate in various aspects of institutional life. Equally important, institutional agents must expect students to be actively involved and make certain that students do not encounter unnecessary obstacles when trying to take advantage of these opportunities (Kuh and Schuh, 1991).

5. *Human-scale settings, characterized by ethics of membership and care:* Large institutions offer few educational advantages over small institutions (Bowen, 1977; Sizer, 1992). Settings with a relatively small number of participants place a greater claim on each member to be a responsible, contributing member (Barker and Gump, 1964). When classes have more than one hundred students, and residences accommodate more than three hundred people, students can too easily be anonymous and shirk collective responsibility for the welfare of others and the quality of their own experience. When people are known by name or face, however, they cannot be anonymous. Belonging to an affinity group of one or two dozen people provides a frame of reference within which to evaluate one's behavior under different circumstances. In human-scale residential settings, it is easier for faculty and staff to make certain that all students—age, race, ethnicity, and gender notwithstanding—feel that they are individuals of worth (ethic of care) and that, as full members of the campus community, they are capable of learning anything (ethic of membership) (Kuh, Schuh, Whitt, and Associates, 1991).

6. *Use of effective instructional approaches:* When teachers use approaches that accommodate students' learning styles, students learn more than when conventional approaches are used, such as lecturing (Chickering and Gamson, 1987; Pascarella and Terenzini, 1991). Active, collaborative learning strategies encourage students to devote more time and energy to educationally purposeful activities and result in higher rates of learning. Similarly, institutional agents who match instructional approaches with student learning styles also produce higher rates of learning.

In addition to learning styles, social class and culture affect learning. That is, what and how students think are influenced by their cultures of orientation (Van Maanen, 1984). For example, many students from disadvantaged social backgrounds lack experience in discussing literature, politics, and the aesthetic qualities of life. Their social marginality is reinforced by the discourse of the classroom and residence hall (Rose, 1989). When faculty, student affairs professionals, and peers use language that certain students cannot command, they feel excluded, out of place, as if they do not matter (Schlossberg, Lynch, and Chickering, 1989).

7. *Programs and services congruent with student characteristics and needs:* As with instructional approaches, campus policies and practices are more likely to have the desired effect when they take into account students' needs and characteristics. Institutions that attract high-ability, self-directed students promote learning and personal development when their policies and practices are flexible and unstructured, within student residences as well as elsewhere on the campus. For example, at Grinnell College and Stanford University, students determine community standards for their residence, and undergraduate resident advisers do not have discipline responsibilities (Kuh, 1991). But residence life policies and practices at institutions that attract large numbers of first-generation, average-ability students may be more effective if they provide lots of structure. In part, this is because such students typically do not have a tacit understanding of college life; therefore, they need guidance as to the behaviors that lead to success in collegiate environments (Kuh, Schuh, Whitt, and Associates, 1991). An example of the latter approach is provided by Xavier University of New Orleans (Andreas, 1991), which sets forth clear policies and procedures for how students are to behave and what kinds of activities can occur in student residences. Neither structure nor the absence of structure is ideal under all circumstances; the goal is to appropriately match educational purposes, programs, and services to students' characteristics.

8. *Freedom to disagree:* Most colleges and universities claim to be places where alternative—sometimes competing—points

of view are freely examined. Yet most institutions have a strong press for cohesion, for getting along. Among traditional-age undergraduates in particular, the press for conformity is often so great that people have difficulty describing their thoughts and feelings. Instead, they repress contrary feelings and opinions to maintain harmony. This trade-off between cohesion and accuracy (Weick, 1983) often is manifested as passive-aggressive behavior, which can be readily observed in many residence halls, Greek houses, and classrooms. So while educationally purposeful residential environments are psychologically safe and inclusive, this does not mean they are free from conflict. Rather, they are places where disagreements occur routinely. These must be resolved with perseverance, wisdom, grace, and hard work.

9. *An ethos of learning that pervades all aspects of the institution:* Taken together, the conditions described above constitute an ethos of learning that characterizes the campus climate. *Ethos* (a word of Greek origin meaning "custom" or "habit") refers to the belief system widely shared by faculty, students, and administrators. An institution's ethos evokes an emotional commitment to the institution and helps people decide what is appropriate (Kuh, 1993b). Ethos is a soft, vague notion. But like it or not, the ethos is a key factor in explaining institutional effectiveness in a variety of areas (Heath, 1981; Kuh and Whitt, 1988).

As is evident from this brief summary, none of the institutional conditions that foster student learning are surprising. In one form or another, these conditions have received attention in the literature over the years. What is less clear is how to redesign an institution, specifically campus residences, so that these conditions are realized more of the time. It is this significant challenge to which I now turn.

An Agenda for Creating a
Learner-Centered Climate in Campus Residences

While a good deal is known about the impact of college on students, it is not clear how much of this information is, in Ewell's (1988, p. 53) terms, "usable knowledge" for informing institutional policy and practice. As many practitioners know, being familiar with information about the conditions that foster student learning and development is one thing; creating these conditions is another.

Each institution is unique. Therefore, the suggestions that follow must be adapted to fit an institution's particular contextual features — mission, philosophy, location, curriculum, student characteristics, and so on. The following list is by no means exhaustive; the reader will surely identify more telling, relevant, institution-specific issues to address.

1. *Institutional agents must acknowledge, and take seriously, their responsibilities in fostering student learning and personal development.* Colleges and universities afford numerous opportunities for learning, both in and out of the classroom. Much of what undergraduates learn during college is associated with experiences outside the classroom (Boyer, 1987; Kuh, 1993d; Moffatt, 1989; Wilson, 1966). Certainly student affairs staff, particularly those who work in residence life, spend more time than faculty in close proximity to students. It would appear, then, that student affairs staff could have more influence on student learning and personal development than the college outcomes literature suggests (Astin, 1992; Pascarella and Terenzini, 1991). Two explanations for the absence of such findings are plausible.

First, student affairs staff probably do make substantial contributions to student learning, but they do so indirectly. Student-faculty interaction and student effort are usually found to be directly related to measures of student learning and personal development (for example, knowledge acquisition, critical thinking). However, student affairs professionals — when they are doing their jobs well — are often invisible, working behind the scenes to create settings in which students take responsibility for their own lives and seize learning opportunities inherent in residential settings. The second explanation is that student affairs staff do not devote enough time and energy to activities that encourage students to think about what they are learning outside the classroom and to apply this learning to their studies and vice versa. Perhaps if student affairs staff better understood what they could do in residential settings to enhance student learning — the central goal of the academy — they would devote more time and energy to those activities.

To create the conditions that foster student learning, all institutional agents must know how students learn and be familiar with the out-of-class conditions that encourage students to take advantage of learning and personal development opportunities. The extent to which higher education and student affairs professional preparation programs address these topics is not clear. Many preparation programs emphasize socialization experiences and devote relatively little attention to issues more central to the academic mission, such as how out-of-class experiences contribute to the goals of general education. The assessment movement offers additional evidence that student affairs has not yet fully embraced its role in fostering student learning. In most institutions, student affairs lags well behind academic units in identifying ways to assess and report student learning outside the classroom. Finally, the vast majority of sessions at national and regional student affairs meetings focus more on "how to" issues than on the substantive aims of student affairs work and whether student outcomes demonstrate the effectiveness of student affairs programs and services.

2. *Institutions should clarify their mission and interpret what the mission means in the context of campus residences.* Colleges differ on what they emphasize, depending on their mission, history, and so forth. Thus, the first step in creating residential settings that foster student learning is to examine the institution's mission and the appropriate role of residence life, given the mission. In this instance, mission does not necessarily refer to what the institution writes about itself in documents such as the catalogue or mission statement, but rather to what faculty, students, and staff actually do (Davies, 1986; Kuh, 1993a).

Menand (1991, p. 55) suggests that some institutions of higher education are trying to be "too many things to too many people." Visitors from abroad are sometimes surprised and confused by the variety of available services and programs. What is the appropriate role of the institution? To be a mental health clinic? A recreational sports facility? A hotel? Or, as Gardner (1990) suggests, an educational village committed to the development of young people? Some institutions may determine that it is consistent with their mission to "arbitrate disputes about democracy and social justice, or govern the manner in which people relate socially to one another" (Menand, 1991, p. 53); at other colleges, such a policy would be out of place.

One way to initiate a discussion about the institution's mission, and the application of the mission in residence life, is to identify the aspirations articulated or implied in the institution's mission statement. For example, if a church-related college says it is "a community of faith and learning," what does that mean for residence life? What is meant by *community*? Whose faith and whose learning are embraced? How are these addressed in campus residences? How should they be addressed?

3. *Colleges and universities should revise their residence life philosophy, policies, and programs so that they complement the academic mission.* This is far from a novel thought (Blake, 1979; Kuh, Whitt, and Shedd, 1987). In institutions where academic and student life policies and practices are complementary, mutual respect between faculty and student life staff have developed over time, based on knowledge, competence, and trust (Kuh, Schuh, Whitt, and Associates, 1991). Because out-of-class experiences make significant contributions to student learning and personal development, complementarity between academic and student affairs policies and practices is essential, as Levine discusses in Chapter Five. According to Pascarella and Terenzini (1991, p. 655), "The enhancement of the educational impact of a college is most likely if policy and programmatic efforts are broadly conceived and diverse. . . . Thus, instead of singular, large, specially designed, and campuswide programs to achieve a particular institutional goal, efforts might more profitably focus on ways to embed the educational pursuit of that goal in *all* appropriate institutional activities."

Yet ambiguity persists concerning the appropriate role of student affairs on the contemporary college campus. Should student affairs staff engage in activities to complement the academic mission, as the National Association of Student Personnel Administrators (1987) asserts? Or should student affairs focus on aspects of student development that tend to be underemphasized in the classroom (for example, decision making, getting along with people who are different)? In some instances, ambiguity is a function of a lack of knowledge about the role of the curriculum and faculty in fostering student learning and personal development. A similar claim can be made about the lack of knowledge on the part of many faculty about the contributions of students' out-of-class experiences to the institution's mission. Ryan (1989, p. 71) likens the relationship between academic and student affairs to a whale and an elephant:

> A whale and an elephant are about thirty yards apart. The elephant, having just entered the water, is using its trunk to throw water on itself when it sees the whale. Both have big eyes and excellent hearing. They watch and listen to each other. The whale, aware of the elephant's presence in its domain, shoots a gigantic jet of water high into the air with a great hissing sound and beats the waves with its flukes. The elephant, hearing and seeing the whale's reaction, retreats to the sand but trumpets loudly to show its own power. The whale and the elephant can see and hear each other, yet neither understands what the other is up to. They agree not to come any closer.

A critical step in moving toward clarity and complementarity between purposes of academic and student affairs is to determine the educational assumptions on which residence hall policies and practices are based. To determine if residence life policies and practices are congruent with the institution's mission and philosophy, faculty and staff must discuss the extent to which their performance and accomplishments indirectly or directly contribute to student learning by helping to create one or more of the nine conditions mentioned earlier known to foster student learning. Institutional factors such as size often determine the nature of policies and practices. For example, large institutions tend to attract students with a wide range of abilities, needs, and developmental levels. Thus, it is improbable that a single, inflexible residence life policy can be established for all undergraduate residences and still promote educationally purposeful behavior. In such settings, student learning is more likely to be fostered with policies flexible enough to respond to changing student characteristics and needs on a residence-specific basis. Flexible, responsive policies, however, may confuse staff members who believe that consistency is a virtue (for instance, many undergraduate resident assistants, some entry-level staff socialized in settings where structure was valued). Therefore, institutions that adopt flexible, responsive policies will have to be selective in staff hiring and training.

Faculty and staff must examine the assumptions that guide their work and the extent to which their assumptions are congruent with the institution's goals for student learning and personal development. Too often, student affairs staff focus on developing measurable objectives, such as implementing a certain number of programs on a given floor or residence during the year. Student learning is more likely to result if staff discuss their assumptions about teaching and learning outside the classroom and develop a coherent philosophy and approach to encouraging students to take advantage of learning opportunities inherent in residential settings.

Educationally purposeful residential environments demand intentional action and constant care and attention. Some immediate steps can tighten the couplings between the academic mission and residential life. For example, the dean of students could annually inform the campus community about the contributions of out-of-class experiences to the institution's mission. This can be done orally at the opening fall faculty convocation (if the institution has such an event), followed by a written document distributed to all faculty, staff, students, and trustees. Periodic presentations by the director of residence life to the community assembly or faculty council during the academic year also are worthwhile. Similarly, inviting faculty and academic administrators to conduct professional development seminars for student affairs staff on topics of common interest also would foster collaboration and mutual understanding.

4. *Institutions must discover the current state of affairs with regard to student learning in campus residences.* The academic mind requires empirical data before being moved to action. Thus, a current, in-depth look at the campus may be necessary before policy

groups will take seriously the challenge of modifying the institution's learning climates (Kuh, 1993a), even though many institutional agents may be aware that certain institutional conditions do not measure up to some of those described earlier. Therefore, a task force made up of faculty, staff, and students should be charged with discovering how the current campus climate contributes to student learning. For this group to have the desired impact and influence, support is required from the highest administrative level (the president) and policy level (the governing board) of the institution. It may be that other imperatives can be used as touchstones to generate campus enthusiasm for the project. For example, a weekend symposium focused on such issues as diversity or health awareness can bring together trustees, faculty, and students to engage in dialogues about the current situation. Using this as a lever for action, the task force can conduct an audit of the conditions known to foster student learning and determine how well the institution measures up.

Student affairs staff will be particularly interested in learning about the degree to which students' out-of-class experiences contribute to the institution's learning and personal development goals. But focusing such an assessment activity exclusively on out-of-class experiences may overlook some of the more important aspects of the undergraduate experience that contribute to the benefits of attending college. Therefore, any effort to understand how the residential experience fosters an ethos of learning must take a wide-angled view of campus life. That is, the institution's culture must be systematically examined with an eye toward modifying policies and practices so that the learning and personal development goals of *all* students are addressed (Minow, 1990).

The audit should also include a focus on the role and contributions of campus residences in establishing a climate for learning on the campus. Two questions are key for focusing the audit: (1) Is the enacted residence life philosophy congruent with the espoused institutional philosophy? (2) Do residence life policies and practices complement other institutional policies and practices and promote student learning? Other questions should be addressed as well. Do faculty and student affairs staff have a shared vision of the institution's educational mission? To what extent are the curriculum and campus residences mutually supporting? Do faculty and student affairs staff share with students responsibility for blurring the boundaries of classroom and residential living? Are students expected to be responsible, and held accountable for, their behavior? Or are students coddled, even though the student code of conduct says students are adults?

Certain combinations of student characteristics (such as personality, age, gender, achievement orientation, ability, academic interests) create distinctive climates in residences; some of these combinations are more conducive to student learning and personal development than others (Moos, 1979). The living environments created by men and women (as well as other groupings of students), and the experiences of various groups of students in these environments, must be monitored on a continuing basis. For example, Astin (1992) reports that, on average, the self-esteem of women *decreased* during college. This is a reversal of earlier findings showing that the self-esteem of both men and women increased during college. To what extent the environments of campus residences contribute to this disturbing finding must be determined on a campus-by-campus basis. Therefore, systematic attention to various subenvironments of the campus is important, including an analysis of the institution's physical properties and psychological climate (Kuh, 1993a; Kuh, Schuh, Whitt, and Associates, 1991).

It is unlikely that the group charged with a campus-level study will have sufficient resources for an in-depth examination of each campus residence. This should not discourage residence life staff from undertaking these projects on their own. Not all residences can be studied at the same time, and so some prioritizing will be necessary. Guidelines for conducting audits are described elsewhere (Fetterman, 1990; Kuh, 1993c; Kuh, Schuh, Whitt, and Associates, 1991; Whitt, 1993).

5. *Residence life staff must be knowledgeable about best practices from the literature and research.* Recent research offers insights into student learning with which student affairs professionals must be familiar. Two findings from Astin (1992) illustrate this point.

First, peers are the most influential group on campus in terms of student learning. This is because the student culture is the single most powerful and credible source of knowledge as far as traditional-age students are concerned, determining whom they spend time with and the values and attitudes they are exposed to (Baird, 1988). Therefore, students must be full participants in any effort to modify their residential environments, for they will ultimately determine the meaning and impact of any institutional policy (Kuh, 1990a).

The second finding of interest from Astin (1992) is that students exposed to diversity (for example, by living with someone from a different racial and ethnic background) exhibit greater gains on items reflecting goals of general education (such as appreciation for human differences and the aesthetic qualities of life). Issues related to diversity will remain high on the student affairs agenda for the foreseeable future (Kuh, 1990b; Levine, 1991). Therefore, familiarity with the current literature about race relations on campus is not only helpful but essential.

For example, consider Weiner's (1992) three propositions about ethnic diversity on campus. First, how students experience ethnic diversity on a campus depends on institution-specific factors, including the history, traditions, and size of the institution, the location of the campus, the relative size of each ethnic group in the student body, students' previous experience with diversity, institutional policies, and faculty attitudes and teaching skills. Thus, the relations among students at a small, geographically isolated, church-related college — where whites are the overwhelming majority — will differ from relations at a large state-assisted institution with substantial numbers of students of color.

Second, understanding interethnic relations among students is extraordinarily complex. Like other groups, students are ambivalent about how they experience diversity. Simple answers are not possible when attempting to understand the interactions of ethnicity, social class, sexual orientation, academic major, and gender. For instance, while ethnicity plays a part in shaping identity, it does not completely determine identity. Knowing someone's ethnic background offers only limited insight into that person's identity because such characteristics as gender, personality, social class, and academic interests are not considered.

Finally, friendship is not sufficient to establish cooperative relations among groups. It is generally assumed that if people from different ethnic groups become friends, stereotypes will erode. But friendships alone do not seem to neutralize stereotypes and myths. While friendships are important, *knowledge* is also necessary—about the economics, politics, sociology, and psychology of racial and ethnic relations (Weiner, 1992). In addition, institutional agents must be sensitive to culture and class in order to encourage students to talk about what they are learning, thinking, and feeling and to seek out new experiences when they are ready.

As campuses become increasingly diverse, institutions must experiment with ways of encouraging students to think and act *inclusively*. In the larger society, people are refusing to remain invisible; old silences are being shattered, such as by those who have been physically or emotionally abused, and long-repressed voices are making themselves heard (Greene, 1993). To embrace a wider range of views, the institution's mission may have to be reinvented and the history of student residences reinterpreted. Policies and practices also must be reviewed with inclusivity as the goal (Weiner, 1992). Do residential practices keep certain groups invisible? Can students room with friends of the same ethnicity and yet have close friends of a different ethnicity?

6. *Student affairs professionals must use effective teaching approaches.* For decades, student affairs professionals have asserted that they are educators (Brown, 1972; Delworth and Hanson, 1989; Miller and Prince, 1976). If student affairs professionals are to more fully realize their espoused educator function, they must use effective teaching techniques, such as active learning strategies that take into account such student characteristics as learning styles, social class, and culture of orientation. Resources that describe effective instructional approaches for novices and experienced educators alike can be found in Angelo and Cross (1993) and Goodsell, Maher, and Tinto (1992).

The use of effective teaching approaches in campus residences has three immediate applications. First, students must be taught how to take advantage of learning resources, both in the residence and elsewhere on campus (for example, in libraries or in the academic skills center) (Kuh, 1992). This is particularly important at institutions that enroll large numbers of first-generation college students who lack tacit knowledge about the undergraduate experience.

The second application is using active, collaborative learning strategies that encourage students to apply what they are studying in class to their lives out of class. This would include such activities as asking students to talk in small groups about how they are applying what they are learning in the classroom to their life in the residence hall and vice versa (Kuh, 1993a).

The third application is teaching students how to disagree with grace and dignity. Indeed, more often than not, the unmet challenges in higher education are social, not intellectual (Rose, 1989). The basic task is to prepare students socially and intellectually to live productive and satisfying lives after college. This is why community building is a goal of most departments of residence life. But often the conception of community is based on traditional assumptions of what constitutes a community, such as a place where people have similar interests and attitudes and usually agree on matters. This view of community is no longer adequate for a world that is becoming increasingly pluralistic (Gardner, 1990). An important ingredient of a good learning community is establishing a climate where people feel free — even obligated — to disagree when their experience warrants telling their truths. Palmer's (1987, p. 20) thinking is helpful here. Community, he says, is "that place where the person you least want to live with always lives." Palmer's corollary to this definition is especially apt for residence life: "When that person with whom you least want to live moves away, someone else arrives to take his or her place" (p. 20).

Thus, students must learn, and institutional agents must know how to teach students, how to disagree while aspiring to common ground. This means that faculty and student affairs professionals must become comfortable and skilled at dealing with the conflicts that arise from attempting to balance the rights of the individual with the press to conform. Finally, unity (working together to achieve the institution's educational purposes) must be clearly distinguished from conformity, which is the failure to appreciate the gift of diversity.

Conclusion

Processionary caterpillars feed on pine needles. When foraging, they move through the trees in a long procession, one leading and the others following — each with its eyes half closed and its head snugly fitted against the rear extremity of its predecessor. After experimenting, a great French naturalist enticed some of these caterpillars to the rim of a large flowerpot, where he connected the first one with the last, thus forming a complete circle, which started moving around in a procession with neither beginning nor end. The naturalist expected that after a while they would catch on to the trick, get tired of their useless march, and start off in a different direction. But not so. Through force of habit, the living creeping circle kept moving around the edge of the pot — around and around, keeping the same relentless pace for seven days and seven nights — which would surely have continued had it not been for exhaustion and starvation. Incidentally, an ample supply of food was in sight, but it was outside the range of the circle. Because of instinct, habit, custom, past experience, or whatever, the caterpillars continued along the beaten path, each one following another blindly. They mistook familiar, routine behavior for accomplishment.

Caterpillars and colleges have some things in common. Members of both must work together to survive. Both caterpillars and colleges rely on experience to guide behavior. And when their worlds change dramatically, the way they usually do things may no longer work. Because of shifting demographics and budget constraints, the worlds of higher education, and residence life in particular, certainly have changed in recent years.

Change brings uncertainty as well as opportunity. Faculty and staff must seize the present moment by affirming the primary purpose of higher education: fostering student learning and personal development (Wingspread Group on Higher Education,

1993). Before an institution can create conditions in campus residences that promote student involvement, faculty, administrators, and others must determine what their institution aspires to be, why these aspirations are important, and whether institutional policies and practices complement the institution's mission and philosophy and are appropriate, given students' characteristics and educational goals. Three key steps are: (1) to develop a coherent institutional philosophy of student learning for the residential system, (2) to discover how the student culture in various campus residences shapes student learning and personal development, and (3) to become proficient in using effective instructional and community-building approaches.

References

Andreas, R. E. "Where Achievement Is the Rule: The Case of Xavier University of New Orleans." In G. Kuh and J. Schuh (eds.), *The Role and Contributions of Student Affairs in Involving Colleges*. Washington, D.C.: National Association of Student Personnel Administrators, 1991.

Angelo, T. A., and Cross, K. P. *Classroom Assessment Techniques: A Handbook for College Teachers*. (2nd ed.) San Francisco: Jossey-Bass, 1993.

Astin, A. W. *Four Critical Years: Effects of College on Beliefs, Attitudes, and Knowledge*. San Francisco: Jossey-Bass, 1977.

Astin, A. W. "Student Involvement: A Developmental Theory for Higher Education." *Journal of College Student Personnel*, 1984, *25*, 297–308.

Astin, A. W. *What Matters in College? Four Critical Years Revisited*. San Francisco: Jossey-Bass, 1992.

Baird, L. L. "The College Environment Revisited: A Review of Research and Theory." In J. Smart (ed.), *Higher Education: Handbook of Theory and Research*. Vol. 4. New York: Agathon Press, 1988.

Barker, R. G., and Gump, P. V. (eds.). *Big School, Small School*. Stanford, Calif.: Stanford University Press, 1964.

Blake, E. S. "Classroom and Context: An Educational Dialectic." *Academe*, 1979, *65*, 280–292.

Bowen, H. R. *Investment in Learning: The Individual and Social Value of American Higher Education.* San Francisco: Jossey-Bass, 1977.

Boyer, E. *College: The Undergraduate Experience in America.* New York: HarperCollins, 1987.

Brown, R. D. *Tomorrow's Higher Education: A Return to the Academy.* Washington, D.C.: American College Personnel Association, 1972.

Cappelli, P. "College, Students, and the Workplace: Assessing Performance to Improve the Fit." *Change,* 1992, *24*(6), 55–61.

Chickering, A. W. *Commuting Versus Resident Students.* San Francisco: Jossey-Bass, 1974.

Chickering, A. W., and Gamson, Z. F. "Seven Principles for Good Practice in Undergraduate Education." *AAHE Bulletin,* 1987, *39*(7), 3–7.

Chickering, A. W., and Reisser, L. *Education and Identity.* (2nd ed.) San Francisco: Jossey-Bass, 1993.

Davies, G. K. "The Importance of Being General: Philosophy, Politics, and Institutional Mission Statements." In J. Smart (ed.), *Higher Education: Handbook of Theory and Research.* Vol. 2. New York: Agathon Press, 1986.

Delworth, U., and Hanson, G. R. "Future Directions: A Vision of Student Services in the 1990s." In U. Delworth, G. R. Hanson, and Associates, *Student Services: A Handbook for the Profession.* (2nd ed.) San Francisco: Jossey-Bass, 1989.

Doyle, D. P., and Pimental, S. "A Study in Change: Transforming the Charlotte-Mecklenburg Schools." *Phi Delta Kappan,* 1993, *74,* 534–539.

Ewell, P. T. "Outcomes, Assessment, and Academic Improvement: In Search of Usable Knowledge." In J. Smart (ed.), *Higher Education: Handbook of Theory and Research.* Vol. 4. New York: Agathon Press, 1988.

Feldman, K. A., and Newcomb, T. M. *The Impact of College on Students.* San Francisco: Jossey-Bass, 1969.

Fetterman, D. "Ethnographic Auditing: A New Approach to Evaluating Management." In W. G. Tierney (ed.), *Assessing Academic Climates and Cultures.* New Directions for Institutional Research, no. 68. San Francisco: Jossey-Bass, 1990.

Gardner, J. *On Leadership.* New York: Free Press, 1990.

Goodsell, A., Maher, M., and Tinto, V. (eds.). *Collaborative Learning: A Sourcebook for Higher Education.* University Park: National Center on Postsecondary Teaching, Learning, and Assessment, Pennsylvania State University, 1992.

Greene, M. "The Passions of Pluralism: Multiculturalism and the Expanding Community." *Educational Researcher,* 1993, *22*(1), 13–18.

Heath, D. H. *Growing Up in College: Liberal Education and Authority.* San Francisco: Jossey-Bass, 1968.

Heath, D. H. "A College's Ethos: A Neglected Key to Effectiveness and Survival." *Liberal Education,* 1981, *67,* 89–111.

Kuh, G. D. *Indices of Quality in the Undergraduate Experience.* ASHE-ERIC Higher Education Report No. 4. Washington, D.C.: American Association for Higher Education, 1981.

Kuh, G. D. "Assessing Student Culture." In W. G. Tierney (ed.), *Assessing Academic Climates and Cultures.* New Directions for Institutional Research, no. 68. San Francisco: Jossey-Bass, 1990a.

Kuh, G. D. "The Demographic Juggernaut." In M. J. Barr, M. L. Upcraft, and Associates, *New Futures for Student Affairs: Building a Vision for Professional Leadership and Practice.* San Francisco: Jossey-Bass, 1990b.

Kuh, G. D. "Student Affairs at Stanford University: Caretakers of the Collegiate Culture." In G. Kuh and J. Schuh (eds.), *The Role and Contributions of Student Affairs in Involving Colleges.* Washington, D.C.: National Association of Student Personnel Administrators, 1991.

Kuh, G. D. "What Do We Do Now? Some Implications of *How College Affects Students." Review of Higher Education,* 1992, *15,* 349–363.

Kuh, G. D. "Assessing Campus Environments." In M. J. Barr and Associates, *The Handbook of Student Affairs Administration.* San Francisco: Jossey-Bass, 1993a.

Kuh, G. D. "The Forgotten Link Between Institutional Ethos and Student Learning." *Liberal Education,* 1993b, *79*(4), 22–31.

Kuh, G. D. "Some Implications of Cultural Perspectives for Student Affairs." In G. Kuh (ed.), *Cultural Perspectives in Student Affairs Work.* Alexandria, Va.: American College Personnel Association, 1993c.

Kuh, G. D. "In Their Own Words: What Students Learn Outside the Classroom." *American Educational Research Journal,* 1993d, *30,* 270–304.

Kuh, G. D., and Coomes, M. D. "Robert H. Shaffer: The Quintessential 'Do-Gooder.'" *Journal of Counseling and Development,* 1986, *64,* 614–623.

Kuh, G. D., and Schuh, J. H. "Conclusions and Recommendations." In G. Kuh and J. Schuh (eds.), *The Role and Contributions of Student Affairs in Involving Colleges.* Washington, D.C.: National Association of Student Personnel Administrators, 1991.

Kuh, G. D., Schuh, J. H., Whitt, E. J., and Associates. *Involving Colleges: Successful Approaches to Fostering Student Learning and Development Outside the Classroom.* San Francisco: Jossey-Bass, 1991.

Kuh, G. D., and Whitt, E. J. *The Invisible Tapestry: Culture in American Colleges and Universities.* ASHE-ERIC Higher Education Report No. 1. Washington, D.C.: Association for the Study of Higher Education, 1988.

Kuh, G. D., Whitt, E. J., and Shedd, J. D. *Student Affairs, 2001: A Paradigmatic Odyssey.* Alexandria, Va.: American College Personnel Association, 1987.

Levine, A. "The Meaning of Diversity." *Change,* 1991, *23*(5), 4–5.

Light, R. J. *The Harvard Assessment Seminars: Explorations with Students and Faculty About Teaching, Learning, and Student Life.* Second report. Cambridge, Mass.: Graduate School of Education and Kennedy School of Government, Harvard University, 1992.

Menand, L. "What Are Universities For?" *Harper's Magazine,* Dec. 1991, pp. 47–56.

Miller, T. K., and Prince, J. S. *The Future of Student Affairs: A Guide to Student Development for Tomorrow's Higher Education.* San Francisco: Jossey-Bass, 1976.

Minow, M. "On Neutrality, Equality, and Tolerance." *Change,* 1990, *22*(1), 17–25.

Moffatt, M. *Coming of Age in New Jersey: College and American Culture.* New Brunswick, N.J.: Rutgers University Press, 1989.

Moos, R. H. *Evaluating Educational Environments: Procedures, Mea-*

sures, Findings, and Policy Implications. San Francisco: Jossey-Bass, 1979.

National Association of Student Personnel Administrators. *Points of View.* Washington, D.C.: National Association of Student Personnel Administrators, 1987.

Pace, C. R. *The Undergraduates: A Report of Their Activities and Progress in College in the 1980s.* Los Angeles: Center for the Study of Evaluation, Graduate School of Education, University of California, 1990.

Palmer, P. "Community, Conflict, and Ways of Knowing: Ways to Deepen Our Educational Agenda." *Change,* 1987, *19,* 20–25.

Pascarella, E. T., and Terenzini, P. T. *How College Affects Students: Findings and Insights from Twenty Years of Research.* San Francisco: Jossey-Bass, 1991.

Rose, M. *Lives on the Boundary: The Struggles and Achievements of America's Underprepared.* New York: Free Press, 1989.

Ryan, E. "The Whale and the Elephant: A Fable for Our Time." *NASPA Journal,* 1989, *26,* 70–76.

Sanford, N. "The Developmental Status of the Freshman." In N. Sanford (ed.), *The American College.* New York: Wiley, 1962.

Schlossberg, N. K., Lynch, A. Q., and Chickering, A. W. *Improving Higher Education Environments for Adults: Responsive Programs and Services from Entry to Departure.* San Francisco: Jossey-Bass, 1989.

Sizer, T. R. *Horace's School.* Boston: Houghton Mifflin, 1992.

Study Group on the Conditions of Excellence in American Higher Education. *Involvement in Learning.* Washington, D.C.: U.S. Department of Education, 1984.

Terenzini, P. T. "On the Road to Community in Higher Education: Myths and Realities About College's Effects on Students." Paper presented to the Council on Academic Affairs and the Council on Student Affairs of the National Association of State Universities and Land Grant Colleges, New Orleans, Nov. 1992.

Van Maanen, J. "Doing Old Things in New Ways: The Chains of Socialization." In J. Bess (ed.), *College and University Orga-*

nization: Insights from the Behavioral Sciences. New York: New York University Press, 1984.

Webster, H., Freedman, M. B., and Heist, P. "Personality Changes in College Students." In N. Sanford (ed.), *The American College.* New York: Wiley, 1962.

Weick, K. E. "Contradictions in a Community of Scholars: The Cohesion-Accuracy Tradeoff." *Review of Higher Education,* 1983, *20,* 20–33.

Weiner, S. S. "'Can't We Just Be Friends?': Student Race Relations." Paper presented at the annual meeting of the American Educational Research Association, San Francisco, Apr. 1992.

Whitt, E. J. "Making the Familiar Strange: Discovering Culture." In G. D. Kuh (ed.), *Cultural Perspectives in Student Affairs Work.* Washington, D.C.: American College Personnel Association, 1993.

Wilson, E. K. "The Entering Student: Attributes and Agents of Change." In T. Newcomb and E. Wilson (eds.), *College Peer Groups.* Chicago: Aldine, 1966.

Wilson, L. S. "Beyond Conservation and Liberation: The Education of Our Aspirations." Thirteenth David Dodds Henry Lecture, University of Illinois, Urbana-Champaign, Feb. 1992.

Wingspread Group on Higher Education. *An American Imperative: Higher Expectations for Higher Education.* Racine, Wis.: Johnson Foundation, 1993.

Seven

Connecting Residence Halls to the Curriculum

Elizabeth J. Whitt
Elizabeth M. Nuss

Previous chapters have discussed the roles of residence halls in undergraduate education and initiatives for promoting student learning in on-campus housing. Each reminded us—implicitly or explicitly—that (1) where and how students live, and with whom, influence student learning and development, and (2) residence halls can make a significant contribution to achieving the educational purposes of colleges and universities. The purpose of this chapter is to consider the next logical step in this discussion: the integration of curricular goals and academic programs in residence halls.

This chapter offers examples of this integration and examines the qualities that enable institutions to make strong and lasting connections between the curriculum and residential education. By understanding the factors that promote these connections, academic and student affairs leaders will be better able to design living-learning communities appropriate to their institutions—communities that fulfill the potential that is often discussed but seldom achieved. Literature on student out-of-class experiences (Astin, 1992; Kuh, Schuh, Whitt, and Associates, 1991; Pascarella and Terenzini, 1991), learning communities

(Gabelnick, MacGregor, Matthews, and Smith, 1990; Smith, 1993), and campus cultures (Kuh and Whitt, 1988) provides a context for exploring how to go about connecting residence halls to the curriculum.

Before proceeding, it is important to define what is meant by "connecting residence halls to the curriculum." For the purposes of this chapter, "connections" between residence halls and curricula are *systematic* and *sustained* efforts to achieve institutional academic purposes and implement curricular goals through residence hall programs and activities. Sometimes the expression "learning communities" is used to denote the integration between in-class and out-of-class experiences, as well as the intellectual and social interaction between students and faculty and among students, that these programs provide (Gabelnick, MacGregor, Matthews, and Smith, 1990; Smith, 1993). Examples of such connections include honors program residences and major-related residence floors. Learning communities as described here are designed, implemented, and endorsed in collaboration between student affairs and academic affairs.

Occasional programs by resident assistants on study skills or current events are not included within the focus of this chapter. Although these are valuable student- or staff-directed educational programs, these activities do not—for the most part—constitute a complete and systematic connection between the curriculum and residential living.

The chapter begins with an overview of the importance of connecting the curricula and residence halls. A description of some colleges and universities that have been successful in making and maintaining such connections follows. An analysis of common characteristics of those institutions and programs is then provided followed by a conclusion with a discussion of implications for practice.

A Rationale for Connecting the Curriculum and Residence Halls

In an assessment of the condition of undergraduate life, Boyer (1987) lamented that on most campuses there was little connection between what was learned in residence halls and the undergraduate curriculum. He pointed to the "great separation, sometimes to the point of isolation, between academic life and social life on campus" (p. 5). At approximately the same time, the National Association of Student Personnel Administrators (NASPA) established its Plan for a New Century Committee to consider the *1937 Student Personnel Point of View* on the occasion of its fiftieth anniversary (National Association of Student Personnel Administrators, 1987). The committee identified the basic assumptions and beliefs of the student affairs profession and asserted that the "academic mission of the institution is preeminent . . . [and] [a]s a partner in the educational enterprise, student affairs enhances and supports the academic mission" (p. 12). Both Boyer and the NASPA committee perceived a need to view the educational purposes of colleges and universities broadly — not as academic and nonacademic experiences in isolation from, or even in opposition to, each other, but as involving all aspects of the student and all aspects of college life.

These concerns of the 1980s are reinforced in recent research on "what matters in college" (Astin, 1992). Astin was clear in his call for systematic connections between the curriculum and residential life. He argued that student learning and development are influenced by the extent to which students are involved in the educational process. As highlighted in previous chapters, student involvement is fostered by interaction with peers in cooperative learning efforts, tutoring, discussions about common academic experiences, and common core curricula. The importance of interactions between students and faculty and among student peer groups for student learning (Astin, 1992; Kuh, 1992; Pascarella and Terenzini, 1991) reinforces the case for establishing learning communities of students and faculty and for finding ways to connect the curriculum with the residential experience.

Throughout the history of American higher education, there has been a fundamental belief in the importance of the education of the whole student and an understanding that to achieve this goal, institutions must find more ways to link the curriculum to out-of-class learning opportunities. Changing roles of faculty and the emergence of student affairs professionals have contributed to some successes and some difficulties in trying to connect residence halls to undergraduate curricula. Colleges and universities continue to be expected to facilitate growth and development of the "whole student" (Bok, 1986, p. 52) and campus residence halls to assist in achieving these goals (Astin, 1992; Chickering, 1974; Jencks and Riesman, 1962). Finding ways to provide common academic experiences through residential programs in deliberate and systematic ways remains a challenge. The following section describes ways in which four colleges and universities have met this challenge.

Current Examples of Connecting Residence Halls and the Curriculum

Today, a number of colleges and universities seek to integrate academic and residential experiences to meet students' educational and developmental needs (Gabelnick, MacGregor, Matthews, and Smith, 1990; Smith, 1993). A brief description of several institutional programs follows. These examples were selected because they illustrate current practices, although they are not necessarily representative of the entire array of efforts underway. These examples include small and large, public and private, and selective and less selective institutions: Earlham College, Stanford University, Michigan State University, and the University of Maryland. Each description captures a small part of the institution at a particular point in time. Nonetheless, these examples provide useful insights about the development and maintenance of learning communities.

Earlham College

Earlham College, located in Richmond, Indiana, is a small liberal arts college founded by the Society of Friends (Quakers). The college's statement of purpose acknowledges connections inherent in all aspects of college life: "The network of human relationships [at Earlham] is sustained by a sense of common purpose, mutual caring and respect. . . . In such a community, the teaching and learning roles are merged, and the curricular and experiential are combined. Earlham is both a sanctuary for reflection and a stimulus to practical action" (Kuh, Schuh, Whitt, and Associates, 1991, p. 44).

Approximately 800 Earlham students live in five campus residences, known at Earlham as dorms, and twenty-two college-owned houses. Residences at Earlham are "intentionally arranged to accentuate" (Kuh, Schuh, Whitt, and Associates, 1991, p. 218) connections between students' out-of-class lives and liberal education and the merger of curriculum and experience decribed in the statement of purpose. In general, students are given a great deal of responsibility for the quality of dorm life, including establishing rules for community living; thus, educational goals of developing critical thinking and responsible citizenship are promoted (Krehbiel and Strange, 1991).

Evidence of specific connections between residence halls and the curriculum can be found in Earlham's Living Learning Humanities Halls. The Humanities Program is required of all first-year students and is intended to provide both an academic and a social orientation to Earlham, introduce concepts of humanistic education, build writing and research skills, and immerse new students in the collaborative and interdisciplinary learning processes valued by the college (Kuh, Schuh, Whitt, and Associates, 1991).

Although all first-year Earlham students participate in the Humanities Program, about one-third (100 students in 1992–93) spend their first term in the program housed in the Living Learning Humanities Halls (at Earlham, the term *hall* refers to a dorm floor). Assignments to the Humanities Halls are made on a first-come, first-served basis, and the demand for the program regularly exceeds the available space (A. Wright, personal communication, April 1993).

Course requirements include reading a book a week from works in history, philosophy, literature, social science — "significant ideas, well expressed" (L. Blake, personal communication, April 1993) — and writing a paper each week on the assigned text. In addition to class time, students and faculty participate in tutorials in which the students review one another's papers with help from the faculty member. Some faculty hold class sessions in the dorms, while others choose to meet in classroom buildings.

Having students in the same class living on the same hall facilitates learning in that conversations about the humanities extend into the residence, thereby increasing opportunities for involvement with the subject matter (A. Wright, personal communication, April 1993). Also, because all students on the hall have a paper due every Monday, collaboration is fostered — faculty say the students "bond very rapidly" — and the papers become a focus of residents' interactions. Faculty find the Living Learning students to be comfortable about speaking in class and willing to help other students as informal tutors. Sharing ideas about the texts for the weekly papers also prompts diverse ways of interpreting the texts and helps students find their own meaning in the works (L. Blake, personal communication, April 1993).

The Living Learning Humanities Halls also enable students to experience the important connections between the subject matter of their humanities course, the Quaker traditions of the college, and the daily challenges of their lives. Decisions in both the Humanities Program and the residences are made by consensus, affirming the Quaker belief that there is a "light of truth" in each individual (Krehbiel and Strange, 1991). Collaborative learning techniques support the Quaker tenet that no single individual can possess all the "truth" and that all sides of an issue must be considered in cooperation (Krehbiel and Strange, 1991).

The Living Learning Humanities Halls are coordinated by a Convener, a faculty member who teaches in the Humanities Program. A committee of faculty members develops a reading list for the course each year, and the faculty of the program meet each week to discuss the text for the following week and to "spend social time together" (L. Blake, personal communication, April 1993). Student affairs staff cooperate with the Humanities faculty regarding room assignments and in other ways as needed.

Stanford University

Stanford University is both a major research university and a rich and involving undergraduate college (Kuh, Schuh, Whitt, and Associates, 1991). Stanford's mission includes a commitment to "bring knowledge and understanding to each new generation of young people; . . . to provide the basis for ethical and responsible lives, productive careers, and contributions to the public welfare . . . [and provide] a campus environment and activities through which students develop attitudes and values in the midst of a diverse population" (Kuh, 1991, p. 48).

This mission is reflected in the goals of Stanford's residence halls: (1) to enhance the intellectual life of the campus and campus residences, and (2) to develop inclusive communities (Kuh, 1991). "By integrating curricular experiences with students' lives outside the classroom, the residential education program is integral to the high-quality, out-of-class learning that characterizes Stanford University" (Kuh, 1991, p. 60). The accomplishment of educational purposes in Stanford's residence halls, commonly referred to as dorms, is facilitated by the small size of its housing units. Stanford dorms house from 30 to 280 students, and the largest are only three or four stories high (Kuh, Schuh, Whitt, and Associates, 1991). Two examples of ways in which Stanford integrates the curriculum and campus housing are the Resident Fellows and the Structured Liberal Education Program.

Resident Fellows. Resident Fellows (RFs) are faculty or staff members who live in Stanford dorms to make clear and practical connections between academic and residence life. Approximately thirty-seven of Stanford's seventy campus residences have RFs, each of whom is expected to be an educational leader in the dorm. She or he provides academic counseling, supervises resident assistants, and serves as a liaison between the dorm and the Office of Residential Education. Furthermore, RFs bring other faculty members into the dorms for debates, presentations, film series, and workshops; RFs also sponsor field trips, fine arts events, and community service projects (Kuh, Schuh, Whitt, and Associates, 1991).

RFs also teach courses in their dorms. Some are instructors for the course required of all first-year students, "Culture, Ideas, and Values." Others provide classes in their special interests. For example, a professor of anthropology engaged his students in developing a multimedia course on Mayan culture and civilization. An RF in Ujamaa, the African-American theme house, taught a course on the Los Angeles riots of 1966 and 1992. RFs build on their own strengths and the strengths and interests of students to achieve curricular goals in nontraditional and innovative ways (A. Supton, personal communication, April 1993).

Regardless of the specific nature of the programs or activities in which RFs are involved, every effort is made to encourage students to see their education at Stanford as seamless (Kuh, Schuh, Whitt, and Associates, 1991): that challenging subject matter, critical thinking, and discussions about cultural, political, and historical events are not restricted to the classroom. An excerpt from the RF job description illustrates this commitment to fostering learning wherever it occurs: "Resident Fellows can also provide invaluable mentoring to undergraduates. Knowing the students as individuals, RFs can influence students' learning by such simple gestures as loaning a book, clipping a newspaper article of interest, bringing together students interested in the same subject, or suggesting avenues of research and faculty contact" (Kuh, Schuh, Whitt, and Associates, 1991, p. 205).

Commitment on the part of Stanford faculty and administrators to the RF program is clear. RFs have received tenure at the same rate as their colleagues who do not serve as RFs. Most important, RFs speak of their work as an essential aspect of the total undergraduate experience at Stanford (Kuh, Schuh, Whitt, and Associates, 1991). The coordinator of the RF program is the director of residential education, who works in cooperation with academic administrators and faculty but is a member of the student affairs staff.

The success of the RF program depends to some extent on the institution's ability to provide attractive housing for the

RFs and some relief from the traditional undergraduate teaching load. In addition, although RFs are expected to respond to emergencies, they are not responsible for long-term disciplinary or personal counseling (A. Supton, personal communication, April 1993).

Structured Liberal Education Program. Stanford's Structured Liberal Education (SLE) Program had two purposes when it was begun in 1974: (1) to provide a focused academic experience for first-year students, and (2) to provide that academic experience where the students lived in order to lessen distinctions between students' in-class and out-of-class lives (J. Reider, personal communication, April 1993). The SLE program continues today as a curricular program based in the residence (A. Supton, personal communication, April 1993).

Students are chosen by faculty to participate in SLE on the basis of their housing applications. Faculty look for students who desire a "highly structured, highly interdisciplinary" academic experience and who are perceived to be serious students. In particular, SLE requires students who want to take ideas, and talking about ideas, seriously and who are willing to bring their coursework into their residence. About eighty-five first-year students were involved in SLE during the 1992–93 school year (J. Reider, personal communication, April 1993).

All SLE students live in Florence Moore Hall, read the same books, and have the same assignments and so engage faculty and one another in a "shared intellectual enterprise" (J. Reider, personal communication, April 1993). All papers are due the same day, and students prepare for oral examinations in collaboration with other students. The Florence Moore Resident Fellow is a SLE faculty member. Classes and discussion groups meet in the dorm, and SLE-related programs are open to residents.

The heart of SLE is the twice-weekly discussion sessions among twelve to fourteen students and a teacher. The focus of these discussions is developing oral skills as students think aloud about books and ideas. Course subject matter focuses on the ancient world, the Renaissance, and the modern world, and texts in history, literature, political science, and philosophy are assigned. No matter what texts are assigned, SLE students and faculty discuss broad issues, such as the nature of a good life and the nature of knowledge and inquiry.

Each SLE student has a tutor; approximately thirty SLE tutors serve the eighty-five SLE students. Many of the tutors are former SLE students who want to "give something back" to the program. Tutors work with students on drafts of their papers and focus on developing ideas and critical thinking.

Students who participate in SLE are described as "empowered in their own education, because they are asked to speak, to write, are heard and responded to, and experience a lot of evaluation." They "think cogently and speak well and show intellectual self-confidence" (A. Supton, personal communication, April 1993).

The success of SLE can be attributed, in part, to one senior faculty member who is credited by others with getting the program going and maintaining a broad institutional commitment to SLE over the past two decades. Also necessary to the program's survival is a small group of founding faculty who continue to be committed to the program, who get along well with one another and enjoy spending time with students, and who have a nontraditional view of academic experiences. The small number of faculty involved in SLE limits the number of students who can participate, but those who are involved believe in the program (J. Reider, personal communication, April 1993). Finally, student affairs administrators who facilitate the integration of SLE into residential education — through room assignments, staff assignments, and program support — are essential.

Michigan State University

Efforts by Michigan State University to integrate living and learning reach back even farther than those at Stanford. In the late 1950s and early 1960s, Michigan State University was a rapidly growing institution under the leadership of then–President John Hannah. Concern for retaining advantages of a small college while making the most of the opportunities of an expanding major university led to the development of three residential colleges in the mid 1960s: James Madison College, Lyman Briggs College, and Justin Morrill College (Waltzer, 1992). At first, the focus of these colleges was first-year students—providing them with access to student services, academic advising, and a majority of their classes within the residence.

Three decades after the founding of the colleges, James Madison College and Lyman Briggs College are still in existence. The programs and policies of both have evolved to meet changing circumstances and requirements, but any changes have been consistent with their original missions (M. Haas, personal communication, June 1993). Although budget cuts have threatened the programs at times, recent attention on the freshman-year experience has affirmed the importance of the residential colleges for Michigan State University.

James Madison College. James Madison is a small residential college that provides rigorous programs in public affairs and social sciences for approximately 1,000 undergraduates interested in law, government, foreign service, and related areas (College of James Madison brochure, 1992–93). The college is housed in Case Hall, a facility that includes classrooms and faculty offices as well as dormitory rooms and lounges for students.

Recent curriculum change in James Madison "carries forward the initial vision of study planned around 'public policy problems,' but is more interdisciplinary and theoretical, more international and comparative" than in the past (Waltzer, 1992, p. 29). The curriculum and the college's administrative structure foster extensive interaction between students and faculty, and the students are described as "liberal thinking" (M. Haas, personal communication, June 1993).

Lyman Briggs School. After Michigan State's fiscal crisis in 1981, Lyman Briggs was reorganized as a school within the Department of Natural Sciences. Its mission did not change, however; Lyman Briggs is an undergraduate residential program for students pursuing broad, science-based fields of study.

"The educational philosophy of Lyman Briggs School is based on the belief that those sharing an interest in science will benefit from learning and living together" (Lyman Briggs School brochure, 1992). By taking much, though not all, of their academic program in the residence hall, students stimulate and enhance one another's intellectual and personal growth. Also, faculty emphasize close working relationships with students. Classes tend to be small and enhance the residential aspects of the school by promoting interaction among students and instructors through discussions of the readings and exchange and evaluation of papers. Labs in some courses operate on an open, or unscheduled, basis, which offers flexibility and independence for students.

All of the Lyman Briggs first-year students and many upperclass students live in Holmes Hall. The residence facility includes living quarters for students, a cafeteria, classrooms, laboratories, faculty and administrative offices, a computer room, a science library, and recreational facilities. Many undergraduate teaching assistants also live in Holmes Hall and are available to tutor students and to facilitate study and review sessions.

The general atmosphere of Lyman Briggs is described as providing important opportunities for the individual student to experience personal and intellectual development through close interaction with other students and faculty. Because students not enrolled in Lyman Briggs are also housed in Holmes Hall, Briggs students have contact with a wide array of student experiences.

Two full-time staff members are funded jointly by the college and residential life to share academic advising responsibilities. These staff members also edit a newsletter and assist with planning and implementing both curricular and cocurricular programs.

University of Maryland, College Park

In contrast to the long-standing residential colleges at Michigan State, living-learning programs at the University of Maryland, College Park, were created only recently. The University of Maryland is a publicly supported, land-grant university dedicated to the educational needs of Maryland residents. Located in a suburb of Washington, D.C., the campus enrolls approximately 22,000 undergraduates, 7,500 of whom live in campus residence halls. The campus goals for undergraduate education were approved by the Campus Senate in 1988: "An education at the University of Maryland at College Park strives to cultivate intellect by teaching students to extend principles and ideas to new situations and to new groups of people. It aims to provide students with a sense of identity and purpose, a concern for others, a sense of responsibility for the quality of life around them, a continuing eagerness for knowledge and understanding, and a foundation for a lifetime of personal enrichment. . . . Specifically, undergraduate education at College Park seeks to enable students to develop and expand their use of basic academic and intellectual tools" (undergraduate catalogue, 1992–93, p. i).

Consistent with this emphasis on intellectual enrichment and development of community are the university's three residential programs that link out-of-class experiences to academic goals: (1) Honors Living/Learning Center, (2) Language House, and (3) International House. Each program is located in a recently renovated building that houses approximately 100–125 students and that has facilities for faculty-in-residence as well as a mix of gathering spaces and classroom facilities. The three living-learning halls are located near one another in the central, academic "core" of the campus.

The programs have been successful because of the campuswide commitment to making them work, including strong and visible support from President William E. Kirwan. As highlighted in Chapter Three, the success of the programs also is attributed to the leadership of academic affairs and student affairs staff. This partnership requires faculty and staff to learn about and understand each other's professional culture and to identify what each of the partners does best — how each can contribute to the educational purposes of the institution through the living-learning programs (P. Mielke, personal communication, March 1993; J. Lawrence, personal communication, May 1993).

Honors Living/Learning Center. The Honors Living/Learning Center has housed students enrolled in the University Honors Program since fall 1992, and the residence "serves as the center of Honors life and as the focal point for excellence in undergraduate education" at the University of Maryland (Anne Arundel Hall brochure, Honors Living/Learning Center, University of Maryland, College Park, 1992). Assignment to the residence is granted by application and is based on several criteria, including academic achievement, involvement in Honors programs on campus, and participation in extracurricular activities. Students may live in the Honors Center for a maximum of two years but must meet the necessary criteria each year. Administrative offices of the Honors Program, faculty offices, classroom space, a reading room/library, and an informal lounge in the residence hall facilitates direct links between the students' academic experience and the living situation. An apartment for visiting scholars provides additional intellectual enrichment opportunities for students.

The Living/Learning Center provides classroom space for one-half (approximately twenty to twenty-five) of the Honors seminars. Lectures and other special social and cultural events offer opportunities for Honors students residing elsewhere, as well as for students not involved in the Honors Program, to benefit from the center.

The Honors Center has completed its second year of operation. Future plans include more extensive publicity about lectures and special activities so that more students are aware of, and can participate in, the events. In describing the first year of the Honors Center, the director noted the importance of mutual understanding of the residence life staff and Honors faculty goals and purposes (J. Lawrence, personal communication, May 1993). She asserted that the Honors Program faculty believe that the primary goal of the center is the students' intellectual development, whereas the residence hall staff are committed to social and personal, as well as intellectual, development. She stated that "as faculty, we believe these students are really smart enough to figure out the social and personal things on their own" (J. Lawrence, personal communication,

May 1993). These differences in priorities and beliefs about students' development could lead to conflictual policies and practices if the faculty and student affairs staff were not in frequent communication.

Language House. The purpose of the Language House is to allow students to immerse themselves in a foreign language. Language House is sponsored by the Division of Arts and Humanities, which assigns a faculty member to live in the residence and direct the program and which supports salaries for the faculty director and academic mentors. The faculty member supervises the academic mentors, the computer laboratory, and the café. State-of-the-art computing facilities and a café in the residence provide many opportunities for formal and informal faculty and student interaction. Students enrolled in language courses work together in the computer laboratory and participate in other academic programs in the house.

International House. International House ("I House") is completing its third year and provides opportunities for students interested in other cultures and international issues to participate in a wide range of activities focused on a common intellectual theme. While the students assigned are not necessarily enrolled in similar courses of study, there is an interdisciplinary approach to international issues, and the students share common academic interests and experiences.

Approximately 60 to 70 percent of the 155 I House residents are U.S. students, many of whom have been raised in bicultural families or have had international experience. Twenty to thirty percent of the students are from outside the United States. Many of the students are studying international business, foreign languages, or political science.

I House residents sponsor lectures, discussions, and other programs. The "soapbox" current affairs series invites faculty to lecture or lead discussions on current affairs, world conflicts, and international political topics. A weekly coffee hour is also scheduled. The residence hall includes an apartment for visiting faculty, and many of those visitors have engaged in programs and activities with students. For example, a Russian scholar served tea in the apartment every night at 10:00 and students dropped by for conversation. Also, there have been joint programs with the Language House, including a session on second-language acquisition.

Students apply to live in I House and are selected by a committee based on an essay. There is a strong tradition of student leadership and governance in I House that distinguishes the program somewhat from other academic residential offerings.

Public access areas of the hall and floor lounges were renovated for the international program. Ground floors have lounges, seminar rooms, and a computer room. Students live on both sides of a corridor and share common bathrooms and study lounges. Floor lounges are used for informal discussions and gatherings.

International Education Services (IES) provides a half-time coordinator to work with the residence life staff and I House student committees (V. Woolston, personal communication, June 1993). The IES adviser has an office in the residence hall as well as in the IES office; therefore, students can consult with the adviser in both locations (R. Barrett, personal conversation, June 1993). The rich diversity of programming is influenced by the tenacious involvement and participation of the staff of IES (P. Mielke, personal conversation, March 1993).

Program leaders believe I House requires close work and cooperation between residence life staff and the IES staff. Both groups have learned from each other, especially about differences in organizational cultures. Some differences in focus exist as well. The IES staff perceive that residence life staff are more concerned about building security than they, and IES would like faculty members to have easier access to the facility. Both groups want to develop better orientation programs for the residents and both plan to explore providing regularly scheduled courses in the hall.

Discussion of Current Examples

Although there is great variety in the programs and institutions just described, common elements have helped these colleges and universities implement and sustain their commitment to connecting residence halls to the curriculum. These common elements are: (1) clarity of institutional purposes and expectations; (2) policies, practices, and environments that connect the curriculum and residence halls; and (3) people committed to these connections.

Clarity of Institutional Purposes and Expectations

Learning communities such as those described here "endure when they fit with the values of the institutional community" (Gabelnick, MacGregor, Matthews, and Smith, 1990, p. 50). In each case, the college or university's mission incorporates a commitment to the development of all aspects of students' lives as a part of the institution's educational purposes. This mission provides a basis for explicit connections between students' in-class and out-of-class experiences, including between the curriculum and residence halls. For students involved in the programs noted, those connections are ready-made and highly visible. For students who are not part of these learning communities — most of the students on these campuses — the connections between residence halls and the curriculum may, in the absence of other intentional efforts to integrate in-class and out-of-class experiences, be left to chance.

The institutional mission also supports clear messages to students about what it means to be a student at that institution, how they should expect to spend their time, and the ways in which their intellectual, social, and emotional development shape one another (Kuh, Schuh, Whitt, and Associates, 1991). There may be gaps between what the institution espouses and aspects of the mission that are enacted, especially at the larger and more complex institutions, yet the learning communities do provide a mechanism to implement high expectations for the students involved in the programs.

Policies, Practices, and Environments That Connect the Curriculum and Residence Halls

Learning communities also "are sustained when the learning community conversation becomes embedded in the daily academic, social, and political discourse about learning" (Gabelnick, Mac-Gregor, Matthews, and Smith, 1990, p. 50). That is, the institution's mission informs policies and practices that create and maintain connections between the curriculum and extracurricular aspects of student life.

Each of the programs described in the preceding section requires ongoing collaboration between academic affairs and student affairs. In most cases, faculty coordinate the programs, but student affairs staff have responsibility for important aspects, such as staffing, room and space assignments, and program development and evaluation. All rely on a shared vision of the educational purposes of the college and how that vision can be achieved.

The living-learning programs also demonstrate that curricular goals can be implemented outside the classroom. Earlham's Living Learning Humanities Halls and Stanford's Structured Liberal Education Program are examples of the integration of general education requirements into residential settings. These learning communities also take an interdisciplinary approach to subject matter and use collaborative pedagogical techniques, such as group projects, oral exams for groups of students, extensive interaction between students and faculty, and teaching of students by other students. Faculty members and administrators at Earlham and Stanford believe that, at least for first-year students, explicit connections between academic and nonacademic elements of life, and common, cooperative, cross-disciplinary learning experiences help achieve the academic purposes of the institution and create an important foundation for the rest of the students' time in college.

Commitment to achieving the eduational mission in residences also influenced, and was influenced by, the physical environments of these institutions. For the most part, living spaces are small enough to promote a feeling of closeness, yet provide gathering places—such as lounges and computing, classroom, and office spaces—to encourage interaction between students and faculty and among students. Thus, facilities are available to create a sense of a small learning community within, yet apart from, the larger residential and institutional communities.

Other policies that facilitate connections between residence halls and the curriculum include housing assignments. Housing assignment procedures at these institutions enable students to express interest in the living-learning programs and allow faculty to participate in decisions about whom to assign to the program space. At Earlham, Humanities Program faculty decide, on the basis of information on the housing application forms, the students who might be interested in the Living Learning Halls. At Stanford, SLE students have roommates who are not involved in SLE, so that both are exposed to a variety of learning experiences.

People Committed to These Connections

"Ultimately, learning communities work because people care enough about them to invest time and energy in them over the long haul" (Gabelnick, MacGregor, Matthews, and Smith, 1990, p. 50). The people involved in the learning communities described here — faculty, staff, and students — are critical to the success of the programs.

Systematic connections between residence halls and the curriculum require faculty who are willing to spend time with students in living-learning programs and to engage in cross-disciplinary coursework. Each of the programs mentioned has faculty coordinators, as well as other faculty who help plan classes, decide on texts, and select student participants. Faculty also cited the importance of senior faculty involvement; senior faculty leadership provides the credibility needed to maintain institutional approval and funding. In some cases, a single faculty member takes ownership for the program and keeps it going on the strength of his or her commitment; the future of the program, then, is threatened if, for some reason, that individual can no longer be involved. And the fact that each of the institutions has only small numbers of faculty in the living-learning programs has limited the amount of possible student participation.

Student affairs staff who can work successfully in partnership with faculty are also necessary. A later section of this chapter discusses ways student affairs staff can learn to define their roles to include achievement of the academic purposes of the institution. Suffice it to say here that student affairs staff play key roles on "the residential side" of the living-learning programs by providing staff support for faculty coordinators, working with faculty to devise program goals and planning out-of-class aspects of the program, and hiring and training staff. These staff also model and affirm the academic values of the institution in their contacts with students and use sound teaching and learning principles as the basis for their work with students.

Perhaps most important to sustaining the living communities described here are students who are willing to integrate living and learning experiences in ways consistent with the educational goals of the institution. They should also be willing to take intellectual risks, willing to take ideas and talking about ideas seriously, and willing to take advantage of connections between academic and residential programs. Also important are student cultures within which these expectations, behaviors, and values are socially acceptable; such cultures may predominate at small institutions, such as Earlham, or find small niches at large universities, such as Maryland. Students who can take advantage of living-learning communities tend to be traditional-age and single; the programs described in this chapter do not easily accommodate older learners or students who for a variety of reasons must commute from home to campus.

Implications for Improving Practice

There are many compelling reasons, including enhancing student learning (Astin, 1992; Pascarella and Terenzini, 1991), to develop and sustain connections between the curriculum and residence halls. This chapter has presented elements that can facilitate those connections. If faculty and staff are interested in making such connections at their institution, how and where should they begin? This section identifies issues to consider in developing systematic and sustained connections between academic programs and residential programs on their campuses.

1. *Institutional assessment:* Astin (1992), Kuh, Schuh, Whitt, and Associates (1991), and others (see Kuh in Chapter Six) have

argued that the more an institution really understands itself—
its strengths and weaknesses, its limitations and its potential—the
more likely it is to be successful in carrying out its educational
mission. The examples discussed earlier imply some form of self-
assessment to determine the extent to which the educational purposes, policies, and structures are consistent with, and institutional leadership and others (students, faculty, student affairs
staff, academic affairs staff) understand and are committed to,
explicit connections between curricular goals and programs of
the institution and residence halls.

Questions to be asked to determine the appropriateness
of living-learning programs or readiness for learning communities include the following: What are the institution's educational purposes? To what extent do these purposes demonstrate
a commitment to the education of the whole student? Do the
institution's mission and people tend to view students' in-class
and out-of-class lives as separate? To what extent can the undergraduate curriculum be implemented in residences? For specific guidelines for conducting campus self-assessments, see Whitt
(1993) and Kuh (1993).

The extent to which these factors exist or can be developed or modified on a campus will influence the institution's
ability to design effective learning communities. The results of
the assessment will guide decisions about how to proceed. Additional assessment issues are identified in the next section.

2. *Unique institutional missions and cultures:* An important
aspect of assessment is consideration of the institution's uniqueness. Achieving connections between residence halls and the curriculum is not possible at all institutions in the same ways or
to the same extent. Campuses should design programs consistent with their mission and institutional cultures. As educators
explore models described in this book, they should consider the
adaptations necessary for their institution. The challenges faced
by Earlham are different from those at Grinnell, for example,
just as those faced by Iowa State are different from those at the
University of Maryland.

As noted earlier, the characteristics of students (for example, their academic interests, their expectations for out-of-
class experiences), as well as the nature of student, faculty, and

student affairs cultures, influence the ease with which living-learning programs can be created and sustained. Issues to consider include these: To what extent do faculty expect to—or *are* they expected to—be involved in residential programs? Do student cultures support or inhibit melding of academic and residential experiences? To what extent do faculty and student affairs staff consider themselves partners in achieving the educational purposes of the institution? To what extent are senior faculty involved in and committed to undergraduate education?

Large institutions with diverse student bodies may face particular challenges in developing learning communities. The examples described in this chapter offer living-learning experiences to a small proportion of students at these institutions, in part because of limited faculty involvement and in part because of the facilities that can be devoted to such programs. Also, the residential nature of the programs limits participation to mostly traditional-age, single students. Connections between in-class and out-of-class experiences may need to be defined more broadly than "connecting residence halls to the curriculum" at many institutions (Tinto, Goodsell-Love, and Russo, 1993), although that is the focus of this chapter.

Research universities also may present barriers to developing learning communities. If all faculty are expected to see themselves as researchers, if undergraduate education is the purview of junior faculty and teaching assistants, and if graduate education is the primary focus of institutional resources, convincing faculty to spend part of their limited time in living-learning programs may be difficult.

Finally, commitments to equal access and egalitarianism at some public colleges and universities may hinder establishing separate residential arrangements and privileges for certain groups of students. For example, Indiana University's Wells Scholars Program provides special seminars and extracurricular opportunities for students enrolled in the program. However, it deliberately does not provide special residential housing opportunities. This decision was based on the desire to have as many students as possible interact with the Wells Scholars who have already demonstrated significant academic and leadership promise. Housing the Wells Scholars together was viewed as elitist and would minimize the potential for them to serve as role models for students in many campus settings (J. Bondanella, personal communication, March 1993).

Therefore, the process of self-assessment must consider the institution's unique history, cultures, and human characteristics in determining readiness for connecting residence halls to the curriculum and the form the connections should take. Programs such as the Humanities Halls at Earlham, the Structured Liberal Education Program at Stanford, Stanford's Resident Fellows, Michigan State's James Madison College, or the Honors Center at Maryland might be suitable on other campuses. Or some other type of integration of in-class and out-of-class experiences may be more appropriate (Tinto, Goodsell-Love, and Russo, 1993).

3. *Institutional leadership:* Commitment of academic and student affairs leadership to living-learning programs is essential to their success. Senior officers play key roles in fostering understanding and support from the various campus constituencies—faculty, staff, students, parents, graduates, trustees—all of whom must understand and support the relationship between educational purposes and the out-of-class lives of students. Formal and informal messages and images should communicate high expectations for students' intellectual life both inside and outside the classroom, for faculty involvement in out-of-class experiences of students, and for mutual respect and understanding among student affairs and academic affairs staff. If leader commitment is not present, key faculty members and student affairs staff may form partnerships to initiate living-learning programs, but sustaining them will eventually require institutional support.

Mutual respect and collaboration among faculty and student affairs staff requires both groups to develop greater understanding and appreciation of their mutual and distinct professional cultures (Kuh, Schuh, Whitt, and Associates, 1991). Common examples of cultural differences between academic and student affairs include the following: faculty members tend to have primary ties to their disciplines and/or departments, whereas student affairs staff tend to have strong institutional loyalties; faculty tend to do research autonomously, often in isolation from colleagues, but student affairs staff prefer to conduct their work in cooperation with other people; and faculty tend to focus on the intellectual development of students, while student affairs staff must focus on the development of the whole student (Clark, 1987; Kuh, Shedd, and Whitt, 1987; Mitchell and Roof, 1989). As Kuh noted in Chapter Six, these differences can contribute to ambiguity and lack of knowledge about the roles that student affairs staff — and students' out-of-class experiences — play in achieving the institution's educational purposes.

For collaboration to occur between faculty and student affairs staff, there must be a willingness to identify and seek common ground. Success is unlikely if either or both approach collaboration as having to be done solely on their own terms. It is important to identify faculty and staff colleagues who share an interest in implementing educational goals in residences and who have a broad commitment to effective undergraduate education.

Student affairs staff should view themselves as educators and not appear to be "rescuing students from the unpleasant rigors of schooling" (Weingartner, 1992, p. 129). They should demonstrate interest and concern for students' intellectual development and not behave as if the students' academic responsibilities are less important than their out-of-class activities. To the extent possible, student affairs staff should suggest courses and extracurricular activities congruent with students' academic goals. Their work should exemplify the basic assumptions and beliefs of the student affairs profession — and acknowledge the preeminance of the institution's academic mission (National Association of Student Personnel Administrators, 1987). They must understand the academic mission of the institution, be knowledgeable about the goals and structure of the undergraduate curriculum, and understand the contributions of both the curriculum and the extracurriculum in fostering student intellectual and personal development. Most important, student affairs staff should examine the ways their actions promote — or inhibit — the institution's educational purposes and identify ways they can be active participants in the teaching and learning process. In

Chapter Six, Kuh also provides suggestions for ways student affairs staff can become more effective educators.

Faculty should consider student affairs professionals as partners in the educational mission of the institution. Faculty also should be knowledgeable about how their courses contribute to the institution's goals for undergraduate education and should provide guidance for students about how to apply course-related skills and knowledge in their daily lives. Greater emphasis on cooperative teaching and learning styles would also be beneficial (MacGregor, 1990; Schroeder, 1993). Faculty should recognize that how the curriculum is delivered is more important than its content and structure (Astin, 1992; Weingartner, 1992). Although the examples of learning communities identified in this chapter are available to only small numbers of students, a true intellectual community requires opportunities for the entire student body to share some portion of the curriculum (Astin, 1992; Tinto, Goodsell-Love, and Russo, 1993); "the decision as to what every student should read and learn is far less important than the determination that all students should have a common curricular experience" (Weingartner, 1992, p. 158). This common experience has positive effects on student learning outcomes and enhances students' intellectual involvement (Astin, 1992).

4. *Physical environments:* Campuses should not underestimate the impact of placement of residences on campus, the size of student rooms, access to instructional technology, and the availability of gathering places on the institution's ability to successfully connect the curriculum to residence halls (Kuh, Schuh, Whitt, and Associates, 1991). Unfortunately, the ways many campus residence halls were constructed prevent students from finding places for the out-of-class academic activities they might wish to engage in with faculty or with one another. In many cases, it is impossible to find suitable spaces for formal activities such as classes, group discussions, or project assembly areas (Weingartner, 1992). Also, at many large universities, such as the University of Maryland, high-rise residence halls are located on the periphery of the campus. Decisions at many universities to build residence halls on the edge of the campus close to the

parking lots may communicate a message about the centrality of residence life to the mission of the institution and the intellectual life of the campus. This is in sharp contrast, however, to the living-learning residence halls at the University of Maryland; they are located in the center of campus, close to the library and classroom and faculty office buildings. Holmes and Case Halls at Michigan State were planned with the residential college model — and needs — in mind.

Flansburgh (1991) advised campus planners that student residential space should reflect the special nature and culture of the college and should be used to enhance the quality of total learning on the campus. Computer technology and access to electronic bulletin boards enable students to share comments and observations on common classes, collaborate on projects, and review feedback from faculty and classmates on written assignments. Room, floor, or hall assignments that group students enrolled in common courses provide increased opportunities to link academic programs and purposes with residential education. These initiatives have the potential to strengthen the bond between in-class and out-of-class experiences and provide students with common intellectual tasks.

Programs such as Stanford's Resident Fellows may also require adjustments to the physical environment. If faculty are asked to live in residence halls, desirable apartment space — including space for families — must be provided. Issues such as accessibility to students, yet protection from noise and traffic, and availability of office and work space must be considered.

In the current economic climate, it will be difficult for colleges to invest the resources for renovations or new construction of residence halls. However, many public institutions with declining numbers of traditional-age students experience high residence hall vacancy rates. As plans for renovation or alternatives for unused space are considered, careful attention should be paid to measures that will enable the institution to provide greater opportunities for making connections between the curriculum and residence programs.

5. *Recognition and rewards:* Consistent with the recommendation to set high standards and expectations for faculty, stu-

dents, and staff is the implementation of appropriate recognition and reward systems. Opportunities to celebrate and affirm the intellectual life of the campus include honors convocations and special departmental activities that recognize faculty, staff, and student achievements (Carnegie Foundation for the Advancement of Teaching, 1990). Learning communities can provide a visible focus for such celebrations.

Faculty involvement in educationally purposeful residence programs should be recognized in the promotion and tenure process and not be viewed as an activity outside the scope of the faculty member's academic responsibilities. Boyer (1990, p. 35) argued that the "time has come not only to reconsider the meaning of scholarship but also to take the next step and consider ways in which the faculty reward system can be improved." Boyer identified four separate, yet overlapping aspects of scholarship: scholarship of discovery (research), scholarship of integration (making connections across disciplines, creating new insights and interpretations), scholarship of application (applying knowledge to problems, creating new understandings), and scholarship of teaching. Research universities have tended to reward faculty members for the scholarship of discovery and to disregard scholarly work not aimed at publication in refereed journals. Boyer encouraged institutions to consider improving undergraduate education by developing ways to evaluate and reward faculty performance beyond the scholarship of discovery. Doing so would create a climate that has the potential to encourage faculty to become involved in living-learning programs because such involvement would be seen as making a valuable contribution to the educational purposes of the institution.

Expanding the definition of scholarship might also help faculty and student affairs professionals find common ground. While most student affairs staff are not actively engaged in the scholarship of discovery, they are actively engaged in the scholarship of integration, application, and teaching. Examples include counseling and advising, applications of student development theory to practice, leadership training, assessment, and program evaluation. A broader conceptualization of what constitutes scholarly activity could provide recognition for the im-

portant contributions that both faculty and student affairs professionals make to the intellectual life of the campus through connections between residence halls and the curriculum.

Conclusion

This chapter began with the assumption that by understanding
the factors that promote connections between residence halls and
the curriculum, student affairs and academic leaders will be better able to design living-learning communities appropriate to
their institutions and that fulfill the educational potential of residence halls that is often discussed but seldom achieved. Those
factors were illustrated in examples of actual living-learning
communities — several successful attempts by disparate institutions to create visible and meaningful links between students'
in-class and out-of-class lives.

Some readers might argue that creating intentional living-
learning communities on their campuses would be too difficult
or expensive to contemplate. They might wonder whether creating systematic connections between the undergraduate curriculum and residence hall is an "all-or-nothing" proposition. That
is, are living-learning communities such as those described in
this chapter the only way to foster such connections, or can
smaller-scale and/or less formally structured programs be effective? One answer to the all-or-nothing question is "of course not."
Recall, for example, Weingartner's (1992) assertion — supported
by Astin's (1992) research — that "all [undergraduate] students
[at one institution] should have a common curricular experience" to enhance learning and intellectual involvement. This
common curricular experience could take many forms, such as
general education orientation courses, and could be implemented,
at least in part, in student residences. A number of such programs exist, although the emphasis of many is academic and
the focus of activities is the classroom. This brings us back to
the point of this chapter: considering systematic and sustained
efforts to achieve institutional academic purposes and implement
curricular goals through residence halls.

Therefore, there is another answer to the all-or-nothing

question: "yes, this *is* an all-or-nothing proposition"—if by *all* one means a firm institutional commitment to promoting and enhancing student learning and development by thorough integration of the institution's educational purposes and curricular goals with residence halls and other aspects of the out-of-class lives of students. The institutional examples offered here indicate that such integration, to be successful, demands intentional living-learning communities.

At a time when colleges and universities are challenged to focus more systematically and deliberately on student learning and the outcomes of a college education, renewed consideration of, and commitment to, creating living-learning communities is appropriate (Wingspread Group on Higher Education, 1993). This chapter asserts that creating such communities requires conducting a careful assessment of institutional mission, goals, and culture; acknowledging and communicating high expectations for faculty, staff, and student performance, including mutual respect, understanding, and cooperation among student affairs staff and faculty; ensuring appropriate facilities, furnishings, and equipment; and implementing appropriate—even creative—recognition and reward systems for faculty, staff, and students.

The failure of colleges and universities to take on and struggle through the difficulties inherent in developing living-learning communities—that is, backing away from the all-or-nothing question—ensures that residence halls will not achieve their full educational potential. Research on student learning and involvement and the experiences of institutions such as those described in this chapter leave little doubt about the potential benefits of connecting residence halls to the curriculum for student development and for fulfilling institutional educational goals; the challenges of choosing "all" are indeed worth facing.

References

Astin, A. W. *What Matters in College? Four Critical Years Revisited.* San Francisco: Jossey-Bass, 1992.

Bok, D. *Higher Learning.* Cambridge, Mass.: Harvard University Press, 1986.

Boyer, E. L. *College: The Undergraduate Experience in America.* New York: HarperCollins, 1987.

Boyer, E. L. *Scholarship Reconsidered: Priorities of the Professoriate.* Princeton, N.J.: Carnegie Foundation for the Advancement of Teaching, 1990.

Carnegie Foundation for the Advancement of Teaching. *Campus Life: In Search of Community.* Princeton, N.J.: Carnegie Foundation for the Advancement of Teaching, 1990.

Chickering, A. W. *Commuting Versus Resident Students: Overcoming the Educational Inequities of Living Off Campus.* San Francisco: Jossey-Bass, 1974.

Clark, B. R. *The Academic Life: Small Worlds, Different Worlds.* Princeton, N.J.: Carnegie Foundation for the Advancement of Teaching, 1987.

Flansburgh, E. "New-Wave Housing." *Planning for Higher Education,* 1991, *19,* 1–10.

Gabelnick, F., MacGregor, J., Matthews, R. S., and Smith, B. L. *Learning Communities: Creating Connections Among Students, Faculty, and Disciplines.* New Directions for Teaching and Learning, no. 41. San Francisco: Jossey-Bass, 1990.

Jencks, C. S., and Riesman, D. "Patterns of Residential Education: A Case Study of Harvard." In N. Sanford (ed.), *The American College.* New York: Wiley, 1962.

Krehbiel, L. E., and Strange, C. C. "Checking on the Truth: The Case of Earlham College." In G. D. Kuh and J. H. Schuh (eds.), *The Role and Contribution of Student Affairs in Involving Colleges.* Washington, D.C.: National Association of Student Personnel Administrators, 1991.

Kuh, G. D. "Assessing Campus Environments." In M. J. Barr and Associates, *The Handbook of Student Affairs Administration.* San Francisco: Jossey-Bass, 1993.

Kuh, G. D. *The Other Curriculum: Out-of-Class Experiences Associated with Student Learning and Personal Development.* Paper presented at the annual meeting of the Association for the Study of Higher Education, Minneapolis, Minn., Nov. 1992.

Kuh, G. D. "Caretakers of the Collegiate Culture: Student Affairs at Stanford University." In G. D. Kuh and J. H.

Schuh (eds.), *The Role and Contribution of Student Affairs in Involving Colleges.* Washington, D.C.: National Association of Student Personnel Administrators, 1991.

Kuh, G. D., Schuh, J. H., Whitt, E. J., and Associates. *Involving Colleges: Successful Approaches to Fostering Student Learning and Development Outside the Classroom.* San Francisco: Jossey-Bass, 1991.

Kuh, G. D., Shedd, J. D., and Whitt, E. J. "Student Affairs and Liberal Education: Unrecognized (and Unappreciated) Common Law Partners." *Journal of College Student Personnel,* 1987, *28*(3), 252–260.

Kuh, G. D., and Whitt, E. J. *The Invisible Tapestry: Culture in American Colleges and Universities.* ASHE-ERIC Higher Education Report No. 1. Washington, D.C.: Association for the Study of Higher Education, 1988.

MacGregor, J. "Collaborative Learning: Sharing Inquiry as a Process of Reform." In M. O. Svinicki (ed.), *Changing Faces of College Teaching.* New Directions for Teaching and Learning, no. 42. San Francisco: Jossey-Bass, 1990.

Mitchell, A. A., and Roof, M. "Student Affairs and Faculty Partnerships: Dismantling Barriers." *NASPA Journal,* 1989, *26*(4), 278–283.

National Association of Student Personnel Administrators. *Points of View.* Washington, D.C.: National Association of Student Personnel Administrators, 1987.

Pascarella, E. T., and Terenzini, P. T. *How College Affects Students: Findings and Insights from Twenty Years of Research.* San Francisco: Jossey-Bass, 1991.

Schroeder, C. "New Students: New Learning Styles." *Change,* 1993, *25*(4), 21–27.

Smith, B. L. "Creating Learning Communities." *Liberal Education,* 1993, *79*(4), 32–39.

Tinto, V., Goodsell-Love, A., and Russo, P. "Building Community." *Liberal Education,* 1993, *79*(4), 16–21.

Waltzer, K. "After 25 Years, They're Still Mad About Madison." *MSU Alumni Magazine,* Fall 1992, pp. 26–29.

Weingartner, R. H. *Undergraduate Education: Goals and Means.*

New York: American Council on Education and Macmillan, 1992.

Whitt, E. J. "Making the Familiar Strange: Discovering Culture." In G. D. Kuh (ed.), *Cultural Perspectives in Student Affairs Work.* Alexandria, Va.: American College Personnel Association, 1993.

Wingspread Group on Higher Education. *An American Imperative: Higher Expectations for Higher Education.* Racine, Wis.: Johnson Foundation, 1993.

Eight

Developing Learning Communities

Charles C. Schroeder

Recent reports on the status of higher education — particularly the reports *Involvement in Learning* (Study Group on the Conditions of Excellence in American Higher Education, 1984) and *An American Imperative: Higher Expectations for Higher Education* (Wingspread Group on Higher Education, 1993) — clearly indicate that promoting student learning is the responsibility of both faculty and student affairs educators. The reports broadly conceive student learning to include such outcomes as understanding of self and others, acquisition of knowledge, mastery of content, development of various skills and competencies, and sensitivity to value issues. Many of these learning outcomes could be achieved by intentionally designing residence halls as learning communities. Within such communities, students would learn self-knowledge, self-confidence, and self-worth. These learning communities would foster patience, tolerance, empathy, responsibility, and interpersonal competence. Such humanitarian values as justice, social responsibility, and intercultural understanding would be components of the "implicit" community curriculum. Students would be encouraged to assume a variety of roles, thereby clarifying their values and identifying their strengths and weaknesses. By working together to achieve various community tasks, students would develop decision-making and consensus-building skills. Obviously, many residential experiences promote the achievement of some of these outcomes, albeit some more by default than by design.

The basic premise of this chapter is that learning communities can be developed in residence halls if staff understand the potent impact of peer-group influences on learning and student development. Astin (1992, p. 398) maintains that "the student's peer group is the single most potent source of influence on growth and development during the undergraduate years." Other research has consistently demonstrated that peer-group influences are primary agents in promoting student learning and personal development (Feldman and Newcomb, 1969; Chickering and Reisser, 1993; Pascarella and Terenzini, 1991; Astin, 1977). Unfortunately, staff often fail to link peer-group influences and educational outcomes. Indeed, many traditional approaches to residence education unintentionally create structures that limit student learning and personal development (Schroeder, Nicholls, and Kuh, 1983).

The goal of this chapter is to demonstrate the importance of developing learning communities that maximize peer-group influences. It delineates conditions and principles that foster peer community development, as well as contrasting traditional approaches to residence life with strategies that promote learning communities. A comprehensive example of an effective residential learning community is presented with a description of four principles essential to the development of such communities. Additional examples of learning communities are illustrated, and new perspectives and roles for staff interested in promoting student learning and development are explained.

Community: A Context for Learning and Development

Although "community" is an essential component of promoting learning and student development, no common understanding of its meaning appears to exist among residence educators. For many, community is "traditionally described as a small number of people living in the same area and linked by common values, practices, and goals" (Spitzberg and Thorndike, 1992,

p. 7). Some theorists suggest that community encompasses a number of components, including the following: sharing goals, responsibilities, and communication (Mable, Terry, and Duvall, 1977), mutually agreed-on purposes, transcendent themes, and social contracts (Crookston, 1980), and peer-group influence, territoriality, and transcendent values (Tollefson, 1975). It is precisely these components — commonality of purpose, unity, transcendent values, and cohesiveness — that distinguish a community from a traditional residential unit. For example, students living on residence hall floors often have difficulty identifying commonality of purpose and seldom regard themselves as a unified, cohesive group. Distinctions between communities and traditional residential arrangements are relatively transparent. But what features differentiate residential *learning* communities from such common residential arrangements as living-learning centers, special group housing, and theme housing?

Defining Learning Communities

Astin (1985, p. 161) defines learning communities as "small subgroups of students . . . characterized by a common sense of purpose . . . that can be used to build a sense of group identity, cohesiveness, and uniqueness that encourage continuity and the integration of diverse curricular and co-curricular experiences." As compared to other residential arrangements, residential learning communities are ones that "encourage continuity and the integration of diverse curricular and co-curricular experiences." These components of intentionality and integration, as well as the characteristics listed below, make them unique and distinctive from other residential units.

The research literature on residence halls is replete with references to characteristics of such learning communities; however, the central theme in all of this research is student involvement. As students' involvement increases, they benefit more from their educational experiences (Astin, 1977, 1992). Effective learning communities are characterized by a high degree of student influence, control, and ownership. Students *matter*. They are central to the enterprise, and their participation in a variety of roles is essential. According to Schlossberg (1989), involvement and mattering are linked in a critical fashion. She claims that "the creation of environments that clearly indicate to all students that they matter will urge them to greater involvement" (p. 14). Learning communities are also characterized by students who share common interests and purposes, high degrees of social interaction, and social stability that ensures continuity of relationships (Blimling and Schuh, 1981; DeCoster and Mable, 1980; Kuh, Schuh, Whitt, and Associates, 1991).

The research on residence halls has likewise identified additional social and physical environmental factors that must be addressed when developing residential learning communities. Social environmental constraints include diversity of student characteristics, group size, absence of peer support, roommate and floormate incompatibility, and an absence of student influence in governance (Moos, 1979; Schroeder and Jackson, 1987). These constraints can be minimized by systematically matching roommates and floormates on the basis of similar characteristics, encouraging the development of peer governance systems, and ensuring social stability by allowing students to live in their units for as long as they desire.

Certain architectural features can also inhibit the development of effective learning communities. Stark institutional atmospheres, isolated and inaccessible "group rooms," and long and narrow double-loaded corridors often combine to isolate students rather than encouraging their social interaction and group identity (Schroeder, 1980, 1981). Sommer (1969) has referred to traditional residence hall architecture as "hard architecture"—architecture that is impervious to human imprint! Such architectural constraints can be overcome by expecting students to personalize their physical environment by painting and decorating, providing centrally located group lounges, and designating single-room options to reduce density and crowding.

To summarize, residential communities that promote student learning and development are characterized by a high degree of student participation and involvement, control of bounded space, common interests and purposes, high degrees of social interaction and social stability, transcendent values, and student influence. In effective learning communities, students know they matter — their participation and involvement are central to their day-to-day experience.

Strategies That Promote Learning Communities

Traditional approaches to residential life usually disregard the significance of essential conditions that foster learning and personal development — such conditions as the creation of reference groups with common interests, shared and controlled space, transcendent values, and broad-based member involvement. For example, unsystematic and random assignment of students to rooms and floors increases the diversity of student characteristics, thereby limiting students' ability to identify commonalities. The time-consuming and often narrow emphasis of staff on developing student governments rarely ensures broad-based student participation in *governance*. Staff-initiated, top-down programming approaches frequently result in activities that are highly valued by staff but often regarded with minimal interest by residents. As Stamatakos (1991) suggests, these "educational programs" usually reflect the latest whim of pop psychology and are rarely linked to specific academic or educational outcomes. Likewise, as described in Chapter One, requiring resident assistants to conduct a certain number of "developmental programs" each semester seems to have a minimum impact on student learning and personal development. While these programs are often beneficial to particular individuals, often they do not involve students in matters essential and enduring for peer-group development.

In the traditional programmed approach to residence life, efficiency and authority are valued, whereas broad-based student involvement, participation, and influence are actually minimized. Staff exert authority through articulating housing goals, monitoring student adjustment to institutional regulations, and designing programs to facilitate students' attainment of housing goals. Natural interaction among students is compromised; peer association is manipulated through community-building programs designed for students by administrators. Certain policies, particularly those that prohibit students from painting or otherwise personalizing their living environment, discourage individual and group responsibility for the environment. Social stability and long-term enduring relationships are jeopardized by the forced mobility of students that results from certain types of assignment policies, procedures, and practices. As a result, peer-group influences are minimized, since group norms must be renegotiated frequently.

Although the traditional approach to residence life has merit, it has certain limitations as well. First, the approach generally focuses on staff and their interests and preferences as opposed to students' needs and aspirations. Second, since control is primarily vested in staff, there is little broad-based student involvement and influence. The result is that students are often more than willing for staff to do for them, as opposed to assuming individual and collective responsibility for their community. In addition, when responsibility for community development is vested primarily in staff as opposed to students, the environment limits opportunities for learning and personal development. Learning becomes limited to short-term staff interventions instead of day-to-day learning activities in which residents are highly invested. Finally, the traditional approach ends up focusing staff attention and programmatic intervention on the needs of the individual resident — usually to the exclusion of the needs of the group.

A number of outcomes are associated with such traditional approaches. If students are systematically denied opportunities to become involved and influence the direction of their lives in their residence halls, they often choose to leave and seek housing off campus. Other outcomes such as excessive damages, hostile versus supportive interaction, frequent judicial cases, poor academic performance, and lack of personal and group responsibility for behavior are often characteristic of a system that restricts broad-based student participation.

In contrast to traditional residence life approaches, strategies for developing learning communities encourage and require grassroots collaboration and cooperation by individual students on each floor. Students are *expected* to assume responsibility for most aspects of their social and physical environments. Obviously, staff are still needed to facilitate group development; however, their primary role is to create conditions that foster commonality of purpose, student involvement, reference-group formation, and collaborative partnerships with faculty and academic administrators.

Since learning communities are fostered by commonality and consistency of purpose, shared values, and transcendent themes, residence life staff can create conditions that encourage the emergence of these elements. Commonality of purpose can be achieved by organizing students' floor units around transcendent themes like engineering, pharmacy, and natural science or by creating units formed on the basis of other common educational interests. As Astin (1992) suggests, keys to peer-group formation are the creation of common ground on which identification can occur and the provision of opportunities for sustained interaction and the integration of diverse curricular and cocurricular experiences.

The following comprehensive example illustrates how the preceding elements and conditions can be combined to create a unique and effective peer learning community for students with similar academic interests and aspirations.

An Effective Residential Learning Community

During the mid 1970s, engineering enrollments on many campuses experienced dramatic declines. Although a number of factors contributed to the problem, nonpersisting engineers expressed concern over the lack of strong peer-group support and the relatively inactive role of upperclass students in helping new students adjust. These concerns prompted a collaborative effort by Auburn University's School of Engineering and the Housing Department to structure a unique learning community for engineering students.

To address the perceived lack of peer-group support and to organize around the students' commonality of interest in the engineering curriculum, three consecutive floors in a men's residence hall were designated for the learning community. To

further facilitate group development, a special lounge was constructed by walling off a previously unused entrance foyer. Wall-
to-wall carpeting was added to the lounge, and students were
encouraged to construct their own furniture. Remote computer
terminals were installed in an alcove of the lounge, and access
to the terminals was restricted to engineering residents and their
guests by the use of a special key.

Additional design strategies included matching roommates
on the basis of complementary personality types (as measured
by the Myers-Briggs Type Indicator) and selecting outstanding upperclass engineering students to serve as resident advisers.
The roommate matching strategy helped create commonality
in the roommate relationship and was important in achieving
an appropriate balance of challenge and support in the residential
unit. Students were *expected* to actively participate in structuring their physical and social environments. Residents were encouraged, for example, to personalize their living areas by painting; wall papering; paneling; adding plants, posters, and drapes;
constructing lofts, bookcases, and other furniture; refinishing
doors; plastering ceilings; and replacing fixtures. Room painting included covering the walls with murals, super graphics,
caricatures, and slogans. Students also marked the entrance to
their engineering lounge by painting the word "Engineers" on
the plate-glass window.

A community governance model was implemented to
structure the social environment. Residents developed and maintained floor standards and even retained the right to remove
a student from the unit if he consistently violated the standards.
The limited numbers of highly coveted private rooms were al-
located by the residents themselves based on seniority and students' contributions to the floor unit. Students managed their
floor funds for projects they deemed worthy of support. Various committees were also formed to handle special tasks, including student recruitment, scholarship, social events, and
physical improvements, most of which were designed to ensure
the social and academic *integration* of members with the learning community. The student recruitment committee established
a recruiting booth on campus during Engineering Day and inter-

viewed prospective residents for the special unit. These interviews were the first steps in creating "anticipatory socialization." They also developed an elaborate orientation program designed to integrate new members through formal and informal rites of passage. The scholarship committee established study hours for the freshmen to ensure that academic goals would be achieved. The social committee distributed football jerseys with "Engineers" emblazoned on the front and encouraged everyone to wear them to classes and special events. This group also organized the engineers' participation in the annual Auburn University blood drive. Traditionally, the engineers had won the award for the highest participation rate among campus living units. The physical improvement committee took responsibility for painting stairwells and hallways as well as supervising the general upkeep of the floors and lounge. This committee also developed a general logo, which was painted at the entrance to each floor. To paraphrase Astin (1985), the committee structures were useful in building the identity and cohesiveness that encouraged continuity and integration of curricular and cocurricular experiences.

In subsequent years, student response to the program was so positive that the learning community was expanded from twenty-seven to fifty-four rooms and occupancy increased from fifty to eighty-six residents. Although residents continued to express high satisfaction with their unique community, increased size appeared to have a detrimental effect on group identity, cohesiveness, and reference-group formation.

One solution to this problem was to place more emphasis on small-group development within the overall community by the creation of a house system. To implement the house concept, one student room within each nine-room house was converted to a group room, which was routinely utilized for peer tutoring, studying, and social interaction. Residents personalized this space by painting, paneling, wall papering, and constructing their own furniture.

To further stimulate a sense of identity within each house, students decided to name their houses after seven of Auburn's most distinguished engineering alumni. House representatives obtained biographical data from the alumni office on twenty-five engineering graduates who had made outstanding contributions to engineering and who represented excellent career role models for aspiring engineers. Following a week of intense debate, seven alumni were chosen for the honor. Among those selected were an astronaut, a past president and chairman of the board of AT&T, a vice president of Eastern Airlines, a renowned chemical engineer and Rhodes Scholar, the president and chairman of the board of TRW Corporation, and two regional presidents of the Bell System. In honor of the distinguished alumni, floors became known as Mattingly House, Shephard House, and so on. A wooden plaque designating the unit (Mattingly House), along with a picture of the distinguished alumnus, was placed at the entrance of each house.

The alumni took an active interest in the engineering students, and many agreed to serve as "alumni in residence" during the year. Alumni also provided direct support to the various units through donations of computer terminals, chemical engineering libraries, furniture, and even monetary gifts.

Results of a longitudinal study indicated that residence in the special learning community was positively associated with a number of educational outcomes. For example, students in the special unit perceived their social climate as emphasizing more involvement, emotional support, academic achievement, and intellectuality than engineering students living on heterogeneous floors. Students in the special unit also achieved significantly higher grade-point averages and persistence rates in engineering than engineers who were not in the special program. Finally, students in the special unit had the highest retention rate of any living units on Auburn University's campus (Schroeder and Griffin, 1977).

Four Essential Principles for Learning Communities

Although the success of the engineering learning community was due to many factors, most of the impact can be explained by the *interaction* effect associated with four essential principles. These principles have been referred to as the four *I's:* involvement, investment, influence, and identity (Schroeder, 1993). In the development of learning communities, the principles are both sequential and cyclical—that is, increased student involvement leads to increased investment, which, in turn, leads to greater influence and eventual identity with the unit. The greater the identity, the greater the involvement, investment, and influence. Since these principles are integral to the establishment of any peer learning community, each element is examined in more depth.

Involvement

A true learning community encourages, expects, and rewards broad-based student involvement. The environment is characterized by an ethic of membership (Kuh, Schuh, Whitt, and Associates, 1991), which impels returning residents to assume major responsibility for orienting and integrating "new" members with the community. The environment is also characterized by a high degree of interaction, with students—*not staff*—assuming a multitude of roles. Members face common problems, share common tasks, and otherwise engage in meaningful activities together. As a consequence, everyone is important, everyone is needed, and everyone matters. Finally, learning communities characterized by a high degree of involvement emphasize supportive interactions, with students naturally helping one another with personal and academic problems.

Investment

Investment is a reflection of psychological ownership. It flows naturally from involvement. Investment is also a consequence of the ethic of care—students clearly care about one another and their group. Boundaries with respect to other groups are clear, and group or institutional property is guarded rather than damaged. Students are simply unwilling to have staff assume responsibility for them—they want to demonstrate their capabilities as the group takes on an ever-widening circle of challenge to enhance the group's status. As evidenced by the engineering learning community example, there are clear variations in status and roles, as well as in longevity of association. Rewards are provided for being a "good" member.

Influence

Influence is essentially a consequence of an ethic of responsibility, where control is vested in group members and students exert maximum influence over their physical and social environments. This principle — influence — is the cornerstone of student governance and a major characteristic of learning communities. In the engineering learning community, residents were expected to personalize their space, recruit and assign members, and develop a social contract whereby group standards were affirmed, both individually and collectively. Interactions are frequent and characterized by gentle confrontation rather than polite or passive-aggressive behaviors. Such groups also exhibit high expectations of one another. Again, in the case of the engineering learning community, residents had established clear goals regarding academic achievement, intramural competition, and participation in social activities. In such units, students feel important, their perspectives are valued, and their contributions are essential to the welfare of the group.

Identity

Learning communities characterized by a high degree of identity are ones that focus on commonalities and transcendent values. Affiliation and identification are a function of commonality of purpose. Students in such communities have shared symbols similar to those exhibited by members of the engineering learning community. In that community, identities were symbolized by wearing engineering jerseys and by marking floor units with house symbols. In such living units, members describe themselves in collective terms such as *we* and *us,* not *I* or *they,* reflecting their emphasis on common purposes and unity.

The four I's are principles *essential* to the development, implementation, and maintenance of learning communities. The principles are more process than content variables — that is, commonality and consistency of purpose (for instance, engineering, agriculture) can vary considerably between and among learning communities, but the four principles should remain relatively constant with regard to the maintenance of these communities.

Additional Examples of Learning Communities

Learning communities can be designed to accomplish a number of important educational objectives (Gabelnick, MacGregor, Matthews, and Smith, 1990). This section highlights a number of examples that accomplish this goal. Although not explicitly stated, the four I's are embedded in each example.

Common Curricular Experiences

One of the more pressing challenges in higher education is to create learning opportunities that provide a degree of coherence and integration for different disciplines. A number of institutions have implemented a variety of approaches for linking courses around a common theme or question so students have opportunities for deeper understanding and integration of the material they are learning, and more interaction with one another and their teachers. The Washington Center (Smith, 1993), for example, has sequenced two classes with the same enrollment and has linked smaller classes to larger ones, providing curricular continuity for students. The center has also sponsored freshman interest groups (FIGs), whereby fifteen triads of courses are offered around "areas of interest." One FIG might focus on prelaw as its "commonality," with students in this group registering for the following *same* three courses: American government, introduction to philosophy (ethics), and fundamentals of public speaking. All of these learning communities have been created outside of the residence halls. They could be even stronger if they were *integrated with* residential living.

Students in large institutions often have the greatest need for reference groups, yet large institutions are composed of huge student bodies with an enormous variety of majors, making it logistically difficult for substantial numbers of resident students to form peer-group relationships based on common interests or on common curricular experiences. The Washington Center model, however, holds promise for addressing this concern. Residence halls in large institutions could create learning communities around such transcendent themes as prelaw, premedicine, natural science, social science, and so on, with students registered for at least three "common courses." Then floor learning communities would develop around these common curricular experiences. Students in such communities would be more likely to help one another with study problems and test preparation and would be more likely to discuss choice of majors and career opportunities. The provision of these courses could be coordinated by faculty teams that would offer a degree of coherence and integration, both within the formal classrooms and as faculty affiliates in the residence hall learning communities. To implement such a program, residence life staff need to develop collaborative partnerships with faculty in particular colleges or departments. Once these partnerships are developed, the registration and course sequencing process is relatively simple. Two examples of this kind of approach are currently underway in the residence halls at the University of Missouri, Columbia. One project focuses on co-enrolling students who live on the same residence hall floors in a minimum of two common courses, usually English, math, psychology, or history. The other project, the Wakonse learning community, emphasizes substantive, ongoing interaction between 10 faculty members and approximately 200 students. Faculty and students participate in common courses in their community and frequently explore a variety of academic and career issues. They also work together in service learning projects and create innovative instructional approaches utilizing computer-enhanced multimedia technology.

Research conducted by the Washington Center on a variety of outcomes of model learning community programs indicates that retention, persistence, degree completion, and achievement have been substantially enhanced. Various active learning approaches have also resulted in increased critical thinking and other forms of intellectual development as well as enhanced student sense of belonging (Smith, 1991). If these results can be obtained through creating learning communities outside the residence halls, the potential educational impact would be even greater if these communities were self-sustaining residential learning communities based on the principles of the four I's and developed around specific academic or curricular themes.

Multicultural Learning Communities

Changing demographics have resulted in significant changes in the composition of student enrollments on many campuses. In particular, the significant increase in the number of African Americans, Hispanic Americans, and Asian Americans has, according to Kuh (1990, p. 85), created "unprecedented challenges to institutions of higher education in general and to student affairs professionals in particular." On many campuses, underrepresented groups band together in ethnic enclaves, maintaining a sense of their own cultural identity and often becoming marginalized in the process. Because of the separation and isolation of members of these groups, many white American students rarely interact with and benefit from associations with people of color. Residential learning communities provide opportunities for natural interaction among diverse students and help students see beyond stereotypes.

Residential learning communities could be structured around multicultural and interracial themes. The learning communities could be intentionally linked to courses that focus on such topics as the history of different cultures, interracial communication, and understanding and appreciation of cultural differences. Students might obtain a fourth academic credit in these classes by participating in a multicultural learning community. As part of the community, students would experience cultural differences in music, food, dress, and other customs. In communities such as these, learning outcomes would include understanding and appreciation of cultural differences, racial understanding, increased cultural awareness, and appreciation of diversity. Students would join the learning community based on their desire to achieve these objectives.

Service Learning Communities

The development of such humanitarian values as justice, altruism, good citizenship, and social responsibility could be achieved by learning communities developed around the theme of service. Although many campuses have encouraged volunteerism through departments of student volunteer programs, the often-fragmented and isolated nature of such programs does not allow for the full academic and social impact on students. This concern is the result of the limited "carry-over" effect that occurs when participation is not coupled with a common residential experience. This limitation can be overcome if learning communities are formed on the basis of supporting ongoing service projects that reflect the collective commitment of residents to altruism, social justice, and community service. An example of such a program is the Adams School project at Saint Louis University (Schroeder, 1993). Students living on various floors of a high-rise building chose to "adopt" Adams School, a predominantly African-American, inner-city elementary school located within ten minutes of the campus. Each day students go to Adams to provide tutorial services for approximately fifty youngsters identified by the teachers as needing special, individualized attention. On weekends, students and members of the housing maintenance staff plaster and paint the interior of the school and work with the parents' association to improve other aspects of the school's physical and educational environments.

Many of the college students participating in the Adams School project have decided to change their majors from premedicine and prelaw to such fields as social work and teaching. This service learning experience has enabled these students to clarify their values and identify their various strengths and weaknesses. The experience has also increased their ongoing commitment to community service and civic responsibility.

With national service high on President Clinton's list of priorities, service learning residential communities should be a major component of a residence education program. By involving faculty and integrating certain courses (community psychology, political science, economics) into the learning community program, students will understand the clear connections between classroom and context, between theory and practice, between giving and taking. In such communities, students might engage in various simulations where they assume the role of mayor or city council member, developing and implementing strategies for addressing problems of health care, unemployment, and city services for the poor.

Addressing the Needs of Undecided Students

Institutions of higher learning are increasingly attempting to identify "students at risk." Although students most likely to be characterized as "at risk" are often underprepared students with poor high school grades, low entrance examination scores, and low class rank, increasingly institutions have found that "undecided students" are often at risk as well. Traditionally, undecided students must find their way to the academic advising and/or career planning offices. On presenting themselves, they are usually linked with a counselor who helps them through a process of values clarification, academic and career exploration, and goal setting.

Residential learning communities could be formed on the basis of helping undecided students "decide." Students could be offered a one-year learning community experience with the explicit goal of deciding on a major by the end of the year. Resources such as academic advising, career exploration, and counseling could be *integrated* into the learning community. For example, each week faculty from different academic disciplines could provide brief seminars and dialogue sessions on opportunities in their disciplines. Recent alums could discuss career opportunities associated with those disciplines. A centrally located room could be converted to an academic/career resource center, which might house computer terminals that run software such as SIGI (Systems of Interactive Guidance and Information), a well-respected computer-assisted career search program. Instead of resident advisers, the learning community could be staffed by peer career counselors under the direction of senior staff from the academic advising and career planning and placement centers. The outcomes associated with such a learning community would include skill development in making appropriate academic and career choices, enhanced academic achievement, stability in vocational choice, and increased retention.

Freshman-Experience Learning Communities

With the significant decline in the number of traditional-age college students, many institutions are realizing it is much more cost effective to retain students than to recruit them. As a result, most colleges and universities are providing intrusive academic and social support to freshmen through the creation of special "freshman-year-experience courses" (Upcraft, Gardner, and Associates, 1989). Although these courses are helpful, many lack coherence and substantive integration with other aspects of the freshman experience, and most are operated as an adjunct to the residence hall experience. Residential learning communities can be created to provide the much-needed integration and coherence. For example, students who participate in freshman seminar groups are often assigned to such groups on a random and unsystematic basis. Since students in these groups are rarely assigned common courses, they have few, if any, opportunities to develop ongoing relationships characterized by high degrees of peer support. Instead of randomly assigning students to freshman seminar groups, homogeneous assignments could be developed from floor rosters in the residence halls. For instance, students living on the same floor would be assigned to the same freshman seminar group. Furthermore, using the Washington Center model, these students could be assigned at least two other courses in common, selected from the general education or "core" requirements of the institution and perhaps team taught by faculty with a particular interest in freshmen. Such a strategy would undoubtedly promote a high degree of social and academic integration, contributing in a meaningful way to enhanced academic achievement, persistence, and greater identification with the institution.

The preceding are but a few examples and strategies for developing learning communities around common purposes and transcendent values. Obviously, numerous other examples could be provided, including learning communities based around the concept of intentional democratic values (Crookston, 1980), values inquiry (Kirby, 1991), and various realms of meaning such as empirical and symbolic modes of inquiry (Shaw, 1975). Regardless of the transcendent values, learning communities should incorporate the following specific principles or themes in their development. Themes one through three are principles characteristic of *both* residential-group communities and learning communities. Themes four through six, however, are associated exclusively with residential learning communities.

1. Learning communities are generally *small,* unique, and cohesive units characterized by a common sense of purpose and powerful peer influences.
2. Student interaction within learning communities should be characterized by the four I's—involvement, investment, influence, and identity.
3. Learning communities involve bounded territory that provides easy access to and control of group space that supports ongoing interaction and social stability.
4. Learning communities should be primarily student centered, not staff centered, if they are to promote student learning. Staff must assume that students are capable and responsible young adults who are primarily responsible for the quality and extent of their learning.
5. Effective learning communities should be the result of collaborative partnerships between faculty, students, and residence hall staff. Learning communities should not be created in a vacuum; they are designed to intentionally achieve specific educational outcomes.
6. Finally, learning communities should exhibit a clear set of values and normative expectations for active participation. The normative peer cultures of learning communities enhance student learning and development in specific ways.

Need for New Perspectives and Roles

Forty years of research on the impact of college on students has clearly demonstrated the centrality of peer influence in promoting student learning and development (Sanford, 1962; Feldman and Newcomb, 1969; Chickering, 1981; Pascarella and Terenzini, 1991; Astin, 1992). Yet, in view of this overwhelming evidence, few housing programs have been designed to fully exploit this important resource. Perhaps one of the most compelling reasons for this neglect reflects traditional housing staff assumptions about students and student learning. If students are viewed as capable, responsible young adults, housing staff will *impel* their broad-based participation in all aspects of their residential experience. At present, such traditional residence hall structures as judicial boards, programming councils, and student government are often simply symbols of involvement. What is needed are expectations, policies, and practices that truly *empower* students, that demonstrate trust in students and their ability to assume major responsibility for their learning and development. If residence life staff utilize the four I's as organizing principles in the design and implementation of learning communities, students will indeed be empowered, because maximum, grassroots participation on their part is absolutely essential.

Perhaps another reason that housing staff have neglected to understand the significance of peer-group influences is that many housing systems have a minimal focus on reference-group development. Programmatic interventions are usually focused at the system or residence hall level as opposed to the smaller, floor-unit group. Furthermore, most residence hall programs focus on individual development (vis-à-vis reliance on Chickering's developmental vectors as the typical entry-level catechism) versus a focus on group or community development. This programming preference is related to the fact that most entry-level student affairs professionals have a background in psychology, not sociology or anthropology. The development and supervision of resident assistants also stress the obligation to focus on individual student development. Perhaps their title should be changed to *community development assistant* and their role changed to that of facilitators of group development. Finally, staff must realize that students' involvement and participation are directly related to group size — that is, as group size increases, opportunities for meaningful participation decline (Barker and Gump, 1964). In the design of learning communities, staff must understand that impact is directly related to group size.

Because of reliance on traditional programmatic approaches that often narrowly focus on individual development, residence life staff have neglected broader perspectives such as campus ecology and environmental management that are essential to the design of learning communities. As previously stated, the development of learning communities involves more than simply assigning students to a unit based on common purpose and transcendent values—it involves creating environmental conditions, both social and physical, that exert a directional influence on student learning and development. Although a multitude of research has demonstrated the powerful impact of environmental influences on student behavior, residence life staff have often neglected to utilize this information in the design of learning communities.

Encapsulated staff roles have also limited opportunities for collaborative partnerships with faculty, staff, and students. Garland (1985) has challenged student affairs staff to become boundary-spanning agents and assume the role of "integrator" by focusing their efforts on integrating student development and institutional development. The integrator role requires housing staff to recognize and respond to major institutional agendas such as promoting active modes of student learning, enhancing academic achievement, supporting multiculturalism, improving retention, and contributing to enrollment management initiatives.

Conclusion

The higher education agenda for the future will be driven by many issues, but three, in particular, stand out—total quality management (TQM), establishing a sense of campus community, and promoting student learning. At first glance, these appear to be separate issues; however, within the context of higher education, there is a great deal of similarity and complementarity between them. With its emphasis on continuous quality improvement, TQM focuses on the question, "What value are we adding to the lives of our students?" Marchese (1993, p. 11) addresses this value issue in stating that "an institution's quality is a function of its contribution to student learning." Learning communities in residence halls can provide the "value-added dimension" by integrating diverse curricular and cocurricular experiences in the service of specific educational outcomes. Furthermore, under the TQM mantle, quality has to be specified and monitored. Translating this TQM principle to residence halls simply means that staff must establish learning communities with clear educational outcomes and use a variety of assessment methods to monitor student progress.

TQM also assumes that people are an organization's greatest resource and that empowering people is what makes a difference in the production of quality. If we value student learning and development, we must also value the important role that students play in the learning process. We must value and affirm broad-based student involvement and participation in the design, development, and maintenance of learning communities, extending our traditional emphasis on student government to embrace a broader and richer conceptualization of student governance.

We must also recognize that student learning is not a spectator sport, and we must evaluate our policies in light of Astin's (1977, p. 298) assertion that "the effectiveness of any educational practice or policy is directly related to the capacity of that policy or practice to increase student involvement." Designing learning communities that promote active modes of student learning will also require collaborative partnerships with faculty colleagues, other staff, and students. For too long, student affairs educators have limited their educational impact by keeping their focus within their organizational boundaries. The design of educationally effective learning communities requires residence life staff to leave the comfort, security, and predictability of their bounded organizational space to build linkages with faculty and academic administrators.

In conclusion, residence life staff must assume a broader educational role if they are to contribute to continuous quality improvement, establishing a sense of campus community and promoting student learning. The development of learning communities in residence halls is a primary mechanism for addressing these important higher education agendas.

References

Astin, A. W. *Four Critical Years: Effects of College on Beliefs, Attitudes, and Knowledge.* San Francisco: Jossey-Bass, 1977.

Astin, A. W. *Achieving Educational Excellence: A Critical Assessment of Priorities and Practices in Higher Education.* San Francisco: Jossey-Bass, 1985.

Astin, A. W. *What Matters in College? Four Critical Years Revisited.* San Francisco: Jossey-Bass, 1992.

Barker, R. G., and Gump, P. V. (eds.). *Big School, Small School.* Stanford, Calif.: Stanford University Press, 1964.

Blimling, G. S., and Schuh, J. H. (eds.). *Increasing the Educational Role of Residence Halls.* New Directions for Student Services, no. 13. San Francisco: Jossey-Bass, 1981.

Chickering, A. W., and Associates. *The Modern American College: Responding to the New Realities of Diverse Students and a Changing Society.* San Francisco: Jossey-Bass, 1981.

Chickering, A. W., and Reisser, L. *Education and Identity.* (2nd ed.) San Francisco: Jossey-Bass, 1993.

Crookston, B. B. "A Design for an Intentional Democratic Community." In D. A. DeCoster and P. Mable (eds.), *Student Development and Education in College Residence Halls.* Cincinnati, Ohio: American College Personnel Association, 1980.

DeCoster, D. A., and Mable, P. (eds.). *Student Development and Education in College Residence Halls.* Cincinnati, Ohio: American College Personnel Association, 1980.

Feldman, K. A., and Newcomb, T. M. *The Impact of College on Students.* San Francisco: Jossey-Bass, 1969.

Gabelnick, F., MacGregor, J., Matthews, R. S., and Smith, B. L. *Learning Communities: Creating Connections Among Students, Faculty, and Disciplines.* New Directions for Teaching and Learning, no. 41. San Francisco: Jossey-Bass, 1990.

Garland, P. H. *Serving More Than Students: A Critical Need for College Student Personnel Services.* ASHE-ERIC Higher Education Report No. 7. Washington, D.C.: Association for the Study of Higher Education, 1985.

Kirby, D. J. "Dreaming Ambitious Dreams: The Values Program at LeMoyne College." *AAHE Bulletin,* 1991, *43*(6), 9–12.

Kuh, G. D. "The Demographic Juggernaut." In M. J. Barr, M. L. Upcraft, and Associates. *New Futures for Student Affairs: Building a Vision for Professional Leadership and Practice.* San Francisco: Jossey-Bass, 1990.

Kuh, G. D., Schuh, J. H., Whitt, E. J., and Associates. *Involving*

188   The Educational Potential of Residence Halls

Colleges: Successful Approaches to Fostering Student Learning and Development Outside the Classroom. San Francisco: Jossey-Bass, 1991.

Mable, P., Terry, M., and Duvall, W. J. "A Model of Student Development Through Community Responsibility." *Journal of College Student Personnel,* 1977, *18*(1), 50–56.

Marchese, T. "TQM: A Time for Ideas." *Change,* 1993, *25*(3), 10–14.

Moos, R. H. *Evaluating Educational Environments: Procedures, Measures, Findings, and Policy Implications.* San Francisco: Jossey-Bass, 1979.

Pascarella, E. T., and Terenzini, P. T. *How College Affects Students: Findings and Insights from Twenty Years of Research.* San Francisco: Jossey-Bass, 1991.

Sanford, N. (ed.). *The American College.* New York: Wiley, 1962.

Schlossberg, N. K. "Marginality and Mattering: Key Issues in Building Community." In D. C. Roberts (ed.), *Designing Campus Activities to Foster a Sense of Community.* New Directions for Student Services, no. 48. San Francisco: Jossey-Bass, 1989.

Schroeder, C. C. "Territoriality: An Imperative for Personal Development and Residence Education." In D. A. DeCoster and P. Mable (eds.), *Personal Education and Community Development in College Residence Halls.* Cincinnati, Ohio: American College Personnel Association, 1980.

Schroeder, C. C. "Student Development Through Environmental Management." In G. S. Blimling and J. H. Schuh (eds.), *Increasing the Educational Role of Residence Halls.* New Directions for Student Services, no. 13. San Francisco: Jossey-Bass, 1981.

Schroeder, C. C. "Conclusion: Creating Residence Life Programs with Student Development Goals." In R. B. Winston, Jr., S. Anchors and Associates, *Student Housing and Residential Life: A Handbook for Professionals Committed to Student Development Goals.* San Francisco: Jossey-Bass, 1993.

Schroeder, C. C., and Griffin, C. R. "A Novel Living-Learning Environment for Freshman Engineering Students." *Engineering Education,* 1977, *67,* 159–161.

Schroeder, C. C., and Jackson, G. S. "Creating Conditions for Student Development in Campus Living Environments." *NASPA Journal,* 1987, *25*(1), 45–53.

Schroeder, C. C., Nicholls, G. E., and Kuh, G. D. "Exploring the Rain Forest: Testing Assumptions and Taking Risks." In G. D. Kuh (ed.), *Understanding Student Affairs Organizations.* New Directions for Student Services, no. 23. San Francisco: Jossey-Bass, 1983.

Shaw, W. B. *The Residence Hall as a Community in Higher Education.* Denver, Colo.: University of Denver Press, 1975.

Smith, B. L. "Assessment That Is Fun, Real, and Stimulating: Washington State's Grass Roots Approach." Paper presented at the annual conference of the American Association for Higher Education, San Francisco, March 1991.

Smith, B. L. "Creating Learning Communities." *Liberal Education,* 1993, *79*(4), 16–21.

Sommer, R. *Personal Space: The Behavioral Basis of Design.* Englewood Cliffs, N.J.: Prentice Hall, 1969.

Spitzberg, I. J., and Thorndike, V. V. *Creating Community on College Campuses.* Albany, N.Y.: State University of New York Press, 1992.

Stamatakos, L. C. "The Great Expectations of Student Affairs and Lessons from Reality: A Contextual Examination." Paper presented at the Virginia Association of Student Personnel Administrators/Virginia Association of College and University Housing Officers Fall Conference, Wintergreen Resort, Va., Oct. 1991.

Study Group on the Conditions of Excellence in American Higher Education. *Involvement in Learning.* Washington, D.C.: U.S. Department of Education, 1984.

Tollefson, A. L. *New Approaches to College Student Development.* New York: Behavioral Publications, 1975.

Upcraft, M. L., Gardner, J. N., and Associates. *The Freshman Year Experience: Helping Students Survive and Succeed in College.* San Francisco: Jossey-Bass, 1989.

Wingspread Group on Higher Education. *An American Imperative: Higher Expectations for Higher Education.* Racine, Wis.: Johnson Foundation, 1993.

Nine

Helping Students Understand and Appreciate Diversity

Marvalene Hughes

College students are becoming an increasingly diverse population as a result of demographic shifts and changes in values and other characteristics. One consequence of the increasing diversity on campus has been fragmentation among student groups. Fragmentation in the student population poses special challenges to community building (Levine, 1993). This chapter describes these challenges and suggests a number of avenues for building a diverse residential community using knowledge from the literature and the insights from a study conducted with residence hall students at the University of Minnesota. A residence hall curriculum on diversity, together with a pedagogical process for implementing it, are outlined.

Residence Halls as Community

Students in residence halls are mirrors of the larger society, but, unlike the communities from which they come, the residence hall setting offers opportunities for students to interact with their peers with greater regularity and more intensity. By planning a curriculum on diversity, residence hall staff can create a community that offers much more than a convenient shelter to simplify students' lives and ensure quick access to classes, campus facilities, and services. This on-campus living environment can become the psychological home and the locus of identity development during the most concentrated and intense learning period in the lives of students. Unlike students who live off campus, those who reside on campus are more likely to develop diverse friendships and to benefit from other concentrated program efforts. This is particularly true with respect to first-year students, since more than two-thirds of first-year students enrolled in public universities live on campus and over 80 percent in private colleges and universities live on campus (Boyer, 1988).

As illustrated in previous chapters, there is considerable evidence that residence halls have profound positive effects on the total college experience. Since freshmen enter the university with some degree of fear and uncertainty about diversity and many other issues, there is a need to introduce a curriculum on diversity early in students' college experience (Dalton, 1991). To develop communities supportive of diversity, the curriculum should be introduced soon after students move into residence halls (Reinerio, 1993). Before designing such a curriculum, educators must understand the various challenges to creating a diverse residential community.

Students, like members of the larger society, are socialized in those values and attitudes that reflect their cultural backgrounds. A curriculum that emphasizes diversity will encourage students to become more knowledgeable about their cultural backgrounds, to push beyond their cultures to understand the cultures of others, and to seek the common bonds of humanity. Residence halls offer the ideal opportunity for students to develop greater appreciation of their cultures, respect for diversity, and commitment to community building; however, challenges posed by an increasingly diverse student population are formidable. Students enter college with limited experience with diversity, yet they believe they are not prejudiced or bigoted (Laramee, 1991). This may be attributed to students' lack of experience with diversity, or they may simply not perceive problems. The popular media, however, often portray the rising incidence of hate crimes and violence against individuals in residence halls. If we are to achieve a sense of community on campus, we must first understand changing demographics and the unique characteristics of different student populations.

Changing Demographics and Group Characteristics

In the fall of 1991, students of color made up 21 percent of total college enrollment (Evangelauf, 1993). In 1993, the *Chronicle of Higher Education* summarized college enrollment by ethnicity and made comparisons over an eleven-year period ("College Enrollment by Racial and Ethnic Group," 1993). The total number of African-American, American Indian, Asian-American, Hispanic, and international students increased by more than 50 percent, from 2,254,000 in 1980 to 3,369,000 in 1991. These data reveal that the largest ethnic "minority" population in college is African-American (1,335,000 in 1991) and the greatest gains over the eleven-year period were observed in the Hispanic (472,000 to 867,000) and Asian-American (286,000 to 637,000) populations. With a slight exception within the Asian-American group, women have outnumbered men in all ethnic groups in college and made the greatest enrollment gains—compared to other time periods—during the eleven-year period between 1980 and 1991. The gender trend is reversed among international students, where men have consistently outnumbered women by approximately 50 percent. These patterns in the international and Asian-American populations are probably due to cultural differences affecting gender roles. However, the gender gap is narrowing with each passing year. A curriculum on diversity must include much more than color and gender. Demographic trends clearly convey the need to expand our definition of diversity in the academy to serve the present and future profile of the student population. For example, today's students range in age from fifteen to over sixty-five, highlighting the need to incorporate the age dimension into diversity initiatives.

African Americans

Today, as in the past, some African-American students maintain an attitude of mistrust toward whites, presumably as a result of historical and continuing discrimination (Thompson and others, 1990). A commonly held belief among African Americans is that they are wise to maintain a level of mistrust. This is thought of as a "healthy cultural paranoia" and often results in social alienation between African Americans and whites. Even when African Americans succeed in the career world and gain middle-class stature, there is evidence that subdued rage lingers (Cose, 1993).

Women

Sexism, sexual harassment, and date and acquaintance rape on university campuses are commonplace (Fitzgerald and others, 1988; Hirsh, 1990; Koss, Dinero, Seibel, and Cox, 1988; Paludi, 1991; Sanday, 1990). The campus climate for women has been described as "chilly" (Sandler, 1986) and insensitive to women's developmental patterns, learning styles, career aspirations, and personal adjustment. Discrimination against women in the academy is attributed to the unquestioned curricular content (Fuehren and Schilling, 1985) and systemic institutionalized gender inequity. Such patterns may be key to the decline in self-esteem for women during college years (Allen and Niss, 1990). It has been reported also that undergraduate women's academic and career aspirations decrease between their freshman and senior years (Astin, 1977; El-Khawas, 1980). Clearly, women students encounter barriers in their efforts to succeed academically. These barriers may pose double jeopardy to women of color, disabled women, and lesbians. Since women outnumber men in college, and the demographic forecast indicates continued growth in the number of female students, a residence hall curriculum that addresses women's needs could compensate for deficits in the campus climate and augment the academic curriculum.

Asian Americans

Since the mid 1960s, the Asian-American population has grown at an explosive rate. Asian groups have had a higher rate of enrollment in educational institutions than other ethnic groups.

This commitment to education is evident at all age levels, although intra-Asian group variations are recognized. However, Asian Americans' pursuit of education has not translated into equity in terms of employment and income (Agbayani and Ching, 1993). Asian Americans must be viewed from their own cultural perspective, which emphasizes values such as interdependence, cooperation, and conformity — in contrast to the mainstream American values of individuality, autonomy, and independence.

American Indians

Native American culture is in sharp contrast to mainstream U.S. values. American Indians are the native inhabitants of the United States, with a history vastly different from all other groups. Theirs is a history of progressive disenfranchisement from the land where their culture evolved. Determined to preserve the essence of their historical roots, where nature, Mother Earth, tribal languages, and the spiritual world are intertwined, many American Indians maintain physical, psychological, and cultural distance from the dominant culture in the United States. American Indian students are considered to be more "at risk" than other ethnic groups, as measured by the low educational level of parents, low family income, high school-dropout rate, low college retention and graduation rates, high rates of substance abuse, and high rate of suicide (R. Hill, personal communication, February 1993). While the number of students entering higher education has increased, only 6 percent of American Indians have completed college, as compared to 23 percent of whites and 12 percent of African Americans (Astin, 1982).

Hispanics

Hispanics have underscored the need to preserve the totality of their roots, including language, religion, and culture, emphasizing that these are inseparable entities. Their participation in higher education is lagging. In 1986, 10 percent of the nation's students were Hispanic, but only 6 percent of the new graduates and 5 percent of all college students were Hispanic (Levine and Associates, 1989). Even though the numbers of Hispanic students are expected to increase rapidly in the fore-seeable future, Hispanic students are highly disadvantaged in the educational system. Levine and Associates observe that these students are less competitive than white or Asian-American students in the high school setting, so that they are often unprepared for the competitive nature of the college environment. And increasing numbers of Hispanic children are growing up in poverty and attending public schools with a high concentration of low-income students. Many cultures and intraethnic differences are prevalent among Hispanics, largely due to vast geopolitical variations. Hence, multiple factors must be addressed to teach numerous cultural identities among Hispanics.

White Americans

White students may also need training in their various cultural identities, although the mainstream curriculum on campus reflects a white perspective. Without a thoughtful training program that helps white students expand their knowledge of their cultures, they could feel left out of the diversity initiative and become disinterested, disengaged, and perhaps disruptive. Although white students represent diverse cultures, minority students are likely to perceive them as constituents of a generic Eurocentric population. Residence hall staff who recognize the need to introduce white identity development into the residential curriculum could offer new perspectives to white and minority students alike.

Disabled Students

Enrollment statistics for students with disabilities depict rapid increases on most campuses. This group can be difficult to track, because some disabilities are invisible and known only to the disabled person and perhaps a close circle of others. For example, learning disabilities such as dyslexia are often invisible to an untrained observer. Even though students with invisible disabilities may be eligible for benefits, many choose not to self-identify. Jarrow (1991) argues that these students wish to avoid the stigma often associated with disabilities. There is a need to demystify the view that disabled people bring with them only a set of medical and access problems. Their culture and history have been hidden in the shadow of our fear and denial, and now it is urgent to promote greater understanding of their cultural and psychological identity development. The most profound student development issues, such as career and life planning, development of autonomy, and social, emotional, physical, and spiritual development, are integral to the total development of disabled college students.

Gay, Lesbian, and Bisexual Students

Campuses are not hospitable to gay men and lesbians. Negative attitudes about lesbians and gay men are widespread (Herek, 1989). Verbally abusing, shaming, and threatening the gay and lesbian populations have been common practices for years, thus demonstrating the pervasiveness of homophobia. Heterosexual men are more negative in their views of homosexuality than are heterosexual women (D'Augelli, 1989), and their perceptions of gay men are more negative than their beliefs about lesbians. D'Augelli (1989) attributes attitudes about gay men to a lack of exposure.

Evans and Levine (1990) point to the growing need to provide institutional support by educating heterosexual populations on campus about homosexual life-styles and cultures. Improvements are needed on campus to create an atmosphere for gays and lesbians to feel physically and psychologically safe (McNaron, 1991). For example, conditions in residence halls have barely changed during past decades, and students are terrified at being "found out" (McNaron, 1991). Nonetheless, gay men and lesbians are increasingly coming out, and "students, staff, faculty, and alumni are more visible and vocal than ever before" (Berrill, 1992, p. 259). There are no precise barometers to gauge the size of the gay, lesbian, and bisexual populations. Based on trends and general statistics, the populations of gay men, lesbians, and bisexuals appear to be larger than those who have "come out."

Knowledge of the characteristics of diverse student populations is essential to the design of a residence hall curriculum on diversity. Furthermore, educators must understand students' attitudes and values in relation to diversity. A recent study conducted at the University of Minnesota provides valuable insights into students' opinions regarding a variety of issues concerning diversity. The following section describes the study and its most salient results.

Insights from the Minnesota Diversity Study

One example of residence hall students' perspectives on diversity is illustrated by the results of a study at the University of Minnesota that included 2,243 students (6 American Indian, 205 Asian/Asian-American, 62 African-American, 32 Hispanic, 1,846 white, 24 biracial, 25 disabled, and 43 gay/lesbian/bisexual/transgender) who resided in campus residence halls during the winter quarter of 1993 (Harrold, Hughes, Reinerio, and Scouten, 1993).

Survey Instruments

The study utilized the Residence Hall Climate Survey (RHCS) to explore attitudes and values in relation to diversity. The study also measured moral judgment, using the Defining Issues Test (DIT) (Rest, 1976) to determine the relationship of moral judgment to attitudes toward diversity. Both instruments were administered to residence hall students (52 percent of the residence hall population) who attended special hall meetings. Total anonymity was guaranteed for all participants.

Residence Hall Climate Survey. This 120-item survey was designed by the Research Division of Student Affairs (Harrold, Hughes, Reinerio, and Scouten, 1993) based on a review of the literature on diversity and a review of diversity instruments. A test of internal reliability was conducted on a thirteen-item diversity scale to measure support for or opposition to diversity, yielding a reliability coefficient of .8770. This instrument was designed to survey attitudes and beliefs about diversity and readiness for multicultural competence.

Defining Issues Test. The DIT is designed to measure people's perceptions of right and wrong and how they think about social problems. This study reported only the p score from the DIT since it represents the simple sum of the higher stages that are versions of principled moral thinking. The test-retest reliability for the p scores are generally in the high .70s or .80s, and the Cronbach's alpha index of internal consistency is generally in the high .70s (Davison and Robbins, 1978). Cross-cultural, gender, and religious differences have been studied to determine if moral judgment scores are biased. Kohlberg (1971) argued that all cultures go through the same sequence of moral development. Rest, Thoma, Moon, and Getza (1986) conducted comprehensive studies to detect biases relative to cultural, gender, and religious differences. Acknowledging the difficulty in translating findings to different cultures, the authors reached the following conclusions: (1) the DIT is culturally sensitive, in that it highlights more similarities than differences between cultures; (2) unlike Kohlberg's instrument, the DIT is not vulnerable to the criticism that it is biased against non-Western populations; (3) in contrast to Gilligan (1982), researchers using the DIT uncovered only a slight gender difference ($d = .21$), with females consistently scoring slightly higher than males; and (4) six of the seven studies on religious affiliation found that liberal religious views are associated with high scores of moral judgment.

Limitations

The findings of this study may have limited generalizability to other campuses, since the study was conducted on a single campus — the University of Minnesota, Twin Cities. Although the sample of 2,243 is substantial, caution must be utilized in determining if the specific results apply to other campuses.

Quantitative Results of the RHCS

Analysis-of-variance and t tests were the predominant statistical methods used for the findings discussed below. A primary insight from the data is the limited nature of students' experiences with diverse groups. However, students reported diversifying friendships among all groups, except African Americans and American Indians, as their years in college increased. Respondents were mixed on whether racism was a problem in the residence halls. It is noteworthy that 76 percent of African Americans strongly perceived racism as a problem, while only 33 percent of the white population shared this view ($p < .01$). Overall, residents tended to be neutral on whether sexism was a problem, but significantly more men (41 percent) than women (28 percent) felt that sexism was not a problem within the residence halls ($p < .001$). Support for diversity was greatest among Hispanics, followed by biracial individuals, African Americans, Asian Americans, and whites ($p < .01$). (The American Indian sample was too small for statistical comparisons.) Gays and lesbians were significantly more supportive of diversity than heterosexuals ($p < .001$), and women were significantly more supportive than men ($p < .001$). Students with disabilities did not differ from those who are not disabled in their support for diversity.

The results of the survey also indicated a slight correlation between principled or moral reasoning and support for diversity ($r = .18$; $p < .01$). Third- and fourth-year students scored higher in moral reasoning than first- and second-year students, supporting Rest, Thoma, Moon, and Getza's (1986) finding that a correlation exists between the level of education and moral reasoning ($p < .05$). Gay/lesbian/bisexual respondents had significantly higher scores for moral reasoning (50.9) than their heterosexual counterparts (39.5; $p < .008$). Throughout this survey, the gay/lesbian/bisexual student population was the most supportive of diversity. No significant differences were found in the moral reasoning scores for men and women, for people of different racial/ethnic backgrounds, or for disabled versus nondisabled individuals.

The quantitative data reveal a relationship between principled reasoning and diversity. This relationship deserves a much deeper examination. The significant difference between scores of the gay/lesbian/bisexual population and the heterosexual population on the DIT suggests that ethical and moral development for this homosexual population has reached a higher level than for their heterosexual cohorts.

Qualitative Themes and Trends: Pro-Diversity and Antidiversity

The strengths of these findings lie in the internal consistency of content between the quantitative and qualitative data. Qualitative results, obtained from an open-ended question that asked students how they felt the residence halls were or were not addressing issues of diversity, provided both positive and negative comments regarding diversity efforts. The strongest antidiversity reactions were anti-gay/lesbian/bisexual and anti–African American. White students, particularly some heterosexual white males, indicated feelings of exclusion and isolation in relation to programs designed to promote diversity.

Students who labeled themselves as conservative — largely those who expressed pro-life views — assumed they were outside the campus mainstream. These respondents raised other issues, such as the following: (1) the fine line between diversity initiatives and reverse discrimination, (2) disbelief that bigotry exists on campus, (3) mistrust of procedures for assigning roommates, and (4) concern about the relationship of diversity and free speech. Pro-diversity comments included: (1) support for strong and swift responses to hate crimes; (2) a need for a greater number of staff and faculty of color; (3) support for instruction about diversity early in students' experiences; and (4) suggestions to focus additional attention on communication, community building, and increasing interaction among diverse groups. Listed below are the seven major themes that emerged from the qualitative data.

1. Polarization Between African-American and White Students.
The study identified a deep chasm between African-American

residents and white residents. Neither group manifested much interest in building bridges to one another's culture. African Americans strongly perceive racism in residence halls (76 percent), yet whites do not perceive a similar prevalence of racism (33 percent).

2. White Students' Commitment to White Friends. Eighty-one percent of white students are committed to exclusively white friendships. Findings indicate that American Indians befriend whites to a great extent, followed by a high percentage of Hispanics and Asian Americans and by a far smaller percentage of African Americans. The gap between African-American and white students should be strategically addressed throughout a diversity curriculum. It is possible that the other groups could have a bridging influence.

3. White Racial Awareness and the Need for Identity Training. There is an unawareness or unacceptance by whites that white racism is a problem. This finding makes a strong case for white ethnic identity training. By focusing on white identity development, white students can affirm their heritage and refrain from defensive posturing. They can make genuine strides in understanding themselves and others. The white students who view racism as a problem within the residence halls could be assembled to glean further understanding about their experiences and perceptions.

4. Allies for Diversity: Female, Gay, Lesbian, and Bisexual Students. Women are featured in the literature as having an ethic of human care and a developmental tendency to connect and affiliate with others (Gilligan, 1982; Lyons, 1983). The Minnesota Residence Hall Climate Survey also identified an ethic of care in the gay, lesbian, and bisexual population. A strategic program featuring these two groups' patterns of identity development and highlighting their values of human care could be instructive. Their support could be galvanized to create a better climate in the residence halls.

5. Stereotypical Attitudes of Heterosexuals Toward Gays, Lesbians, and Bisexuals. A gulf appears to exist between the heterosexual and homosexual populations, suggesting that it will be extremely difficult to ensure that the gay, lesbian, and bisexual populations are treated with dignity and respect in residence halls. Transcending stereotypes and judgments about homosexuals' "religious violations, immorality, and mental illness" will continue to challenge residence hall staff. History has perpetuated psychological images and beliefs that will be difficult to erase. Nonetheless, residence hall staff must be vigilant and unconditional in their support of the rights of homosexuals.

6. The Need for Empathic and Cross-Cultural Communication. The qualitative data suggest that students would be more receptive if residence hall staff were less "pushy" with their agendas and more responsive to students' interests in learning to listen to one another and communicate empathically. To promote diversity, staff must apply the knowledge that already exists in teaching communication. Students expressed a strong desire to learn how to communicate with each other. They encouraged "positive interactions instead of forcing diversity." This points to the need for an emphasis on community building by teaching empathic understanding and communication and argues for a strategy that embodies principles of community and interactions rather than emphasizing fragmentations.

7. White Heterosexual Males' Identity Issues. Some white heterosexual males feel isolated from the focus on the diversity agenda and are reluctant to raise their voices. Unless residence hall staff create a strategy that is inclusive of these concerns, they risk exacerbating the problem, contributing to the backlash, and creating toxic tension. Remarks presented in the qualitative data represented a plea for recognition and a need for white racial identity training. It is important to note that some of these remarks were not written in angry tones and did not have racial overtones. But a few statements reflected resentment about perceived reverse discrimination. Two examples of pleas from white heterosexual males follow: "I need sessions to help me feel better about my identity as a white heterosexual person." "Whites are beginning to feel like the minority. We get no attention." White students who harbor these unaddressed feelings are not likely to support efforts to create a diverse climate, as indicated in this study.

A Residence Hall Curriculum on Diversity

It is not enough to offer generic programs on diversity that focus on historically marginalized groups. In fact, this traditional generic approach may contribute to a widening gap between majority and minority groups. Some students are rebelling, others are confused, and still others are less sophisticated in their efforts to cope because they believe the university is forcing the diversity agenda on them. In particular, white students often feel that they are not central to the diversity plan as currently defined. This group must become an integral part of the curriculum on diversity. Planning must be strategic and dynamic, and programs must be created to address the developmental needs of all students.

To plan strategic programs requires that residence hall staff utilize timely and relevant information on diversity issues and develop cultural awareness training grounded in student development theory. The latter requires careful attention to staff development and staff selection. The literature suggests, for example, that male resident assistant candidates are more homophobic and are more likely to express abusive comments than female resident assistant candidates (D'Augelli, 1989). Strategic programming would identify this problem, employ rigorous standards in the selection process designed to screen for homophobic candidates, and introduce a systematic training program to address the issues. Most residence hall staff are students and young entry-level professionals who are also dealing with their own identity development at a critical point in their lives. It is, therefore, important to recognize their developmental needs and limitations.

Diversity has created disequilibrium in the academy by disrupting the traditional patterns that governed education. It has raised questions about the manner in which we organize, implement, and manage education. Minnich (1991) encourages us to welcome the disruptions that diversity introduces and suggests that we must ask the right questions if we are to be effective as educators. The key questions are "How can people who once excluded others from their communities now work and live and learn with them as equals?" and "How can people who once were excluded from those communities enter into and fully participate as equals, bringing their own cultures, identities, and interests with them?" (p. 5). If we simply focus on how to get along, Minnich (1991) believes we will miss the core issue.

If we are to understand cultures other than our own, we must acquire information about the cultures and take the next important step to understand how people view themselves in relation to their cultural identity (Jones, 1990). Everyone is influenced by their cultural identity, and this cannot be ignored in any aspect of residential programming. Residence hall staff must understand the ethnocentric features of all cultures and aggressively plan educational programs using ethnocentricity as a context for understanding cultural differences and promoting diversity (Jones, 1990). To better relate to African Americans, for example, one must be willing to gain knowledge of Afrocentric culture. Lessons learned about diversity while living in residence halls will be of value to students while they are within the academy as well as when they exit the academy and pursue their individual life paths. Such lessons are learned most effectively from a well-designed curriculum on diversity.

Essential components of a residence hall curriculum on diversity include the following: fostering cultural identity awareness, affirming human commonalities, teaching responsible free speech and civility, preventing polarization through conflict management and mediation, developing a diversity portfolio, and organizing allies as trainers.

Fostering Cultural Identity Awareness

Identity development of all residential college students is influenced by residence hall education. To educate all students, it is important to examine how residence hall programs can utilize research on identity development and promote appreciation for differences. Minorities in the United States who seek mainstreamed life paths are compelled to engage with the majority culture (Wong, 1992). While the majority population has not faced the same pressures in the past, it is abundantly clear that today's majority group would benefit from knowledge about minority groups' identity development (Wong, 1992). Serious errors are made when we teach and develop programs that limit majority students' experiences to their monoculture. White students must be encouraged to become equal participants in multicultural understanding. This will require a fundamental shift away from patterns and norms in Western culture.

It is essential to integrate into our diversity planning assurances that no group's culture will dominate the others. Breaking out of the traditional dominator model will require white students to pursue "heightened levels of awareness about the dynamics of racism. White students should be challenged to create attitudinal and behavioral change that results in an atmosphere that promotes positive race relations" (Bourassa, 1991, p. 19). The presence of privilege and power for whites will figure prominently in their identity training.

Identity development within a context of diversity is both an essential and frightening prospect for many students. To successfully create an atmosphere that transcends racism, sexism, and homophobia, professionals must create programs that depart from the mere reconstitution and recycling of old beliefs. There is a clear mandate to conceptualize and actualize transforming programmatic models that promote commonalities among all students.

Affirming Human Commonalities

In addition to the need for cultural identity awareness, there is a related need for cultural identity affirmation. The fundamental need for individuals and groups to affirm cultures other than their primary group affiliation is central to achieving a diverse community. Identity affirmation offers benefits such as the following:

- Promoting self-esteem and a sense of pride for group members
- Expanding opportunities for people to learn from one another
- Affirming the importance of primary group identity
- Recognizing the multiple identities that contribute to the larger human community
- Challenging assumptions that any culture is superior and dominant
- Supporting a deeper inner search for the common core of humanity

Teaching Responsible Free Speech and Civility

The residence hall curriculum on diversity is incomplete unless hate crimes and First Amendment rights are addressed. When intended to harm others, hate speech must not go unchallenged. Hate crimes potentially create serious psychological damage to targeted groups. Administrators who remain silent during hate crimes may miss the teachable moment to challenge perpetrators to critically examine their stereotypes. A curriculum on responsible free speech will allow universities the opportunity to challenge students' values and teach civility. Institutions that miss opportunities to teach civility and compassion for all students cannot expect their campus environments to attract, nurture, and retain students and faculty who are traditionally marginalized. By not answering hate crime and bigotry with an institutional perspective of civility and public ethics, the opportunity to engage students in critical thinking and ethical reasoning is missed. Unless the ethical dimension of hateful and hurtful expressions is raised at the top level and throughout the campus community, the targeted group is further demeaned and members of the majority group may assume they are part of a community that promulgates and condones bigotry.

Free speech and open inquiry are essential components of a climate for learning, but when used to hurt or harm members of the campus residential community, participants in the community should not tolerate this behavior. An ethical community will not endorse hate crimes or any act that denigrates others or denies equal access and equal opportunity to individual productivity.

Preventing Polarization Through Conflict Management and Mediation

Students, staff, and society, in general, are not equipped to acknowledge and manage conflict. The presence of conflict is healthy and natural, and the acknowledgment of conflict in any organization is a symbol of strength and health in the organization. Conflict, when appropriately managed, encourages members to raise questions, challenge, disagree, examine, probe, and even agree. Conflict management training is a crucial part of the residential curriculum on diversity. When opposing voices assert, staff must be prepared to manage the disequilibrium by assisting students to engage in communication strategies to transform feelings of despair, isolation, and confusion into collaborative solutions.

Developing a Diversity Portfolio

Records of students' participation in the curriculum on diversity could be formally acknowledged by preparing a portfolio to reflect the competencies they have acquired. For example, at the University of Missouri at Columbia, students can record their involvement in various diversity and multicultural experiences on their Student Involvement Record, which serves as a companion piece to their academic transcript. Because most companies are seeking college graduates who can work effectively with diverse populations, a diversity portfolio is very beneficial when students become job seekers.

Organizing Allies as Trainers

Potential allies for promoting diversity were identified in the Minnesota diversity study. Having gained an understanding and appreciation of their own cultures and the cultures of others and having acquired effective communication skills, allies in the residence halls and elsewhere on campus can be selected for leadership in teaching the diversity curriculum. As part of the diversity team, these allies could serve as advisers, advocates, peer counselors, and leaders for the curriculum. When their residential peers encounter crises, team members can assist them by building bridges to the cultures of others. They may also help residential staff respond to and prevent crises in the hall. One way to involve students, faculty, and staff in such a program would be to design a reward system. Awards may include special recognition on bulletin boards and in hall newsletters, certificates, and even monetary benefits.

A Pedagogical Process for the Residential Curriculum

A variety of pedagogical processes are needed to implement the residence hall curriculum on diversity. Hughes (1992) offers a model that posits that one function of education is to challenge complacency. When challenged, some students follow the channel of resistance, which occurs when their minds are closed to new perspectives and ideas. An alternative path to resistance is receptivity to change. A function of education is to challenge strongly held stereotypes that promulgate fragmentation. Education should facilitate openness to change, acceptance of new knowledge, commitment to action, and transforming behaviors (Hughes, 1992). When new paths to knowledge are resisted, change and growth are stifled. Students who choose to challenge their socialized beliefs and complacency are likely to see people and the world in a new light. Three pedagogical strategies are offered to assist residence hall staff and students in implementing a diversity curriculum: (1) recognizing the paradox of diversity and unity; (2) distinguishing between healthy tension and toxic tension, and (3) developing communication skills.

Pedagogical Strategy 1:
Recognizing the Paradox of Diversity and Unity

Efforts to promote diversity reflect a paradoxical need to honor and promulgate differences while still encouraging community building (Hughes, 1993). Because unity and diversity seem inconsistent, staff must legitimize the contradictions and confusions that students will inevitably encounter. The dilemma highlights inherent contradictions between diversity and community, but when the contradictions are properly managed, they offer the potential to create a new community that will challenge previously static and homogeneous states (Hughes, 1993).

In actuality, living with a paradox can be stressful, painful, frightening, joyful, and exhilarating, all in relation to the same phenomenon. A paradoxical state can contribute to the transformation by creating the tension to forge the evolution of new forms, new ways of being, new structures, and new ideas. Paradoxes have created transforming opportunities throughout history. In *The Chalice and the Blade: Our History, Our Future* (1987), Eisler reviews centuries of history to offer her perspective on ways cultures have been transformed over time. Using the concepts of partnership and domination, Eisler traces cycles in the past where the course of history shifted from a dominator society to a partnership society as a result of the strong tension between those two contrasting dynamics. When one faction—either the dominator or the partnership—gained strong momentum, the other reasserted itself to bring balance. This is true with respect to diversity as well. When unlike minds meet, the dissonance can potentially create a new reality. Viewed in this light, diversity is forging a transforming society that will not condone traditional stereotypical boundaries.

Programs in the residence halls can facilitate students' understanding of the dilemma and explain their inner turmoil. Students must be challenged to look inside themselves and find their human kinship. By motivating students to become stewards focused on the greater good of humankind, residence hall staff can make a vital contribution. Astin (1992) alludes to a positive aspect of this paradox in citing what can happen when a strong orientation program on diversity is introduced. The program may stimulate protest against diversity. This, in turn, could cause proponents to rally for diversity. In this manner, bigotry on campus may ultimately advance the progress of diversity initiatives.

Pedagogical Strategy 2: Distinguishing Between Healthy Tension and Toxic Tension

Efforts to bridge the chasms created by a curriculum on diversity must attend, first and foremost, to the need to build community. An essential step in creating the new community is to differentiate between "healthy tension" and "toxic tension" (Hughes, 1993), while recognizing that some form of tension is inevitable in a heterogeneous, dynamic society.

A toxic tension syndrome occurs when bigotry is interjected into the community by internal or external factions. Selective and irresponsible media (on and off campus) may contribute to toxic tension. Unhappy consumers, such as parents, alumni, and students, as well as groups external to the university, may fuel the toxicity on campus. Toxic tension results from those who resort to harassing, intimidating, and demeaning strategies designed to assert their ethnocentrism or sexism and demean others unlike them. Actions and attitudes such as hate crimes, racial epithets, anti-Semitic slurs, sexual harassment, homophobia, and xenophobia may represent purposeful efforts to create toxic tension.

Healthy tension, on the other hand, acknowledges the possibility that opposing perspectives can be identified, discussed, and managed to create necessary changes. The results of the Minnesota diversity study suggest the possibility of toxic tension between African Americans and whites, and between homosexuals and heterosexuals. By employing a pedagogical strategy to understand the difference between healthy and toxic tension, majority and minority groups may find their common ground. Diverse communities can produce the healthy tension to create change. Our task, as educators, is to help students identify and design models of healthy tension and to understand that they can grow from tension, if it is managed appropriately.

Pedagogical Strategy 3:
Developing Communication Skills

Communication is essential to the creation and maintenance of authentic communities. Conflict cannot be examined, toxic tension cannot be managed, and transformations cannot be effected unless there is open and empathic communication. Residence hall staff must be skilled communicators to advance the goals of diversity, and they must assist residents in developing communication skills. Listed below are various measures that staff can employ in implementing the curriculum on diversity; all involve communication skills.

• *Create common tasks.* Rather than perpetually being driven by fragmentations, residence hall staff should design common projects and tasks to attract diverse groups. One option would be to create multicultural learning communities like the ones suggested in Chapter Eight.

Learning to communicate with and develop respect for other cultures can best be promoted in natural task-oriented situations as opposed to the typical crisis modality. Residence hall staff can create meaningful simulations to encourage healthy communication and avoid toxic tension. For example, residence life staff at the University of Missouri at Columbia use adventure education to promote racial understanding. Heterogeneous groups of African-American and white students confront novel problems on the Alpine Tower and team challenge course that can only be solved through a cooperative effort.

• *Teach empathy.* It is important to teach empathy. Empathic communication is not new; it was central to the work of Carl Rogers (1977). It has equal potency today in enabling individuals to suspend judgment about other cultures and try to enter into and deeply experience the world of another. We can never achieve an appreciation for diversity unless empathy becomes a way of life.

Empathy training is one component of human relations workshops provided to residence hall students at the University of Missouri at Columbia. As part of the "MU to the Future" initiative, student, staff, and faculty trainers create a learning climate that allows residence hall students to examine biased concepts and behaviors, perceptions of themselves and others with regard to differences, and discriminatory behaviors. A primary goal of this program is to create a framework for accepting and embracing the diversity of the residence halls and university community.

• *Teach students to ignore.* To ignore is to deliberately employ inaction. Inaction may be the strongest action to apply to a situation. An example of the decision to ignore and strengthen one's position may be to ignore a separatist group and all the media and public outcry that it is capable of generating. Although this is a passive strategy, ignoring can be a powerful response. Ignoring an outcry may reduce or diffuse the situation. Communicating this decision to the residents and enlisting their support are extremely important preventive measures.

• *Support constructive activity.* When an activity in the halls has momentum that is viewed as compatible with university goals and is considered healthy and constructive, another purposeful action is to support the momentum. Support may be demonstrated in such forms as fiscal assistance, staff augmentations, recognition, or deliberate behaviors acknowledging the importance of the action. It is easy to forget the value of reinforcing an activity when a positive climate exists, yet reinforcement is an important strategy. An example of supporting an activity is represented in the University of Minnesota's small-grants programs, which fund proposals that promote community and proposals for immersion experiences in diverse cultures. Accordingly, those interested in building community and promoting diversity may apply for grants from the Office for Student Affairs. Applicants may include faculty, staff, and student groups. A campuswide selection team evaluates proposals and awards grants in amounts of $2,000 or less.

• *Negotiate to modify/redirect goals and behaviors.* Occasionally, administrators should review an existing situation or action to decide to modify, redirect, or change it. In this case, stakeholders must be identified early to assess their motivation, rationale, and commitment to the plan. Assessing stakeholders is critical to this category, since their support must be cultivated before any change can be initiated. Administrators who choose to modify or redirect actions initiated by stakeholders must be extremely careful to ensure that ownership remains with the stakeholders. Astute negotiations and collaborations are required for this approach.

• *Initiate constructive programs.* Residence hall staff must take initiative for planning and marketing programs. This is where a diversity planning team establishes its credibility. Initiatives must be based on a stated philosophy and set of values that the residence hall staff wishes to promulgate. An example of this strategy is the initiation of the Student Diversity Institute at the University of Minnesota. Founded in 1992, the institute is currently staffed by three full-time student affairs professionals who are in great demand by all constituencies on campus for diversity training. The staff includes a mobility-impaired female, a lesbian, and a Hispanic male.

- *Extinguish toxic behaviors.* When an event has taken a life of its own and seems unproductive, the choice to extinguish it can become extremely difficult. Everyone would choose to extinguish toxic tension as soon as possible, but it is unlikely to happen by fiat. Swift, strong, and assertive actions are often needed.

Conclusion

Residence hall staff who plan generic programs on cultural diversity training for students may innocently infuse the system with toxic tension, or they may totally miss the mark. Generic programs are primarily based on assumptions that represent the staff's experiences and knowledge. We must rethink our assumptions, structures, and strategies to create diverse communities in residence halls. For example, data must be gathered on residents to determine the demographic profiles, attitudes, and values of students. Programmatic strategies can then be designed to meet the developmental needs of students and prepare them for the future society.

The traditional focus on multiculturalism may be inadequate and incapable of transforming a climate where students will learn to live peacefully together and honor each other's dignity. The Minnesota diversity study revealed that many white students feel excluded when multiculturalism explains deficits and invalidates their cultural experiences. Apparently they do not see themselves in the multicultural picture, since staff generally teach the multiple cultures of minorities and marginalized groups. On the other hand, marginalized groups react strongly against the majority group's efforts to uphold the centrality of their culture as the cornerstone for all peoples' identity. Thus, a backlash may surface unless the situation is carefully managed.

Diversity will become a reality when individuals and groups are encouraged to assert their identity and at the same time to recognize and respect the cultural identity of others. Only then can we transcend the fragmentations on campus to search for the common threads of humanity and to encourage students to build community. The primary group identity and the common identity that bonds humans must never replace one another; they must coexist and reinforce each other.

Principles of diversity and community explain why we must value differences to learn to live together. The ultimate goal in designing the residence hall curriculum on diversity is to create a human community that respects individual identity, primary group identity, the identity of other groups, and the bonding qualities of humanity.

References

Agbayani, A., and Ching, D. "Asian and Pacific Americans in Higher Education." Paper presented at the annual conference of the National Association for Student Personnel Administrators, Boston, Mar. 1993.

Allen, B., and Niss, J. "A Chill in the College Classroom?" *Phi Delta Kappan,* 1990, *71*(8), 607–609.

Astin, A. W. *Four Critical Years: Effects of College on Beliefs, Attitudes, and Knowledge.* San Francisco: Jossey-Bass, 1977.

Astin, A. W. *Minorities in American Higher Education: Recent Trends, Current Prospects, and Recommendations.* San Francisco: Jossey-Bass, 1982.

Astin, A. W. *What Matters in College? Four Critical Years Revisited.* San Francisco: Jossey-Bass, 1992.

Berrill, K. T. "Organizing Against Hate on Campus: Strategies for Activists." In G. M. Herek and K. T. Berrill (eds.), *Hate Crimes: Confronting Violence Against Lesbians and Gay Men.* Newbury Park, Calif.: Sage, 1992.

Bourassa, D. M. "How White Students and Students of Color Organize and Interact on Campus." In J. G. Ponterotto, D. E. Lewis, and R. Bullington (eds.), *Affirmative Action on Campus.* New Directions for Student Services, no. 52. San Francisco: Jossey-Bass, 1991.

Boyer, E. L. *College: The Undergraduate Experience in America.* New York: HarperCollins, 1988.

"College Enrollment by Racial and Ethnic Group." *Chronicle of Higher Education,* Aug. 25, 1993, p. 13.

Cose, E. *The Rage of a Privileged Class.* New York: HarperCollins, 1993.

Dalton, J. C. "Racial and Ethnic Backlash in College Peer Culture." In L. V. Moore (ed.), *Evolving Theoretical Perspectives on Students.* New Directions for Student Services, no. 51. San Francisco: Jossey-Bass, 1991.

D'Augelli, A. R. "Homophobia in a University Community: Views of Prospective Resident Assistants." *Journal of College Student Development,* 1989, *30,* 545–552.

Davison, M., and Robbins, S. "The Reliability and Validity of Objective Indices of Moral Development." *Applied Psychological Measurement,* 1978, *2*(3), 391–403.

Eisler, R. T. *The Chalice and the Blade: Our History, Our Future.* San Francisco: HarperCollins, 1987.

El-Khawas, E. *Differences in Academic Development During College. Men and Women Learning Together: A Study of College Students in the Late 1970's.* Providence, R.I.: Office of the Provost, Brown University, April 1980.

Evangelauf, J. "Number of Minority Students in Colleges Rose by 9% from 1990 to 1991, U.S. Reports." *Chronicle of Higher Education,* Jan. 20, 1993, p. 30.

Evans, N., and Levine, H. "Perspectives on Sexual Orientation." In L. V. Moore (ed.), *Evolving Theoretical Perspectives on Students.* New Directions for Student Services, no. 51. San Francisco: Jossey-Bass, 1990.

Fitzgerald, L., and others. "The Incidence and Dimensions of Sexual Harassment in Academia and the Workplace." *Journal of Vocational Behavior,* 1988, *32*(2), 151–175.

Fuehren, A., and Schilling, K. "The Values of Academe: Sexism as a Natural Consequence." *Journal of Social Issues,* 1985, *41*(4), 29–41.

Gilligan, C. *In a Different Voice: Psychological Theory and Women's Development.* Cambridge, Mass.: Harvard University Press, 1982.

Harrold, R., Hughes, M., Reinerio, J., and Scouten, E. *Survey to Assess the Residence Hall Climate for Diversity*. Minneapolis: Students Affairs Research Office, Division of Student Affairs, University of Minnesota, 1993.

Herek, G. M. "Hate Crimes Against Lesbians and Gay Men: Issues for Research and Social Policy." *American Psychologist,* 1989, *44*, 948–955.

Hirsh, K. "Fraternities of Fear: Gang Rape, Male-Bonding, and the Silencing of Women." *Ms. Magazine,* April 1990, 52–56.

Hughes, M. "Global Diversity and Student Development: Educating for World Citizenship." In M. C. Terrell (ed.), *Diversity, Disunity, and Campus Community*. Washington, D.C.: National Association of Student Personnel Administrators, winter 1992.

Hughes, M. "Reinventing Community." Invited presentation at the annual conference of the American Association of Higher Education, Washington, D.C., Mar. 1993.

Jarrow, J. "Disability Issues on Campus and the Road to ADA." *Educational Record,* 1991, *72*, 26–31.

Jones, W. T. "Perspectives on Ethnicity." In L. V. Moore (ed.), *Evolving Theoretical Perspectives on Students*. New Directions for Student Services, no. 51. San Francisco: Jossey-Bass, 1990.

Kohlberg, L. "Stages of Moral Development." In C. Beck, B. Crittenden, and E. Sullivan (eds.), *Moral Education*. Toronto: University of Toronto Press, 1971.

Koss, M., Dinero, T., Seibel, C., and Cox, S. "Stranger and Acquaintance Rape: Are There Differences in the Victim's Experience?" *Psychology of Women Quarterly,* 1988, *12*(1), 1–24.

Laramee, W. A. "Racism, Group Defamation, and Freedom of Speech on Campus." *NASPA Journal,* 1991, *29*, 55–62.

Levine, A. "Diversity on Campus." In A. Levine (ed.), *Higher Learning in America: 1980–2000*. Baltimore, Md.: Johns Hopkins University Press, 1993.

Levine, A., and Associates. *Shaping Higher Education's Future: Demographic Realities and Opportunities, 1990–2000*. San Francisco: Jossey-Bass, 1989.

Lyons, N. P. "Two Perspectives: On Self, Relationships, and Morality." *Harvard Educational Review,* 1983, *53*, 125–145.

McNaron, T. "Making Life More Livable for Gays and Lesbians

on Campus: Sightings from the Field." *Educational Record,* 1991, *72,* 19–22.

Minnich, E. K. "Discussing Diversity." *Liberal Education, 77,* 1991, 2–7.

Paludi, M. (ed.) *Ivory Power: Sexual Harassment on Campus.* Albany: SUNY Press, 1991.

Reinerio, J. *Diversity in the Residence Halls.* Minneapolis: Department of Educational Policy and Administration, University of Minnesota, 1993.

Rest, J. "An Assessment for Moral Judgment." *Moral Education Forum,* 1976, *1*(3), 1–4.

Rest, J., Thoma, S., Moon, Y., and Getza, I. "Different Cultures, Sexes, and Religions." In J. Rest (ed.), *Moral Development: Advances in Research and Theory.* New York: Praeger, 1986.

Rogers, C. R. *Carl Rogers on Personal Power.* New York: Delacorte Press, 1977.

Sanday, P. *Fraternity Gang Rape: Sex, Brotherhood, and Privilege on Campus.* New York: New York University Press, 1990.

Sandler, B. *The Campus Climate Revisited: Chilly for Women Faculty, Administrators, and Graduate Students.* Washington, D.C.: Project on the Status and Education of Women, Association of American Colleges, 1986.

Thompson, C. E., and others. "Cultural Mistrust and Racism Reaction Among African-American Students." *Journal of College Student Development,* 1990, *31,* 162–168.

Wong, F. F. "Diversity and Our Discontents." *American Association of Higher Education Bulletin,* 1992, *45,* 7–12.

Ten

Increasing Student Involvement Through Civic Leadership Education

Susan R. Komives

Leadership for the twenty-first century will require members of all types of groups to be responsible, involved, educated, and empowered to make a difference in their communities. "The need to establish a sense of community is one of the most critical issues facing higher education during this decade" (Schroeder, 1993, p. 523). As "working civic communities" (Morse, 1989, p. 4), residence halls provide a unique experience for the people who live there to learn and to practice the challenges of shared leadership. This shared leadership must be built on the foundation of each resident's responsibility as a citizen of that environment to influence the character of the living experience.

This chapter will explore the important link between individual residents and their residential communities through leadership involvement strategies. An assessment of the recent developments in the conventional paradigm—which discouraged civic leadership in residence life—is presented, along with a discussion of the emergent agenda promoting empowered civic leadership. Empowering practices that encourage civic leadership among both residents and staff are described.

The Individual and the Whole:
The Contextual Vision

Understanding the responsibilities of individual residents for shared leadership within their residential communities requires an understanding of the assumptions embedded in the relationship of the individual and the whole. The 1980s emphasis on individual differences was a necessary, evolutionary step toward creating more effective, inclusive communities. Tolerant, effective, inclusive, celebrative communities are not likely to develop without an awareness of what perspectives, needs, and talents individuals bring as building blocks of community systems. The dominant American cultural norm is strongly embedded in valuing individualism, yet it is insufficient to focus only on individual difference; effective communities must reframe the understanding of difference as a step toward building a new whole.

The most essential perspective for residents to develop as they assume their responsibilities in the residential environment is to see the multiple realities of their commitments to self and others. Individual residents therefore must continually ask themselves three questions:

- How am I like no one else here?
- How am I like some others here?
- How am I like everyone here?

Harvard sociologist Charles Willie (1992) challenges resident life staff to design residence life systems that encourage both contributive justice and distributive justice. Contributive justice is the responsibility of the individual to the group, whereas distributive justice is the concurrent responsibility of the group to the individual. Care, commitment, energy, and attention flow in both directions — from individual to group and group to individual. When fostering contributive justice, residents expect to identify their individual interests, needs, and expectations, link with others in multiple subcommunities (with such common interests as sports, arts, similar majors, or needs identified by gender, race, or ethnicity), and shape and contribute to the common purpose and vision for the larger community unit. Concurrently, promoting distributive justice, community members must keep a common vision and purpose in front of all residents of why they are here, what they expect as a shared experience, how they can link with others like themselves, and how they can be individually nurtured within this context.

As stated in Chapter Eight, residence hall communities are intentional collections of individuals who come together for common purposes. Individual residents must have an understanding of the common purposes in residential living and must develop commitment to the common good. In this context, residential "community is the binding together of diverse individuals committed to a just, common good through shared experiences in a spirit of caring and social responsibility" (National Leadership Symposium, 1991, p. 19). An explicit objective of the residential experience must be that students become residential citizen-leaders who commit to learning how to create, nurture, and advance their shared community through empowering leadership that values each resident's role in building the shared community.

According to Harriger and Ford (1989, p. 27), "It is not nearly enough to teach students how the world *is*. We must also encourage them to think about how it *ought* to be. Without some hope for a better world it is all too easy to think only of oneself and all too easy to leave the responsibilities of citizenship to others." Clearly, community is not someone else's responsibility, it is a commitment from each resident. Successful resident life systems must position residents in a central leadership role in building their communities.

Examining the Conventional
Paradigm of Residence Life Systems

Reasserting a leadership role for residents in their living-learning communities requires a reflective examination of the changing context of students as residents and of residence life systems in the last twenty-five years of higher education. The changing orien-

tation of students to the inner world of self-interests and the concurrent shift in residence halls as social institutions to become
staff-dominated environments have led to community living environments in which leadership is held by few instead of many.

In the last twenty-five years, traditional-age student generations have exhibited a strong individualistic orientation. Following an era of strong commitment to the welfare of others
and to the individual citizen's responsibility as a change agent
in the 1960s, the "me" generation of the 1970s and 1980s became more inward oriented. The times forced an emphasis on
vocational development, and the harsh economic realities led
to a "me-first" mentality. This movement was reflected in a
dramatic national student decrease in search for a meaningful
philosophy of life and a corresponding increase in the value of
striving to be well off financially (Astin, Green, and Korn, 1987).
This "reactive generation" (Strauss and Howe, 1989) grew up
in an underprotected time requiring them to develop survival
skills and a strong sense of individual determinism.

During the same time frame, many residence life systems
became dominator paradigm cultures, in which students were
sadly depersonalized with little room for individual differences.
The paradoxical transition in the early 1970s upended commonly
accepted control practices such as curfews, no intervisitation,
single-sex halls, and residency requirements. The seeming liber-
alization of residence life systems brought on by such developments as the death of in loco parentis and the sexual revolution
actually launched a reframing of control in which residence
life administrators sought order out of chaos. Seeking answers
to such questions as "What is the nature of our relationship
with students?", a major emphasis on a new system of controls
emerged, having been brought on by a plethora of federal regulations, campus protest, Title IX, contractual relationships, and
a new emphasis on due process. In an admirable quest for "fair-
ness," too many residence life systems assumed that policies and
procedures must be the same for all, when the concept of same-
ness may actually be inherently unfair.

In addition, the newfound 1970s focus on applications of
student development theory was a hopeful movement for resi-

dence life staff, who assumed roles of professional developmental educators. Yet in too many cases, the elevated role of the resident assistant (RA) as a peer counselor and developmental programmer led to the practice of doing even more for students, rather than encouraging them to do for themselves. Instead of valuing such processes as the RA advising a floor leadership or programming group toward shared objectives, expectations shifted to such direct RA outcomes as a specified number of programs per semester as an RA job requirement. A shift from rewarding community building processes to defining success as specific events for which the RA was accountable has perhaps created a disincentive for RAs to spend the time and patience to develop contributive justice among members of the floor community.

Even in a benevolent bureaucracy where a "student-as-customer" model is in effect, well-intended staff tend to do things *to* or *for* students and not *with* them. As a result, residents can have a passive experience, expecting things to be done for them instead of doing for themselves. Pseudocommunities might develop through staff initiatives, but lacking true commitment and involvement from residents, they become passive environments instead of true, authentic communities (Hrubala, 1989; Peck, 1987; Schroeder, 1993).

The prevailing paradigm of leadership education that evolved in this period placed strong emphasis on management skills for the small group of residents who held such positional leader roles as officers or members of the formal residence hall government system. This training often stressed processes like goal setting (not visioning), programming and services (not change agentry and participation), and Robert's Rules of Order (not consensus models). True developmental leadership education was usually found only in training programs for RAs. RAs were often the only residents who did feel empowered as students, yet in their roles, RAs were rewarded for their outcomes and not for process. Most residents usually had no opportunity to develop their leadership skills. While they were encouraged to be responsible floor community members, this expectation valued compliance with rules, not creative initiative. Participation in activities was usually encouraged, however. Many residence life systems urged residents to be active participants in their residential communities, yet this participation was not framed as a leadership development experience. Table 10.1 compares and contrasts the conventional, more controlling paradigm of residential life to the emerging, newer paradigm of empowering residential civic communities.

Promoting a New Paradigm: Civic Leadership

Just as the heightened involvement of citizens in their country must be grounded in local, smaller settings (Woyach, 1991), greater involvement in the campus community must be activated through such settings as the smaller, residential community. A primary strategy for overcoming the passivity, apathy, and isolation so prevalent in large, complex environments is identity with subcommunities: "The only solution to the alienating effects of giantism may well be a vibrant localism" (Woyach,

**Table 10.1. Contrasting Paradigm Views
of the Roles of Residents and Staff.**

Conventional paradigm	Emergent empowering paradigm
Role of residents	
Passive, compliant followers	Active, change agents
Isolated	Involved
"Do your own thing"	Responsible for self and others
Expect apathy	Expect participation
Dispassionate/unconcerned	Caring/concerned
Value independence/"I"	Value community/"We"
Promote social community	Promote civic learning community
Role of staff	
Staff do to or for residents	Staff do with residents
Staff are responsible	Residents assume responsibility
View residents as a nuisance	View residents as central
Controlling	Empowering
Guard information	Share information
Resist change	Continuous improvement
Announce/proclaim	Facilitate/teach/reflect
Create policy/procedures	Implement resident-created policies
Emphasis on outcome	Emphasis on process

1991, p. 26). Residence education systems have a moral imperative to involve students in all aspects of creating and governing their own communities as citizens of dynamic local communities.

When asked about citizenship, most students think of voting, rights and freedoms, and joining a political party. Few students think of the responsibility of citizenship. Murchland (1991a, p. 3) sadly notes that few students recognize that "a citizen is someone who has an active voice in the government of his country or in shaping the values of his society." Residents might likewise need help in translating the concept to their residential experience as students who have an active voice in the government of their residence hall and in shaping the values of the campus culture.

Active citizenship requires individuals to seek the public good. This kind of civic leadership means "living in a manner that actively promotes the public welfare" (Sawyer, 1991, p. 16). Residents must wrestle with the issues inherent in defining what is the common good on the floor or in their residence hall and must try to find the balance between private interests and a genuine concern for the health of the civic community. This challenge moves most residents from passive, isolated floor members to floor citizens with a responsibility for participating in the leadership equation for the shared public life.

Civic leadership emphasizes three salient competencies among participants:

- Understanding the fundamental processes needed to maintain the appropriate interaction between government and its citizens
- The ability of individuals and groups to talk, listen, judge, and act on issues of common concern
- The capacity to imagine situations or problems from all perspectives and to appreciate all aspects of diversity [Morse, 1989, p. 4]

In this context, leadership is a relational process: people working collaboratively together toward shared purposes. Leadership is broader than the positional leader roles of RA, floor representative, or hall president. The outmoded passive notion of followers must be replaced with the active role of members empowered to share leadership. Explicitly linking leadership to the responsibility of community members toward their shared purposes will generalize to students' responsibility to the broader campus community, their other organizational commitments, and their eventual off-campus residential and professional communities.

It is encouraging that the generation of traditional-age students coming to campuses in the late twentieth and early twenty-first century will be the "civic generation" (Strauss and Howe, 1990). Born between 1961 and 1981, this outer-oriented generational cycle follows the more inward "reactive generation." Forecasts suggest that this civic generation is concerned for the greater public welfare, committed to community service, and seeks connections between their individual interests and the interests of others.

Civic Leadership Education: Expanding the Agenda

In any public community, each citizen must *know* something, must *do* something, and must *believe* something (Murchland, 1991a). In the context of residential living, residents must (1) *Know:* Residents must know themselves well, including the strengths and weaknesses they bring to residential living. They must understand the purposes and developmental benefits of campus residential life. They must acknowledge the interdependent nature of residential living. They must know there are multiple perspectives brought by each individual from which to develop the common good. (2) *Do:* Residents must be action-oriented, change agents. They must be willing to dedicate some time and energy to the community and to the subcommunities with which they identify. They must be expected to work in service to others in some way. They must develop the civic discourse skills to understand multiple realities, because community thinking requires deliberative talking (see below). They must be willing to compromise individual preference and personal interest for the common good. (3) *Believe:* Residents must believe that most other residents truly seek a meaningful community. Residents must believe that communities are enhanced by connected, caring people, and they must be willing to be these people. Residents must believe there are common purposes to be found in student residential learning communities. Residents must believe in the obligations of social responsibility.

This kind of civic leadership that connects people to each other and to a shared vision is empowering leadership. Empowering leadership is an emergent paradigm in leadership philosophy that replaces the traditional leader-follower dichotomy with shared leadership and collaboration (see Table 10.1). Current practices in the study of leadership are still very leader-centric; a movement toward each member's role in the leadership dynamic is more fruitful for highly relational civic communities.

The complexities of rapid change and complex social issues mandate replacing the rigid, industrial models of management with more flexible, creative systems of leadership. Tinkering with old systems is less fruitful than reframing the leadership paradigm to relate and lead differently. Vaill (1989) encourages today's leaders to work collectively smarter, to work reflectively smarter, and to work spiritually smarter. All group members (that is, floor residents) need to understand their connections with others, stand back and think and process to make meaning from their experiences, and identify the values and beliefs that guide their individual and collective judgments toward more effective outcomes.

Kouzes and Posner (1987) identify five themes in empowering leadership practices exhibited by leaders and members in effective organizations. When applied in the residence hall setting, leaders and members (1) challenge the process by always asking how things could be improved for residents' benefit; (2) inspire a shared vision by asking what it is we are hoping to accomplish or what we want this experience to be for each of us; (3) enable others to act by sharing information and linking floor members in subcommunities with similar interests, needs, and involvements; (4) model the way by expecting and contributing the highest possible community standards; and (5) encourage the heart by boosting morale in stressful times, empowering others, and celebrating accomplishments. These are leader behaviors, whether performed by formal floor or hall leaders or by individual residents — everyone together "doing leadership" builds community.

Each residence life system needs a philosophy of leadership on which its educational efforts and procedures are built. Expanding the civic leadership agenda within the theoretical frame of Kouzes's and Posner's (1987) empowering leadership practices holds promise for building residential civic communities.

Challenging the Process. Citizens need to know that their participation has the possibility to create change (Harwood, 1991). Residents must know their interests and needs are being taken seriously, both by their peer governance groups and by housing administration. Town meetings and open forums for feedback and discussion impel residents toward community action and encourage them to become citizen change agents on issues of concern within housing, the campus, the local community, and the larger society. "Residential life programs seem strategically placed to challenge students to think about their social and citizenship responsibilities and to provide opportunities for *action* on their convictions" (Winston and Anchors, 1993, p. 44).

After decades of having few heroes, today's students show great admiration for citizens whose actions have made a difference — from rescuing victims of natural disasters, to starting neighborhood cleanup programs, to promoting recycling. Their heroes need not be major world leaders or entertainers; in fact, they are often disillusioned by those figures. Instead, nearly 75 percent of today's students report that they admire and can emulate local change agents (Levine, 1993). Feeling empowered to make a difference is an essential civic leadership skill that needs staff support, so that activities can be channeled toward meaningful outcomes. Further, staff have to be open and responsive to students' questions and criticisms, even when these challenge the housing system and housing processes.

Inspiring a Shared Vision. It is not enough for staff to periodically proclaim a vision with statements such as the following: "The vision of our residential living experience is to support civic communities in which all citizen-residents share responsibility for a caring, learning environment." Vision cannot be proclaimed; it must be created and recreated regularly by the people drawn toward it.

A major impediment to creating effective vision is the lack of social stability created by high turnover rates and absence of continuity in the current formal government structures within residence life systems (such as hall councils or interresidence hall associations). Focusing socialization activities on recreating a residential vision and building commitment among new residents and new members is essential.

New interventions in anticipatory socialization to prepare students for the experience of being in residence or being a council member are critical. What special orientation activities would build a shared vision and establish commitment to community? What member orientation and team-building activities must regularly be offered to include newcomers and enhance their effectiveness within the organization? More flexible participation systems may be needed to connect residents comfortably to community leadership. For example, a floor coordinating committee might be established each semester around changing interests and needs of residents. High turnover is often undesirable, but it may create more opportunity for sharing leadership. Empowerment and belongingness often come from being appropriately and realistically prepared to take part in the new system as a member or new leader. The shared cultural message needs to become, "Even though we may take turns assuming leadership on the floor, we all have a responsibility to be involved in what goes on here."

Enabling Others to Act. Civic leadership strategies include diverse ways to link, involve, and develop the talents of residents. Such strategies may include linking residents to subcommunities of interest. Annual needs and interest assessments can identify differential involvement levels for new and continuing residents around interests in the halls and in the campus at large, resulting in various involvement or leadership options. Given a set of activities like community service, intramurals, recycling efforts, or fitness programs on an interest survey, residents could select such responses as "want to lead/teach/organize this," "want to actively participate/join," or "want to attend if I have time." Student leaders can then facilitate a planning meeting among those who indicate a high commitment and interest (for example, want to teach/lead/organize an activity), and they become empowered to initiate more involvement.

Residential leaders must look beyond the involvement opportunities only in the residence life system and link residents to the rest of campus as intrusive outreach. Minority student leaders often do not stay involved in the residence life system, not because it is unwelcoming, but because the empowerment learned through good leadership education in the halls may catapult those leaders into such groups as the Black Student Union or the campus newspaper. Linking residents with each other around any common purpose is an opportunity for leadership development.

Enabling others to act also requires the preparation of citizens to assume a thoughtful role in accomplishing change. Essential to this role is sharing information so that residents understand the context and the dimensions of a problem or dilemma, and the opportunities and challenges in alternatives. Sharing information is essential to enabling residents to be meaningfully involved. The supreme responsibility of all educators is to bring students into intimate contact with the knowledge and processes they need to influence change. Electronic networking may aid in informing and educating residents and in linking them with others through specialized networks.

Modeling the Way. Empowering leaders walk the talk. Those who shape the culture of the floor, the hall, and the entire system must model being active, committed community members themselves.

One of the most complex skills that empowering leaders must model for civic leadership is deliberative talking (Morse,

1992). Staff must learn these skills to model and teach them to residents. These enhanced communication skills for the complexities of diverse living-learning communities go well beyond "please turn your stereo down." The pace of a rapidly changing world brings keen awareness of multiple salient perspectives on complex issues. Instead of problems to solve, residents now are faced with paradoxes and dilemmas. Individual residents and effective leaders must learn civic dialogue skills that identify the values and assumptions embedded in differences, always seeking the shared common objective and the multiple realities possible in each issue.

The continued oppression of any minority view or voice certainly must be avoided in the quest to truly be an inclusive, shared community. Residence educators will have to constantly use cognitive reframing skills to help students understand multiple realities; this means asking questions such as "How could we look at this differently?" or "How would this seem different to a resident who has a disabling condition, or who is older, or who is gay, or who is a science major?" Clearly, one of the most difficult paradoxes in the academy is the passionate commitment to freedom of speech and the desire for civility. That paradox alone provides many opportunities for case-study discussions of handling seemingly opposing views yet living in harmony in community. Resident education programs emphasizing listening and understanding should be a regular feature of a leadership education program.

Leadership is relational, and relationships are built on listening and understanding the values, beliefs, and assumptions of others as a basis for discussion and action. "Public deliberation is a skill that must be learned" (Morse, 1992, p. 17). The process of consensus requires promoting an environment supportive of dissent. Student communities should have dialogue around the community's distributive values of being taken seriously, of being heard and understood, of having a voice, and of reaching a decision that heard all views even if not all could be addressed adequately. Positional leaders in the community must model this expectation.

Practices that "model the way" are grounded in the values

and principles of moral, ethical leadership. Discussions of ethical issues will be increasingly important in the development of moral leadership. Residence life staff and resident student leaders must establish and uphold ethical codes as building blocks of effective community. Residents holding other residents accountable to shared community standards through effective, caring mediation options and judicial processes support ethical community (Winston and Anchors, 1993).

Encouraging the Heart. Perhaps the strongest empowering practice present in most residence life systems is the celebration of individual milestones and group accomplishments. Floor birthday parties, decorations for holiday recognition, and banners for intramural team wins abound. These activities are valued and pervasive. New celebratory activities will need to be directed to the goals of civic leadership. Special recognition is needed for those who excel in service to others, who are admired for the changes they undertook on behalf of the greater good, and who labored tirelessly for the welfare of fellow residents. These behaviors currently do not get the recognition needed to shape the cultural norm of this civic commitment.

Leadership Development

Elements in a new agenda for resident leadership education clearly must go beyond teaching students such management skills as how to run effective meetings, plan events, or raise money. Civic leadership education in residence units involves both content and process dimensions. Processes include such arenas as self-awareness of personal talents, interests and needs, team building, socialization to issues, commitment setting, conflict resolution, change agentry, visioning, values identification, and targeting leadership development to underrepresented groups. Content includes such aspects as identification of community needs, envisioning a shared experience, and understanding residence life issues.

Many student development initiatives in residence halls can be reframed, indeed even repackaged, as empowering civic leadership education experiences. From recruitment brochures to community living agreements, residents need to see their opportunities and obligations for leadership within these civic learning communities. Leadership development interventions should be varied; possibilities include short-term education in special workshops, orientation sessions, forums on campus issues and broader social issues, skill-building sessions, and long-term development through leadership classes and community service commitments. Target populations include subcommunities of residents like whole floors as well as subgroups such as athletes, graduate students, clusters by academic major, and student employees like RAs, desk workers, food service personnel, and student security. RAs and upperclass mentors must redirect their energy to bringing each resident into the responsibilities of citizen involvement, empowering each through strategies like "What would you like your experience to be?" and "What would you like to do about that?"

The prevailing paradigm of professional residence life systems managing *for* student residents will have to shift to a newer paradigm of intentionally developing leadership among residents and empowering them to lead and to shape their own communities. This will require shifting the staff focus within an empowering leadership model valuing a facilitative, inclusive, educational role for all levels of staff. Staff should shift from hierarchical, power models to empowering, inclusive theories. By becoming principle-centered managers (Covey, 1991), staff will realize that residents have more "creative energy, resourcefulness, and initiative than their [roles] presently allow or require" (p. 179).

A 1992 national study of RAs' effectiveness on seven campuses found that RAs who were assessed to be most effective by their hall directors, their residents, and themselves exhibited all five of the empowering leadership behaviors noted above more frequently than did those assessed to be low in effectiveness (Posner and Brodsky, 1992). RA development seems to have moved toward an emphasis on empowering leadership (Komives, 1993) more readily than have professional staff behaviors. Staff and students need to be collaborators, indeed partners, in leading residential communities. Unless the prevailing power relationships are reframed, however, efforts to involve students in a participatory role in their own communities will be depowering rather than empowering. The paid staff must consult, not dictate; educate, not protect; and trust, not avoid.

Support of Flexible Resident Governance Systems

An essential element of successful community in residence halls is a flexible student governance system vesting significant responsibility in residents to lead their communities (Anchors, Douglas, and Kasper, 1993). Table 10.2 illustrates the contrast between leadership paradigms of conventional resident government systems and those that promote the empowering civic leadership agenda.

Any system of residence hall leadership must include a student-selected governance system with clear authority and accountability for salient aspects of leading the resident community. Decision making should be internally delegated to the

Table 10.2. Contrasting Leadership Paradigms
in Resident Organizational Systems.

Conventional paradigm	Emergent empowering paradigm
Hierarchial structures	Flexible systems
Highly centralized	Decentralized
Emphasis on programming	Emphasis on civic leadership
Uninformed new members	Talent development strategies
Bounded and constrained	Empowered
Value uniformity and consistency	Thrive on ambiguity and diversity
Exclusive "in group"	Inclusive "all welcome"
De facto homogeneity	Strive for heterogeneity
Late start each fall	Emphasis on continuity
Internal focus only	Both internal and external focus
Management training	Leadership development
Adviser centered	Adviser facilitated
Isolated training events	Ongoing leadership development
Recommending power	Deciding power
Uphold status quo	Challenge processes
Emphasis on short term	Emphasis on both tradition and future
"We can't"	"How can we?"

lowest possible level to encourage involvement, meaning, and commitment (Bowling [Komives], 1980). For example, individual floors should decide their quiet hours, programming events, and use of common space like floor lounges or kitchens. Hall governments could decide visitation hours, use of such shared space as weight rooms and piano practicing hours, and new student welcome events. The interresidence hall association should decide policies and processes that influence the entire resident community like room change policies, facilities renovation priorities, and options for new meal plans. Student input must be involved in every aspect of housing and residence life, ranging from actually deciding and being accountable for the decisions to making recommendations and helping others with their own decision-making process.

The emergent paradigm of resident organizational systems and processes would promote more flexible, empowering approaches. Maximum involvement occurs by decentralizing all functions to be closer to residents. Some structure will be useful for continuity, yet elaborate hierarchies will not likely encourage empowering involvement. Parallel systems with ad hoc committees, task forces, interest groups, focus groups, town meetings, forums, and other flexible methods for resident involvement will enhance participation.

Inclusive Involvement. Because traditional structures frequently do not adequately involve the views and voice of underrepresented residents, alternate systems should be established to empower this voice. The value of honoring the diversity within community is essential to inclusive community building. Minority advisory councils, designated minority representation on steering committees, and other targeted interventions may all assist with hearing these voices and building links between subcommunities and a common purpose.

Broadened Focus. Successful resident government associations in the future should expand their role to an outward focus. Many current interresidence hall associations have little interface with the campus at large, preferring instead to focus internally. The size of many residence life systems makes them a powerful lobbying group on campus issues and a major contributor to campus programs. Expanding the view may invigorate interresidence hall associations that need new involvements. Because residence halls are known for some of the more enlightened diversity awareness programming on campus, reaching into the campus culture at large may facilitate the development of a supportive, inclusive campus community culture. Interresidence hall associations must recognize their role as organizational members of the larger campus community in both the distributive and contributory justice model.

Historically staff attention has focused on traditional-age undergraduate residence leadership settings. Staff must expand that outmoded notion to include leadership development in family housing, apartment housing, graduate student units, and specialty or theme housing. The primary purpose remains the same: residents must take responsibility for their own communities. The structures and strategies may vary dramatically; they can include mayor's councils, child-care center parent boards, ad hocracies instead of permanent structures, and informational forums. Although the residents in these units may be older and have competing priorities, their organizations still have high turnover and low knowledge of university structures, necessitating staff advising for continuity and empowerment.

Administrative Commitment. Central student affairs staff—including the vice president for student affairs and central housing administration—must recommit to students being responsible and accountable for meaningful residence leadership systems. Instead of focusing on "What can we shift (or give back) to students?", staff should use a zero-base approach in a study group or task force with student leaders and ask "If we were building a new system, what is the nature of involvement (or accountability) that students must have in various aspects of residence life?" Around the agenda such a process generates, staff can then negotiate, delegate, and set parameters for resident involvement.

A central investment in student governance is reflected in the commitment of key staff as advisers. Studies of formal residence student government associations (Tucker and Komives, 1993; Wyatt and Stoner, 1984) identify a transcendent theme among empowering staff that students matter, that students absolutely have to be centrally involved in leading their communities, and that staff must have the patience and commitment to work with students to keep the residence life organization successful. Staff have to be hired who value a student self-governance philosophy and who make their leadership education and advising role central in their tasks. All staff must be flexible enough to work with the inconsistencies that will result. Staff at all levels in the campus system must be able to say "A strength of our residence life program is that students lead and manage their own living communities even if we do not agree with all of their decisions."

As important as it is that residents handle their own governance structures, the paradox is that the primary continuity for many of these student organizations is the adviser who concurrently serves as historian, facilitator, and leadership educator. Effective advisers honor the resident role in self-governance, have a keen sense of what issues have to be brought to the student system for decision or counsel, and champion the student perspective within the formal administrative system. Far from being paternalistic, the dynamic reciprocity of this relationship models the city council and city manager system where a responsibility of the paid staff member is to keep the elected leaders informed and prepared to do their role thoughtfully.

In balance, residence life systems are not, nor should they be, true democracies. The infrastructure of staff and systems needed to provide housing services and developmental education to students is a responsibility of the host college. Yet promoting community must be residents' responsibility. Promoting active student involvement and the intentional development of leadership must be an explicit outcome of residential living, not a serendipitous second-order consequence.

Barriers to Developing Empowering Civic Leadership

The assumptions and paradigms individuals bring to their view of how people relate to others are complex. These assumptions may also include a range of attitudes and expectations about the nature of community, the responsibility of students, or the role of residence halls. These assumptions lead to attitudes and behaviors that can be difficult to change. Barriers to shifting to a citizen leadership model may exist from the larger campus community and from among residents themselves.

Residents May Resist Involvement. Residence halls are not for all students; if students were to receive a grade for their effective group living and learning efforts, some would fail "Residence Life 101." Campuses with required residency find a diversity of motivations and commitment levels among those required to live-in. In voluntary residency systems, high turnover often results in the residential population being skewed toward younger students whose developmental skills may not be refined sufficiently to handle all aspects of the responsibility of residential citizenship. In either case, commitment-setting strategies are needed to center residents on their responsibilities for these environments.

Upper-Level Administrators May Expect Control. It is not sufficient for residence life educators and residence life administrators to reframe their practices and empower residents toward civic leadership if the rest of the institution, particularly the vice president for student affairs or the college president, expects predictability and practices control. Certainly, some administrative benefits of control are compelling and less control can be frightening, but the educational benefits of control are limited, and less control enhances critical thinking and civic leadership.

Conclusion

A group of leadership educators have proposed a national standard for student leadership programs that is being considered by the Council for the Advancement for Standards. This standard supports a comprehensive multimethod leadership program that includes training, education, development, and experiential modes of leadership education designed around a set of assumptions or purposes to be developed by each campus. An individual institution must determine the role of leadership education within its own mission and develop a vision for leadership education and the many ways it would be developed throughout the campus. Residential communities likely have the strongest potential to develop leadership among more students than any other component of the collegiate learning environment.

Residence life programs have an opportunity, indeed an imperative, as working civic communities to develop leadership skills and community commitment in and among residents, whether as part of a broader campus mission or as an independent initiative. The civic learning experience should enable each resident to say, "I know I can make a difference in my community and I have an obligation to be involved and active in our shared vision for the greater good." Through residential civic leadership development, colleges can rise to the challenge posed by Thomas Jefferson when he wrote, "I know no safe depository of the ultimate powers of the society but the people themselves; and if we think them not enlightened enough to exercise their control with a wholesome discretion, the remedy is not to take it from them, but to inform their discretion by education" (cited in Morse, 1989, p. 51).

References

Anchors, S., Douglas, K. B., and Kasper, M. K. "Developing and Enhancing Student Communities." In R. B. Winston, Jr., S. Anchors, and Associates, *Student Housing and Residential Life: A Handbook for Professionals Committed to Student Development Goals.* San Francisco: Jossey-Bass, 1993.

Astin, A. W., Green, K. C., and Korn, W. S. *The American Freshman: Twenty Year Trends.* Los Angeles: Higher Education Research Institute, University of California, 1987.

Bowling [Komives], S. R. "Student Governance and Leadership." In D. A. DeCoster and P. Mable (eds.), *Personal Education and Community Development in College Residence Halls.* Washington, D.C.: American College Personnel Association, 1980.

Covey, S. R. *Principle-Centered Leadership.* New York: Summit Books, 1991.

Harriger, K., and Ford, M. "Lessons Learned: Teaching Citizenship in the University." In S. W. Morse (ed.), *Public Leadership Education: Preparing College Students for Their Civic Roles.* Dayton, Ohio: Kettering Foundation, 1989.

Harwood, R. C. "Where Citizens Participate in Public Life." In S. W. Morse (ed.), *Public Leadership Education: Practicing Citizenship.* Dayton, Ohio: Kettering Foundation, 1991.

Hrubala, S. D. "A Change of Pace: The Student's Role in Educating for Citizenship." In S. W. Morse (ed.), *Public Leadership Education: Preparing College Students for Their Civic Roles.* Dayton, Ohio: Kettering Foundation, 1989.

Komives, S. R. "Leadership." In G. S. Blimling (ed.), *The Experienced Resident Assistant.* (2nd ed.) Dubuque, Iowa: Kendall Hunt, 1993.

Kouzes, J. M., and Posner, B. Z. *The Leadership Challenge: How to Get Extraordinary Things Done in Organizations.* San Francisco: Jossey-Bass, 1987.

Levine, A. *A Portrait of College Students in the 90s: Taking Responsibility for Educational Management.* Paper presented at the annual conference of the National Association of Student Personnel Administrators, Boston, Mar. 1993.

Morse, S. W. (ed.). *Public Leadership Education: Preparing College Students for Their Civic Roles.* Dayton, Ohio: Kettering Foundation, 1989.

Morse, S. W. (ed.). *Politics for the Twenty-first Century: What Should Be Done on Campus?* Dubuque, Iowa: Kendall Hunt, 1992.

Murchland, B. "Knowledge, Action, and Belief." In S. W. Morse (ed.), *Public Leadership Education: Practicing Citizenship.* Dayton, Ohio: Kettering Foundation, 1991a.

Murchland, B. (ed.). *Higher Education and the Practice of Democratic Politics: A Political Education Reader.* Dayton, Ohio: Kettering Foundation, 1991b.

National Leadership Symposium. *Proceedings from the 1991 National Invitational Leadership Symposium.* College Park: Division of Student Affairs, University of Maryland, 1991.

Peck, M. S. *The Different Drum: Community-Making and Peace.* New York: Simon & Schuster, 1987.

Posner, B. Z., and Brodsky, B. *Leadership and Effectiveness: A*

Noticeable Difference. Paper presented at the annual meeting of the Western Academy of Management, San Jose, Calif., Oct. 1992.

Sawyer, D. "Marriage and Citizenship." In S. W. Morse (ed.), *Public Leadership Education: Practicing Citizenship.* Dayton, Ohio: Kettering Foundation, 1991.

Schroeder, C. C. "Conclusion: Creating Residence Life Programs with Student Development Goals." In R. B. Winston, Jr., S. Anchors, and Associates, *Student Housing and Residential Life: A Handbook for Professionals Committed to Student Development Goals.* San Francisco: Jossey-Bass, 1993.

Strauss, W., and Howe, N. *Generations: The History of America's Future, 1584 to 2069.* New York: Morrow, 1990.

Tucker, G., and Komives, S. R. "Successful Residence Hall Government Associations: Themes from a National Study of Select Hall Government Structures." In N. Dunkel (ed.), *Advice for Advisors: The Development of an Effective Residence Hall Association.* Columbus, Ohio: Association of College and University Housing Officers–International, 1993.

Vaill, P. B. *Managing as a Performing Art: New Ideas for a World of Chaotic Change.* San Francisco: Jossey-Bass, 1989.

Willie, C. V. *Achieving Community on the College Campus.* Paper presented at the annual conference of the Association of College and University Housing Officers–International, Boston, July 1992.

Winston, R. B. and Anchors, S. "Student Development in the Residential Environment." In R. B. Winston, Jr., S. Anchors, and Associates, *Student Housing and Residential Life: A Handbook for Professionals Committed to Student Development Goals.* San Francisco: Jossey-Bass, 1993.

Woyach, R. B. "Strengthening Citizenship." In B. Marchland (ed.), *Higher Education and the Practice of Democratic Politics: Political Education Reader.* Dayton, Ohio: Kettering Foundation, 1991.

Wyatt, K. W. and Stoner, K. L. "A NACURH 'White Paper' on Residence Hall Government." *Journal of College and University Student Housing.* 1984. *14*(1), 3–6.

Eleven

Integrating Living
and Learning in
Residential Colleges

Terry B. Smith

Residential colleges, the oldest concept in Western higher education, are experiencing a renaissance. Dozens of colleges and universities in North America are rediscovering the venerable benefits of teachers and students living, dining, and studying in the same building. This chapter explores the nature and history of residential colleges and the benefits of the residential college experience to faculty, staff, and students. Programs at a private and public university are highlighted, while current challenges to residential college programs are enumerated. The chapter concludes with a discussion of where the movement stands and where it is headed.

The Evolution of Residential Colleges

Why do residential colleges exist? Historically they were a logical solution to the problem of transmitting knowledge when higher learning left the monasteries at the end of the Dark Ages. Teachers went to the cities and hung out their shingles, and students came to cloister with these scholars in an environment

Note: The author gratefully acknowledges the contributions of Mark Ryan and the Fulbright Scholarship Program in the preparation of this chapter.

in which there was no separation between the living and the learning. When the students were pronounced learned they went forth and did likewise, spreading education throughout Europe (Oakley, 1992). But in twentieth-century higher education, the residential college approach has a hint of anachronism, certainly inefficiency. Mass higher education in America can be delivered only by warehousing students on one side of campus and faculty and classrooms on the other, causing a type of schizophrenia for the academy. Undergraduates are expected to leave their brains outside the residence hall and leave their personal lives outside the classroom door. America has educated tens of millions of students this way since World War II, but not without psychic cost to individuals and campuses. Residential colleges are increasingly seen as a way to heal some of these psychic costs. They facilitate intense faculty-student interaction in a comprehensive, inclusive fashion, integrating in a coherent fashion students' intellectual and personal lives. Furthermore, well-developed residential colleges address critical higher education issues: involvement, community building, diversity, retention, bridging the gap between ideal academic standards and actual student performance, fostering faculty and student interaction, and enhancing the freshman experience.

In this chapter, the residential college concept is defined. Benefits of this arrangement are presented, examples of effective programs are provided, and future directions for residential colleges are suggested.

Defining Residential Colleges

It is vital first to distinguish a residential college from a residence *hall*, then to carefully describe what is meant by a residential college. "College residence halls exist to provide relatively low-cost, safe, sanitary, and comfortable living quarters; to promote the intellectual, social, personality, physical, career, educational, and moral development of those who live there; and to supplement and enrich students' academic experiences" (Winston, Anchors, and Associates, 1993, p. xix).

Residential colleges exist *primarily to supplement and enrich students' academic experiences, if not to actually create them.* If the primary and explicit goal of a college housing facility is something other than to promote academic development, that facility is not a residential college, whatever else occurs there.

While the distinction between residential colleges and residence halls may be straightforward, there is no consensus on the definition of the term *residential college.* This term has three connotations, however. The generic usage means an institution on whose campus most of its enrolled undergraduates live, as opposed to one with a large commuter or off-campus student population. There are hundreds of these small, primarily private liberal arts schools, usually self-contained, residential, undergraduate, and often located in small towns. The generic term *college* has its American origins in the nineteenth-century notion that a college is more than a curriculum, a library, a faculty, and students — it is residential and respectful of quiet rural settings, dependent on dormitories and committed to dining halls, and permeated by paternalism (Rudolph, 1991). The dormitory — a new concept in the nineteenth century — that characterized these fledgling colleges was a mixed blessing, however, and helped establish the philosophical and historical foundations for many of the nonintellectual purposes of the American college (Rudolph, 1991). This type of school continues to be called a residential college, but in reality, it does not conform to the classic definition as set forth below.

A second, more restrictive usage includes those institutions at which significant traditional academic programming occurs in residential facilities. About sixty-five institutions in North America report intensive programming of this sort (Smith and Raney, 1993). These programs are commonly called "living-learning" or interest units. The living-learning center features an array of academic support services such as classrooms and classes, tutoring, and study skills centers occupying residential hall space. The academic interest unit is often nothing more than a group of students with an academic commonality — a foreign language, an academic discipline, a devotion to interdisciplinary studies — residing in the same proximity, forming a learning community. Living-learning centers and interest units challenge the traditional barrier between faculty and student but do not fully cross it. While they introduce intellectual activity into the residential setting and, as will be described, make a positive difference in the life of the undergraduate, they usually are administered by student affairs staff; faculty are typically conspicuous by their absence.

Currently fewer than thirty institutions have the third type, the "classic" residential college, characterized by faculty and students sharing living and working space. The classic residential college first appeared in the Islamic world in the eleventh century and became Europeanized in the twelfth century in Paris and Oxford (Oakley, 1992). Oxford and Cambridge colleges evolved in medieval England to serve largely upper-class young men in a holistic way—body, soul, and intellect. The American Puritans exported Calvinist inspiration and Oxbridge form to the colonies as the foundation of their colleges, both to train minds and mold character (Smith, 1990). Colleges patterned after English models were founded in the colonies in the seventeenth and eighteenth centuries at, among other places, Harvard, Princeton, and William and Mary.

It was at the college at New Haven that the collegiate ideal was most eloquently defended in the Yale Report of 1828. The report endorsed the classic seven liberal arts, the facilities designed for their instruction, and the accompanying ethos: "The parental character of college government requires that students should be so collected together, as to constitute one family; that the intercourse between them and their instructors may be frequent and familiar" (Ryan, 1993, p. 9). These connections created by living arrangements were the key to the English experience, but the "parental superintendent" role never prevailed in America for financial reasons. Few colleges could afford the architectural prerequisites, such as a complete quadrangle with a single exit, a commons, an all-member dining hall, or staffing essentials such as the porter guarding the single exit (Rudolph, 1991). Nonetheless, fragments of the English experience—faculty and students sharing living quarters, blended intellectual and religious instruction, bucolic surroundings—still exist at institutions that join living with learning. Many current programs have residential faculty. Others are values driven or values seeking, providing a sectarian education (such as Brigham Young) or a classic liberal arts experience (for example, St. Lawrence). Still others, such as at Appalachian State and Northeast Missouri State, are found at rural institutions (Smith and Raney, 1993).

As the nineteenth century progressed, American infatuation with the Germanic model of higher education, emphasizing research and independent study, eroded the rationale of the residential college and gave rise to the argument that schools could spend more on faculty and libraries if they spent less on residences (Ryan, 1993). For some decades, the university, with its specialized faculty and curriculum, large student bodies, and typically urban setting, represented the ideal of American higher education. In the late nineteenth century, Charles Eliot, Harvard's president, led the effort opposing close communities of learning and moral guidance of students in residence halls (Ryan, 1993). Eliot's idea was the antithesis of the collegiate model, so in some ways contemporary residential colleges are a reaction to the Germanic scheme. A number of large research institutions have in fact established and nurtured residential colleges in response to the depersonalization and alienation caused by mass higher education.

Early in this century, a revival of collegiate values took place, led by Woodrow Wilson, Princeton's president, who spoke of the need to awaken the whole person (Ryan, 1993). Wilson failed to create at Princeton a classic system of colleges, one characterized by a quadrangle with a dining hall, commons room, and resident Master, while Harvard and Yale succeeded to an extent. Harvard's houses, of largely Georgian architecture, were considered luxurious, with student suites of a bedroom, living room, and bath. Fine cuisine was served by uniformed motherly Irish women (in order not to stimulate the libidos of the undergraduates) (Smith, 1990). Yale built neo-Gothic colleges, reproducing the architecture if not the curriculum of the past. Yet even Harvard and Yale were ultimately unable to realize their potential and were more successful in reviving the social and moral climate of the collegiate way than in sustaining any marked intellectual improvement (Rudolph, 1991). Nonetheless something important was created—collegiate units within the modern university—joining the British college to the American dormitory (Ryan, 1993). Harvard and Yale gave contemporary American higher education a sense of the possible. All that remained for the renaissance of residential colleges were the will and resources to proceed.

Only a few universities have created totally residential college campuses. Some, such as Harvard, Yale, and Rice, flourish, while others—Princeton, Northwestern, Miami (Florida), Pennsylvania, Stanford, and Northeast Missouri State—do well on a large-but-less-than-total-campus scale. California–San Diego and California–Santa Cruz have reportedly failed as residential college campuses after being overwhelmed by entrenched academic disciplines (Smith, 1990). Other large institutions (Illinois, Indiana, Southern California, Colorado, Miami (Ohio), Virginia) have residential colleges that subdivide these universities into small, more humane communities in order to preserve liberal education.

During the period of greatest upheaval in modern American higher education (the late 1960s and early 1970s), a number of colleges and universities experimented with "cluster colleges" as a response to internal and external demands for reform (Gaff, 1970). While most were curriculum based and were separate only in the organizational sense, a few were residential colleges or living-learning centers. Some founded during that time continue to this day (James Madison College at Michigan State University, the Residential College at the University of Michigan, Unit One at the University of Illinois), though many have failed or lost their identities as residential colleges. A number were experimental and collapsed after their utopian adventure spent itself (Gaff, 1970).

Since 1982, at least thirty-one institutions have started new programs, and several others are strongly considering it (Smith and Raney, 1993). Underlying the revitalization of the residential college idea is a parallel renaissance of the liberal arts on many campuses and the emergence of the concept of involvement as a catalyst for promoting the building of learning communities. Coincidentally, these developments have received extensive analysis in recent higher education literature, albeit not explicitly in the context of living-learning. Two recent books explore the impact that the substance and process of higher education have on the participant. Pascarella and Terenzini (1991) comprehensively review the literature on the subject, and Kuh, Schuh, Whitt, and Associates (1991) formulate their concept of involving colleges based on inspections of a number of American campuses. To encourage involvement, campuses must create a sense of belonging as well as a supportive and valuing environment, and they must acknowledge and nurture the perception of most undergraduates that in-class and out-of-class experiences are seamless (Kuh, Schuh, Whitt, and Associates, 1991). The residential college is a special type of residence hall that introduces explicit academic activity into the student living environment. The classic residential college has the live-in faculty presence. The living-learning center/interest unit has intentional academic programming such as classrooms, classes, advising, tutoring, study skills centers, and libraries, but faculty do not live with students. The literature does not differentiate between pure residential colleges and living-learning programs, but it does suggest that the higher degree of involvement fostered by both is associated with positive educational outcomes (Pascarella and Terenzini, 1991).

Benefits of Residential Colleges

While the preponderance of the literature discusses benefits of residential college environments to students, there is evidence that faculty and student affairs staff also reap dividends from working in them. Faculty benefit primarily by having a broader and deeper level of involvement with students, and, in many residential colleges, by having the opportunity to experiment with curriculum. The first benefit gives faculty and students the ability to see each other from nonstereotypical, less formal, multidimensional perspectives. Kuh, Schuh, Whitt, and Associates (1991) describe several schools where informal residential college contact has positive results for faculty, who report improved teaching skills growing from the experiences. The natural affinity of faculty for their discipline motivates their interest in the academic component of residential colleges. By contrast, the involvement of student affairs staff in the academic component of residential colleges is often superficial, because their academic endeavors are seldom grounded in a traditional discipline.

Faculty seem to especially appreciate the opportunities offered by those residential colleges with unique curricula. They report positive attitudes about working closely with colleagues from other disciplines (Stark, 1993) and about taking unique approaches, giving special emphasis to traditional subjects, and experimenting with team teaching (Arndt, 1993). They report relief from the curse of hyperspecialization and pleasure from confronting the "irony of expertise," the concept that knowledge does not grow until authority for it is shared (Cornwell and Guarasci, 1993). Furthermore, faculty affiliated with residential colleges tend to be more supportive of innovation and experimentation (Martin and Wilkinson, 1970; Gaff, 1970). In the most global sense, these faculty tend to be more concerned with and more knowledgeable about the larger institutions' educational philosophy than unaffiliated faculty (Martin and Wilkinson, 1970).

The first benefit of residential colleges to student affairs/residential living staff is direct engagement with the instructional mission of the institution, and its corollary, collaboration with faculty on academic programs. In most residential colleges, student affairs staff, not faculty, coordinate in-residence delivery of academic services and are therefore obligated to work closely with faculty and academic staff (Hart, 1991). Student affairs/residential living staff often contend that "we are educators too; students just don't get academic credit for what they learn from us." This claim is both true and important. Faculty and academic administrators tend to view only credit-bearing academic activity as legitimate; therefore, any cooperative endeavor supporting the formal academic mission, the core activity of the enterprise, is viewed by faculty as at least nontrivial and often central to the academic mission. Such services, when they measurably benefit institutional objectives such as retention, cast student affairs in favorable light (Hart, 1991).

The second benefit to student affairs is a derivative of the first: when academic development is seen as a significant component of a student development model, student affairs/residential living objectives and programming are transformed and the "false dualism" of student versus academic affairs is exposed (Cornwell and Guarasci, 1993). Because faculty are often narrowly focused on their disciplines, student affairs staff are frequently better able to model the liberal arts, the connectedness of learning. Staff systemically integrate what undergraduates come to the institution to do—take classes and maintain at least satisfactory progress toward a degree—into the other parts of their lives. They model how students can respond effectively to opportunities and responsibilities present in an academic community; few faculty have the temperament and training to do this (Pascarella and Terenzini, 1991). Students are better able to understand how their formal learning fits into the larger picture of personal, social, and ethical growth. They thereby see staff in a primary, rather than ancillary, role in their education. The chief academic affairs and student affairs officers have vital roles as well. By working together on the common ground of the residential college, they show that the priorities of academic and student affairs can complement each other if both acknowledge their common commitment to the institution's mission (Pascarella and Terenzini, 1991).

Students also benefit in diverse ways. Research generally indicates that students residing in an environment where living and learning are explicitly blended show more autonomy, intellectualism, and personal growth, although the effects may be indirect rather than direct, mediated by the nature and frequency of the interactions that living-learning centers promote with faculty and peers (Pascarella and Terenzini, 1991). Generally, when environments are created to nurture serious academic work, students living in those environments do better academically. It is therefore not surprising to find residential college settings associated with satisfaction with academics (Stark, 1993) and greater gains in intellectual orientation, critical thinking, and cognitive development (Pascarella and Terenzini, 1991). The faculty presence positively influences the intellectual atmosphere. Positive faculty interaction with students such as book loans, bull sessions, and research prompts have a different hue and texture in the residential environment. Frequency and quality of contact with faculty increase. Students often come to know faculty members for the first time as multidimensional human beings, not as detached scholars living on pedestals or in ivory towers. The "you leave me alone and I'll leave you alone" arrangement becomes shallow and banal (Kuh, Schuh, Whitt, and Associates, 1991).

Students benefit nonintellectually as well. Researchers find higher cultural and aesthetic interests, higher family independence scale scores, increases in liberalism and social conscience, positive effects on self-reliance, self-understanding, interpersonal skills, and personal discipline (Pascarella and Terenzini, 1991), better multicultural expression and sensitivity (Cornwell and Guarasci, 1993), and improved personal growth generally (Gaff, 1970). All of these factors tend to interact to increase persistence rates of students in residential colleges (Pascarella and Terenzini, 1991; Stark, 1993). They are by design "involving" environments that promote many practices prized by advocates of quality higher education. In addition, colleges that exist exclusively or primarily for first-year students provide benefits unavailable in traditional residential environments, such as immediate and intimate involvement with regular teaching faculty and early, multifaceted exposure to mainstream academic activity (Smith, 1993).

Exemplary Residential College Models

Two residential college programs in particular illustrate the range of goals, staffing arrangements, facilities, and challenges as well as their impact on students, faculty, and staff: Yale University (which began residential colleges in 1933) and Northeast Missouri State University (which initiated its program in 1988). Yale exemplifies a mature, well-established, campus-dominating program, while Northeast represents a new, aggressive, innovative, evolving program.

A Traditional Model: Yale

Yale opened ten residential colleges in the 1930s and added two more in 1962. In the vision of the founding donor, these "quadrangles" — all built, like the colleges of Oxford and Cambridge, around courtyards — created manageable communities in the modern university, reviving some of the "social advantages" of the intimate Yale College that he knew as a student. Each college, with its affiliated freshman dormitory, houses 375–400 students, a college master (normally a tenured member of the faculty), a dean (usually a junior member of the faculty), and two resident faculty fellows. Freshmen are assigned to a college at admission and affiliate with it through graduation. Most, however, do not live in the quadrangles until sophomore year, spending their first year on the "Old Campus," Yale's Freshman Quad. Nevertheless, in Yale's student culture — and in part because of the university's college-orientation procedures — college affiliation quickly becomes central to a student's sense of identity at the institution. First-year students are ceremoniously welcomed by college masters and deans, received by college-affiliated resident counselors, and attend several college-centered orientation events. "From the time I was accepted, I got letters from the college," one student commented recently. "When I arrived, I got a key to the college. My 'big sibling,' wearing a college T-shirt, was there to greet me. There was a freshman cookout in the college courtyard with upperclassmen flipping burgers for us. I didn't feel like I really met Yale until later."

The sense of belonging is reinforced by the services that students receive through their colleges and the facilities that these units offer. First-year students are advised by college-affiliated faculty fellows; they take meals in the college dining hall, which becomes a center of their social life; and they quickly find their way into an array of college organizations, including intramural sports teams, student government, music and drama groups, and social and educational committees. For many students, masters — who oversee the college life — and deans — who are academic advisers — become personal counselors as well as resident authorities and essential guides to the otherwise potentially baffling array of university resources. Residents can make use of numerous other facilities housed in the colleges, typically including a small library, computer rooms, squash courts, an exercise room, a student-operated snack bar, a game room, and such specialized facilities as music practice rooms, a darkroom, a woodshop, even a printing press. A current challenge for the residential colleges at Yale, however, is millions of dollars of deferred maintenance; these elegant neo-Gothic and neo-Georgian halls have sizable infrastructure problems. A renovation program is currently underway, though it is moving more slowly than many would like.

Yale's colleges are largely social institutions: they offer little in the way of curriculum. Attempts over the years to enhance their academic component have failed to win essential support from the academic departments. Each college, however, offers a handful of "residential college seminars" taught primarily by outside instructors and graduate students. These seminars are chosen by a student-fellow committee of the college and meet in the college's classrooms; priority in enrollment is given to the sponsoring college's students. With the presence of residential college deans and faculty fellows, the colleges are centers of academic counseling. College-affiliated tutors in writing and in the sciences, and noncredit programs such as senior essay workshops overseen by faculty fellows, enhance the colleges' cocurricular role. Prominent visitors occasionally deliver college-sponsored lectures or, more frequently, join in informal discussions at teas in the stately masters' houses. The dining halls and common rooms become the setting for plays, concerts, and other cultural events, often involving student performers. For the faculty, college fellowships offer an opportunity or social contact across departmental boundaries. Each college draws its fellows from across the spectrum of academic fields, and some fellows have offices in the quadrangles. Although the level of faculty participation varies from one college to another (and often is seen as wanting), some fellows meet for dinners as often as weekly, typically in wood-paneled fellows' common rooms. A free lunch program encourages faculty to dine with students, and with one another, in the college dining halls.

To the students, however, the most significant element of college life is the strong bonds of friendship promoted in these close-knit communities. Such ties, reinforced over a student's four years, help explain the high level of student satisfaction at Yale, as well as the ongoing alumni involvement. "You feel like you're living in a small community," one student recently said, "even though you have all the resources of Yale. You don't feel lost. You are living with all sorts of different people, but you get to know them really well. You feel a shared spirit and energy, and that gives a sense of continuity." College members— students, faculty, staff—"accept the educational value of community life, strive to develop the whole psyche, and accept the principle that students educate each other fully as much as they are educated by the faculty" (Ryan, 1993, pp. 14–15). Yale's is surely the archetypal residential college system in North America, oft-emulated. To be sure, it faces the challenges of a mature system, needing periodic personnel and programmatic revitalization, but it also has the extraordinary advantages of a world-class reputation, healthy endowment, breathtaking buildings, and a program that is inseparably a part of the campus culture (Smith and Raney, 1993).

An Emerging Model: Northeast Missouri State

Northeast Missouri State is one of Yale's emulators. Northeast, once a teachers' college, became the state's public liberal arts and sciences institution in 1986. It created four residential colleges in 1988 to increase the academic atmosphere of the residence halls and to promote the new mission. Each of its four colleges (two coed, two single-sex female) house 300 (60 percent freshman, 25 percent sophomore, 15 percent junior and senior); collectively, the colleges house 40 percent of the on-campus students. Living in each college is a faculty member whose assignment is split between teaching two courses per semester in an academic discipline and advising 90 freshmen from a variety of majors. More than half of Northeast's freshmen receive their advising in a residential college; the advising process begins with specially trained undergraduate peer advisers prepping the freshmen who live in their sections about the mechanics of course registration, thus allowing the resident faculty adviser to deal with larger issues during the academic guidance appointment. "Getting advised in my college is a real benefit," said one freshman. "My adviser's around a lot, even during odd hours, and is really knowledgeable. Advising seems like a more natural process in the college, more a part of the total experience." Another freshman said, "I was skeptical about my peer adviser being able to advise me about classes. Not only did she give good information, but by taking care of the basics, she allowed me to spend time with the Assistant College Professor [resident faculty adviser] talking about goals and what he calls 'the existential concerns.'"

College members receive their new-student orientation through the college during a week that immediately precedes the start of the fall term and includes a for-credit minicourse. The orientation deeply involves faculty and among other things helps develop more sophisticated conversation skills (a skill too often overlooked) and expedites the transition from high school to college by humanizing faculty (Hohenbary, Bryan, Cross, and Cruse, 1993). Members also take general education and interdisciplinary courses in-college; the residential colleges are the only academic units that offer interdisciplinary courses. Two benefits accrue: residents cannot easily find an excuse to skip class if they do not even have to put their shoes on, and faculty have a good reason to be in the building — their presence is not invasive. Faculty are able to find expression for their academic interests in ways not allowed in their regular teaching assignments; often the interdisciplinary course is an amalgam of faculty and student interest ("Baseball Literature," "Reading the Nature Writers," "To Be Young, a Woman, and a Scholar") (Hohenbary, Bryan, Cross, and Cruse, 1993). "One of my best classes was 'Contemporary Issues,'" said a sophomore. "Three upperclass students developed the course under the supervision of the Assistant College Professor, but we selected the topics. It was intense and rigorous but we totally owned the class. It was 'empowering,' as they say, and I really sharpened my thinking about abortion and capital punishment and racism, to name just three." Members do not, however, dine in a facility used exclusively by them, and the facilities (large residence halls built in 1963 and modestly renovated in 1988 to create faculty offices and larger faculty apartments) do not fully support the program — there are but two small seminar rooms and no space for all college members to dine privately or meet as a college.

Northeast's colleges did not come into being as part of a rational, collegial planning process but rather by well-intended but nonconsultative administrative action. Faculty and students felt little ownership of the process and therefore the product; hence, many faculty ignore the colleges, a few are hostile, and those who are interested in involvement have few incentives, especially those leading to tenure and promotion. In contrast to the situation at Yale, the Northeast undergraduate culture and the residential college culture are not synonymous. Nonetheless, Northeast faculty see its colleges as venues for curricular experimentation and innovation, as well as a place to engage students in unconventional, interesting ways. The primary benefit of in-college faculty-student interaction is that it is organic and unforced. The programming that results meets the "relevance" criterion and therefore illustrates in a supremely natural way that learning indeed occurs elsewhere (Hohenbary, Bryan, Cross, and Cruse, 1993). A senior peer adviser said "living in a residential college brings classroom education and life education under one roof." The residents of the colleges have higher persistence rates, make better grades, and in surveys express more general satisfaction with university programs and services. Despite these successes, however, the long-term future of Northeast's colleges is not guaranteed. There is continuous competition for scarce resources, an insecure power base for the colleges, and the view by some that an academic presence in the residence halls can be provided more cheaply with more traditional student affairs models. Northeast's colleges are probably better appreciated off campus than on (Smith and Raney, 1993).

Current Challenge and Future Prospects

Residential colleges face philosophical and political obstacles that account for their relative rarity. Some contend that residential colleges represent a return to the days of in loco parentis, with too much integration and intrusiveness. The potential exists for students not to be empowered to do things for themselves and for students to believe that the extras provided by the residential college are norms for the institution. Parents may also have greater expectations of staff responsibilities toward their children living in residential colleges (Platt, 1992). Ironically, the converse of too much in-college faculty and staff involvement can be alienation from the institution of which the college is a part. This alienation can interfere with the learning process and cause isolation from the intellectual life of the institution and the inhibition of some aspects of cognitive growth (Pascarella and Terenzini, 1991), although at least one study suggests that residential colleges decrease alienation generally (Cornwell and Guarasci, 1993). Indeed, some residential colleges have become insulated subsystems, isolated and alienated from the rest of campus. The well-intended personalization has led to student "preoccupation with existential concerns," creating a cloistering effect, sometimes accompanied by alternative life-styles well outside the campus mainstream. Further, some have eschewed normal institutional bureaucratic expectations, alienating campus majorities. The very spirit of innovation and experimentation can be threatening to the larger community and can attract faculty and students who are malcontents (Gaff, 1970).

Student affairs/residence life staff, who are central to the success of a residential college program, often believe themselves marginalized by faculty and academic administrators in a residential college setting and therefore may be less than enthusiastic about the prospects of helping run a program. There is some circularity to the marginality argument. For example, Zeller, Fidler, and Barefoot (1991) propose thirteen "Goals for the First Year Experience in College and University Residence Halls," yet in only four of them is the word *faculty* or *academic* or *scholar* found. Faculty and academic administrators reviewing these goals might not see student affairs/residence life staff as major players in efforts to build learning communities for first-year students.

Residential colleges are not cheap. Many have been abandoned early or strangled later by financial neglect (Gaff, 1970). Others persist at the pleasure or whim of administrators who have chronic funding problems and continually cast about for "nonessential" programs to eviscerate. No constituency naturally "claims" a residential college. Faculty tend to see residential colleges as "housing stuff." Student affairs/residence life professionals tend to see them as "untrained faculty horning in" and posing a philosophical threat to traditional student development models and programming (Creeden, 1988).

Perhaps the largest obstacle to the vitality of residential colleges is the increasing trend of faculty loyalty to their academic discipline, rather than to the institution and the well-being of the undergraduate (Hart and Smith, 1993). The trend is reinforced by institutional incentive structures that reward research and scholarly activity in the disciplines in promotion and tenure decisions. Compounding the faculty loyalty problem is the increasing number of part-time faculty being hired, especially by urban institutions (Kuh, Schuh, Whitt, and Associates, 1991).

Finally, neither student affairs, nor housing, nor academic affairs, nor faculty discipline professional groups have residential college caucuses. In fact, it was not until 1992 that a network of residential college professionals was formed, a group whose creation all agreed was long overdue. This group held its first conferences in 1992 and 1993 and has among its key resources the 1992 conference proceedings (Smith, 1992), a directory (Smith and Raney, 1993), a monograph on the benefits of residential colleges to first-year students (Smith, 1993), and a growing group of consultants. Because the network is in its infancy, it is only beginning to struggle with challenges long settled in other arenas. How do interested faculty, staff, and students start a residential college? Get support for it? Get other faculty involved in it? Evaluate it? Revitalize it when it is tired? The traditional academic disciplines have wrestled with these issues for centuries. Residential colleges have collectively tackled these issues systemically for mere months, and have done so during a period of enormous change and instability in higher education.

Despite all of the obstacles, residential colleges are having a renaissance, as noted. One of the greatest benefits of the new network of residential colleges is its pool of talent available to help others who are considering creating a residential college. The following tables illustrate current residential colleges and living-learning centers in North America, arrayed by date of founding (see Table 11.1) and proportion of total campus residential population housed in the residential college/living-

Table 11.1. Date of Founding of Residential Colleges
and Living-Learning Centers by Type and Size of Institution.

Total enrollment	Private	Public
0–2,999	Whitman (1970) Macalester (1972) Susquehanna (1975) Gettysburg (1984) Ohio Wesleyan (1987) St. Lawrence (1987) Briar Cliff (1988) Dickinson (1989) Whittier (1990) [Wooster (N/A)]	
3,000–9,999	Rice (1957) Dartmouth (1970) Vanderbilt (1972) Creighton (1977) Princeton (1982) Puget Sound (1982) Emory (1983) Lehigh (1984) Miami (Florida) (1984) Bucknell (1986) Butler (1989) Scranton (1989) St. Thomas (Minnesota) (1991)	California–Santa Cruz (1963) Vermont (1973) Maryland–Baltimore (1988) Northeast Missouri State (1988) Winona State (Minnesota) (1991)
10,000–19,999	Yale (1933) Stanford (1965) Cornell (New York) (1970) Northwestern (Illinois) (1972) Fordham (1987) [Dayton (N/A)]	California–Irvine (1965) SUNY–Binghamton (1968) North Carolina–Greensboro (1970) Appalachian (North Carolina) (1972) Miami (Ohio) (1974) SUNY–Stony Brook (1984) Virginia (1986) Cal Poly–San Luis Obispo (1987) Wisconsin–Oshkosh (1987)
20,000+	Pennsylvania (1972) Southern California (1983) Brigham Young (1985)	Michigan (1962) Massachusetts–Amherst (1964) North Carolina State (1966) Michigan State (1967) Colorado (1972)

Table 11.1. Date of Founding of Residential Colleges
and Living-Learning Centers by Type and Size of Institution, Cont'd.

Total enrollment	Private	Public
		Illinois (1972)
		Indiana (1972)
		Penn State (1973)
		South Carolina (1982)
		North Carolina–Chapel Hill (1986)
		Florida International (1987)
		Arizona State (1988)
		Kent State (1988)
		California–Berkeley (1989)
		Maryland–College Park (1989)
		Missouri–Columbia (1989)
		British Columbia (1991)
		[California–Davis (N/A)]

Source: Smith and Raney, 1993, p. 82. Used by permission.

learning setting (see Table 11.2). The renaissance is attributed
to three factors: renewed efforts by large universities to create
smaller and more successful learning communities; attempts by
prestigious private institutions to gain a marketing advantage
in tight economic times; and efforts by state colleges to offer
safe, academically oriented, compact communities in a non-
urban setting to prospective students from metropolitan areas.
Each successful new venture is characterized by clearly identified need, support from the top, fit-to-institutional-mission,
a distinctly academic focus, assiduous involvement of the faculty,
and clear exposition of the uniqueness of the enterprise to all
constituencies—faculty, staff, administrators, and students. Educators promoting involvement and the nurturing of learning
communities support the residential colleges concept. The authors of the definitive compendium of research findings practi-
cally endorse residential colleges and urge their presence on more
campuses (Pascarella and Terenzini, 1991). Educators who promote "psychologically small" communities within larger ones also
support the residential college concept, as do educators who promote communities with commonalities of purpose.

Table 11.2. Percent of Total Campus Undergraduate
Resident Population Housed in Residential Colleges and
Living-Learning Centers by Type and Size of Institution.

Total enrollment	Private	Public
0–2,999	Whittier — 100% Dickinson — 33 St. Lawrence — 25 Briar Cliff — 20 Gettysburg — 20 Susquehanna — 12 Whitman — 10 Macalester — 9 [Ohio Wesleyan — N/A] [Wooster — N/A]	
3,000–9,000	Rice — 100% Miami (Florida) — 76 Princeton — 50 Butler — 33 St. Thomas — 20 Creighton — 18 Scranton — 14 Lehigh — 8 Dartmouth — 4 Puget Sound — 3 Vanderbilt — 2 Emory — 1 [Bucknell — N/A]	Northeast Missouri State — 39% Maryland–Baltimore — 33 Winona State (Minnesota) — 24 Vermont — 15 [California–Santa Cruz — N/A]
10,000–19,999	Yale — 100% Stanford — 65 Cornell (New York) — 50 Northwestern (Illinois) — 25 Fordham — 14 [Dayton — N/A]	SUNY–Binghamton — 80% Wisconsin–Oshkosh — 16 Virginia — 15 Cal Poly–San Luis Obispo — 15 Appalachian State (North Carolina) — 5 North Carolina–Greensboro — 4 Miami (Ohio) — 3 [California–Irvine — N/A] [SUNY–Stony Brook — N/A]
20,000+	Brigham Young — 100% Pennsylvania — 49 Southern California — 20	California–Berkeley — 45% Kent State — 15 Michigan — 12 Arizona State — 8 Florida International — 8 Illinois — 8 Massachusetts–Amherst — 8

Table 11.2. Percent of Total Campus Undergraduate
Resident Population Housed in Residential Colleges and
Living-Learning Centers by Type and Size of Institution, Cont'd.

Total enrollment	Private	Public
		Missouri–Columbia — 8
		South Carolina — 8
		North Carolina State — 7
		Indiana — 6
		Maryland–College Park — 6
		North Carolina–Chapel Hill — 6
		Penn State — 5
		British Columbia — 4
		Michigan State — 3
		[California–Davis — N/A]
		[Colorado — N/A]

Source: Smith and Raney, 1993, p. 84. Used by permission.

But involvement, community building, intimacy, and evidence of intellectual and personal development are but preludes to the next stage of development of the residential college idea. On the near horizon, institutions will be faced with more students with hugely diverse backgrounds, fewer faculty, chronically tight resources, ever-increasing expectations about what higher education should be and do, and mandated accountability. How can residential colleges respond?

Residential colleges can continue to be incubators for innovation. Most American residential colleges were founded in the spirit of experimentation; many remain the venue for trying new educational concepts where success can be reinforced and exported and failure does not cripple. There is an implicit benefit returned to the residential college because it is a testing ground: "Students and faculty bring with them a high degree of courage and commitment — they are, after all, taking risks — and in turn, the college that has been forced by its circumstances to be self-conscious, critical, and definitive has something special to give these faculty and students" (Martin and Wilkinson, 1970, p. 178).

Residential colleges can serve as catalysts for campus cultural integration. Some residential colleges nurture diverse constituencies and empower special interest groups. Other programs consciously integrate these same diverse constituencies into the larger living-learning community. Schools with different missions have divergent philosophies about how to support increasingly diverse campus populations; hence, no one approach is right. Residential colleges can even be an agent for effective service to a nontraditional student population. In the land of medieval and indescribably tradition-bound residential colleges — England — the Master of one "red brick" (new) program is reinvigorating his program by recasting its mission to provide moral and logistical support for the increasing numbers of mature nontraditional and part-time students he intends to recruit (Burnet, 1993). No North American residential college is known to have such a mission, though the argument is compelling and the constituency is large and growing. But residential college sites for innovation, diversity empowerment, and nontraditional student support are possible in the future only if residential college leadership keeps as its first priority being part of the academic mission of the institution. Emulating the successful 1992 Clinton presidential campaign, residential college leaders need a sign in the office that says, "It's academics, stupid."

Conclusion

The 1991 annual report of Monroe Hill College of the University of Virginia contains a statement that encapsulates the residential college philosophy: "There must be a richer experience for students at the university than to be left entirely to their own devices, and rewards for all in conversation across the gulf of age and habit. The cultivation of common ground is significant educational enterprise. In the process we might see signs of the value of work; a higher level of civilized behavior; greater interest in intellectual work; a greater degree of engagement in the university's wealth of cultural variety; more effective guidance of youth; and deeper respect and sympathy on all sides" (*Annual Report,* 1991, p. 3).

How are educators to realize this ambitious yet essential goal of a more sublime and ennobling undergraduate experience, one that lifts up students, faculty, and staff alike and together? We must heed the voices of history, remembering why residential colleges came into existence in the first place, remembering why American higher education leaders either succeeded or failed to marry Oxbridge (why isn't it ever Camford?) to Old Siwash or to Large State University. We must heed the voices of faculty, who point to their reward structures when we seek their greater involvement in our programs. We must heed the voices of staff, dedicated and well trained but feeling left in the backwaters of traditional academic life; residential colleges cannot run without them. And we must heed students, who urge us to proceed from living to learning — not the other way around — to bridge to their academic environment without making them feel overdosed on education; to stay relevant (Hohenbary, Bryan, Cross, and Cruse, 1993).

In 1991, the author and his college-age children visited a residential college at an English university. After spending a day on the campus and talking with college members, the author's daughter observed: "They sure do cherish their students here, don't they?" "Cherishing" is our majestic mission: giving special care, empowering the whole student, while mindful of why higher education emerged from the monasteries in the Late Dark Ages to begin with: academics. Residential colleges embody a commitment to academics by providing an educational environment that values students and their holistic development.

References

Annual Report, 1990–91. Charlottesville: Monroe Hill College, University of Virginia, 1991, 13.

Arndt, F. "Making Connections: The Mission of UNCG's Residential College." In T. Smith (ed.), *Gateways: Residential Colleges and the Freshman Year Experience.* Columbia, S.C.: National Resource Center for the Freshman Year Experience, 1993, 49–54.

Burnet, F. "Time Travel in British Higher Education." In T. Smith (ed.), *Gateways: Residential Colleges and the Freshman Year Experience.* Columbia, S.C.: National Resource Center for the Freshman Year Experience, 1993, 73–79.

Cornwell, G., and Guarasci, R. "Student Life as Text: Discovering Connections, Creating Community." In T. Smith (ed.), *Gateways: Residential Colleges and the Freshman Year Experience.* Columbia, S.C.: National Resource Center for the Freshman Year Experience, 1993, 41–48.

Creeden, J. "Student Affairs Biases as a Barrier to Collaboration: A Point of View." *NASPA Journal,* 1988, *26*(1), 60–63.

Gaff, J. (ed.). *The Cluster College.* San Francisco: Jossey-Bass, 1970.

Hart, D. "Encouraging the Retention and Academic Success of First Year Students Through Residence Based Academic Support Programming." In W. Zeller, D. Fidler, and B. Barefoot (eds.), *Residence Life Programs and the First Year Experience.* Columbia, S.C.: Association of College and University Housing Officers–International/National Resource Center for the Freshman Year Experience, 1991, 49–56.

Hart, D., and Smith, T. "Residential Colleges: Vestiges or Models for Improving College Residence Halls?" In T. Smith (ed.), *Gateways: Residential Colleges and the Freshman Year Experience.* Columbia, S.C.: National Resource Center for the Freshman Year Experience, 1993, 25–31.

Hohenbary, J., Bryan, R., Cross, B., Cruse, L. "Us and Them." In T. Smith (ed.), *Gateways: Residential Colleges and the Freshman Year Experience.* Columbia, S.C.: National Resource Center for the Freshman Year Experience, 1993.

Kuh, G. D., Schuh, J. H., Whitt, E. J., and Associates. *Involving Colleges: Successful Approaches to Fostering Student Learning and Development Outside the Classroom.* San Francisco: Jossey-Bass, 1991.

Martin, W., and Wilkinson, J. "Making a Difference." In J. Gaff (ed.), *The Cluster College.* San Francisco: Jossey-Bass, 1970.

Oakley, F. *Community of Learning: The American College and the Liberal Arts Tradition.* New York: Oxford University Press, 1992.

Pascarella, E. T., and Terenzini, P. T. *How College Affects Students: Findings and Insights from Twenty Years of Research.* San Francisco: Jossey-Bass, 1991.

Platt, D. "Student Affairs in James Madison College." In T. Smith (ed.), *Proceedings of the First Annual Conference of Residential Colleges and Living-Learning Centers.* Kirksville: Northeast Missouri State University, 1992.

Rudolph, F. *The American College and University: A History.* (rev. ed.) Athens: University of Georgia Press, 1991.

Ryan, M. "Residential Colleges: An Historical Context." In T. Smith (ed.), *Gateways: Residential Colleges and the Freshman Year Experience.* Columbia, S.C.: National Resource Center for the Freshman Year Experience, 1993, 11–18.

Smith, P. *Killing the Spirit: Higher Education in America.* New York: Viking, 1990.

Smith, T. (ed.). *Proceedings of the First Annual Conference of Residential Colleges and Living-Learning Centers.* Kirksville: Northeast Missouri State University, 1992.

Smith, T. (ed.). *Gateways: Residential Colleges and the Freshman Year Experience.* Columbia, S.C.: National Resource Center for the Freshman Year Experience, 1993.

Smith, T., and Raney, B. *North American Directory of Residential Colleges and Living-Learning Centers,* 2nd ed. Kirksville: Northeast Missouri State University, 1993.

Stark, J. "Putting the College Back in University." In T. Smith (ed.), *Gateways: Residential Colleges and the Freshman Year Experience.* Columbia, S.C.: National Resource Center for the Freshman Year Experience, 1993, 55–60.

Winston, R. B., Jr., Anchors, S., and Associates. *Student Housing and Residential Life: A Handbook for Professionals Committed to Student Development Goals.* San Francisco: Jossey-Bass, 1993.

Zeller, W., Fidler, D., and Barefoot, B. (eds.). *Residence Life Programs and the First Year Experience.* Columbia, S.C.: Association of College and University Housing Officers–International/National Resource Center for the Freshman Year Experience, 1991.

Part 3

========

Strengthening
Educational Impacts
of Residential Life

During the past ten years, colleges and universities have been increasingly expected to demonstrate that students achieve certain educational outcomes. This emphasis on accountability has compelled educators in both academic affairs and student affairs to utilize a variety of assessment strategies for demonstrating educational impacts. Assessment is a powerful tool for determining how residence halls contribute to the desired outcomes of student learning and personal development. It is also an essential element in making residential education more intentional.

In Chapter Twelve, David H. Kalsbeek uses metaphors to examine widely varying perspectives on the educational role of residence halls. He presents six different metaphors, describing the residence hall as a consumable, a classroom, a catalyst, a climate, a culture, and a community. These metaphors provide different mental models or "frames of reference" that influence our approach to assessing the residential experience and various educational outcomes associated with that experience.

In Chapter Thirteen, Charles C. Schroeder and Phyllis Mable describe five transcendent themes from the previous chapters and utilize these themes to derive implications and recommendations for realizing the educational potential of college residence halls. They make fifteen recommendations for implementing a residence hall curriculum based on these five themes.

They also challenge educators in academic affairs and student affairs to demonstrate three forms of leadership—conceptual, educational, and administrative—necessary to achieve the full educational potential of residence halls.

Educators who achieve and demonstrate mastery of residence hall education will have a profound impact on the education of their students and the vitality of their institutions. By providing integration between the instructional environment and various out-of-class experiences of students, residence halls can be centers of effective undergraduate education.

Twelve

New Perspectives for Assessing the Residential Experience

David H. Kalsbeek

The scene is the chancellor's conference room at a Midwestern university. The campus' accreditation review committee has appointed an outcomes assessment committee to develop assessment strategies to comply with recent recommendations from a North Central Association review.

> "Now on to the next topic on the assessment agenda," says the faculty chairperson of the outcomes assessment committee. "Let's see: the residence experience. I'm not sure how the dorms really fit in an assessment of educational outcomes. Any ideas?"

> "Well, it's important that students be satisfied with the services we provide," suggests the college's chief business officer. "That's an outcome that can be assessed by surveying students to measure their satisfaction with the dorms. Or maybe we should assess how adequately our current facilities and meal plans are meeting student needs."

"We need to think more broadly," urges the student development specialist. "We should begin by reviewing both cognitive and psychosocial theories of student development and instruments to assess student growth. If we compare the scores of residents and commuters, we can see the developmental impact of campus living."

"But what's really more important in our assessment of educational outcomes," argues the director of residence life, "is showing how much students are learning from the programs the RAs are doing in the halls, like on gender-role stereotypes, wellness, and alcohol abuse."

"Don't you think we first need to assess how residents *perceive* their residential environment, like the level of social interaction? Or maybe assess the behavioral norms or values that are apparent in the residence halls?" asks the dean of students.

"And what about our students' sense of community responsibility? I think we need to show how involved the students living on campus are in campus life," says the campus minister. "After all, involvement is the key to the educational impact of campus life."

"Hmmm, I guess these all have some possibilities," the faculty chairperson ponders aloud. "I certainly hadn't thought of some of these perspectives on the role of residence halls in our educational outcomes. It seems to me that what we first have to do is define exactly what is the residential experience and how that fits with the college's educational outcomes. Surely that won't be too difficult . . . or will it? Does anyone know where to start?"

This hypothetical scene actually occurs with increasing frequency in American colleges and universities. *Assessment* has emerged as one of the critical issues now facing higher education, one that presents both a timely opportunity and a set of substantial challenges for educators. Erwin (1991) builds on the work of Rossmann and El-Khawas (1987) in noting that the momentum propelling the assessment of educational outcomes has its roots deep in the prevailing political, economic, social, and educational milieu. Therefore, as a result of the convergence of these and other factors, the assessment juggernaut will be a defining characteristic of higher education in the 1990s and beyond and will determine how we think about "realizing the educational potential" of our colleges and universities — and our residence halls.

Two noteworthy trends in the assessment field relate directly to the educational role of residence halls. First, the need to assess that role arises from the general affirmation that campus "environments" and student experiences are as prominent in an assessment program as are developmental changes or progress toward educational outcomes among students. The assessment of the campus environment in general, of the residential environment in particular, and of the full scope and quality of the student experience outside the classroom has emerged as a necessary component of student outcomes assessment (Ewell, 1988; Hutchings, 1989; Baird, 1988; Baldwin and Thelin, 1990). "Conversations" such as the one previously described are occurring on campuses nationwide as assessment committees respond to this call.

Second, outcomes are now being defined more broadly than academic, course-based learning and cognitive development. New perspectives include a wider range of out-of-class experiences and broader dimensions of student growth. Several taxonomies and frameworks for what should be included in an assessment of educational outcomes have been presented in the literature (Ewell, 1988; Terenzini, 1989). These outcomes include not only knowledge but skills, attitudes, values, behaviors, and a full range of cognitive and noncognitive development with emotional, moral, and psychosocial dimensions (Ewell, 1988; Erwin, 1991). As the definition of student outcomes expands beyond that which is purely "academic," there is opportunity for positioning strongly the out-of-class experience and particularly the residential experience in the overall assessment of student outcomes.

The purpose of this chapter is to address both the opportunities and challenges this assessment movement presents for educators committed to realizing the educational potential of residence halls. This chapter will illustrate one approach for responding to the question posed by the faculty chairperson of the hypothetical outcomes assessment committee: "Does anyone know where to start in defining what the residential experience really is?" This approach is intended to bring to the surface the widely varying perspectives present on our campuses regarding the educational role of residence halls. By doing so, educators can first explore and articulate and subsequently demonstrate through assessment how residence halls contribute to educational outcomes.

Use of Metaphor

The first instruction in publications on assessment is often to define one's terms and specify precisely what is to be assessed (Erwin, 1991; Ewell, 1988; Terenzini, 1989). This was also the suggestion of our hypothetical assessment committee chairperson after she heard some widely varying perspectives on the outcomes of campus residence. However, before one defines anything, it is important to wrestle with an underlying web of assumptions about the educational process, about how various factors affect that process, and about how to come to an understanding and evaluation of that process through assessment. These assumptions naturally determine the conceptual and methodological parameters within which assessment questions are posed and answered. Any discussion of assessment in general and of assessment of the educational impact of the residential experience in particular should begin by surfacing and then untangling those assumptions about the residence halls that prescribe what and how to assess.

How can our hypothetical committee chairperson begin to tease out the varied and competing perspectives that came up in that short dialogue? Silverman (1981), Lakoff and John-

son (1980), and Morgan (1986) offer some clues and avenues
for approaching that task. Lakoff and Johnson suggest that the
conceptual constructs and assumptions that shape what we perceive and how we make sense of the world are fundamentally
metaphorical. Metaphor, rather than being an ordinary linguis-
tic device, is the essential manner in which human thought processes are structured. They suggest that "the essence of metaphor is understanding and experiencing one kind of thing in
terms of another" (p. 5). If in fact "our conceptual system is
largely metaphorical, then the way we think, what we experience, and what we do every day is very much a matter of metaphor" (p. 3). Their essay shows the pervasiveness of metaphor
in the way we think and act and the importance and usefulness
of recognizing and appreciating the implications of the "metaphors we live by." They suggest, in other words, that the divergent perspectives among the members of our outcomes assessment
committee may reflect alternative metaphors for understanding
residence halls and their educational influences.

Silverman (1981) notes that the process of exploring alternative metaphors for any given phenomenon is evocative,
freeing the knowledge generation process from the constraints
of unquestioned assumptions, perspectives, theoretical models,
or methodologies. In a similar vein, Morgan (1986) shows just
how potent metaphors can be as tools for coming to a fuller understanding of any phenomenon and for generating new understandings that may run counter to taken-for-granted ideas.
Both introduce the pragmatic value of metaphor, offering metaphor as a useful heuristic device for surfacing alternative frames
of reference.

In the hypothetical meeting described above, the comments and divergent perspectives offered by the committee members seem to suggest a number of alternative metaphors. Exploring those metaphors could be provocative and productive
grist for the committee's deliberations as they respond to the
chairperson's concern about how to clarify their collective thinking. Likewise, in responding to the similar assessment challenges
on our own campuses, perhaps we can be more aware of the
metaphorical nature of our assumptions and explore the meta-

phors that consciously or unconsciously shape our definition of the residential experience, that frame how we define its relationship to educational outcomes, and that determine the range of assessment strategies we consider appropriate.

This chapter presents six different metaphors for the college residence hall: the residence hall as a consumable, a classroom, a catalyst, a climate, a culture, and a community. Each was reflected in comments offered in the hypothetical committee discussion. Each has implications for how to define and understand residential facilities, the students who reside in them, the range of activities, services, programs, and policies that constitute the collective residential experience, and the role of the residence halls in the overall educational enterprise. Comparing and contrasting those metaphors can be a process by which our assumptions are surfaced as well as a creative process for provoking consideration of various educational roles of residence halls and for generating insights into alternative approaches to assessing the educational outcomes of that experience.

The Residence Hall as a Consumable

When all other purposes and intentions are set aside, residence halls are dormitories, physical facilities in which students are housed while enrolled in college. In addition, residence halls provide a wide range of services as part of the contractual arrangements with the tenants. Those services and the physical accommodations are provided as part of the ancillary programs and services for students that have emerged as such a dominant part of American higher education; the management and delivery of such services has become a specialty in higher education administration. The literature in the college and university housing area has long encouraged residence life professionals to view their work in this way, noting even in the late 1970s that there needed to be more concern about students as *consumers* as residence life programs seek to respond to student needs (Phillips and Schuh, 1979).

Viewed in this way, the residence halls are consumables and the students are consumers or tenants, purchasing and consuming services, facilities, and programs. Their residential experience is substantially divorced from the educational enterprise or any educational purposes, or is tangential at best. The intent is to provide basic and satisfactory services that facilitate and never interrupt the student's academic pursuits. The interaction between the student and the residential environment is basically a contractual relationship and is a function of services offered being responsive to services demanded. A business perspective prevails. Educational outcomes are difficult to identify; student use of and satisfaction with services is emphasized over student learning per se as the dominant outcome.

Assessment Strategies. Considering the residence hall as a consumable suggests an assessment approach that would be analogous to consumer research. For example, it would focus on *needs assessment,* gauging the needs, interests, or level of demand for various housing options, services, or programs. It would focus on *service marketing research,* including questions about the perceived benefits of campus residence relative to its costs. It would focus on *consumer behavior and satisfaction,* including assessments of what services students actually use, the quantity and quality of services, programs and facilities, and the level of student satisfaction with the range of services and goods provided. This metaphor also focuses attention on *program evaluation,* questions related to the effectiveness of various programs and activities in achieving their goals, routine evaluations of residence life staff, housing rules and regulations, and social activities. Finally, much of the work in the campus ecology or campus *ecosystems* area reflects this metaphor of the residence hall environment as a consumable, focusing on the dynamic interaction between the student with certain needs and the environment with certain available resources to meet those needs and offering numerous examples of instrumentation and methods for ecosystems assessment (Schuh, 1979).

The Residence Hall as a Classroom

Residence life professionals frequently define their role as "educational" and "instructional," arguing that they are partners in the educational process and that "residence educators are teachers"

(DeCoster and Mable, 1974, p. 34). Thus, they call on their peers to equate their roles with those of the faculty and the academic curriculum (Blimling, 1981). The emergence of the living-learning center concept further encourages the consideration of the residence hall as a classroom.

Many graduate programs in student personnel prepare entry-level residence life staff to develop and implement educational programming efforts. Staff are encouraged to develop programs that engage residents in exploring topics, issues, or concerns that are predictable or natural for certain student populations. For example, educational programs are developed to address the predictable student concerns that arise as they establish autonomy from their family or explore their sexual identity. A similar orientation toward residence halls is reflected in values clarification and other exercises designed to instruct residents in issues such as tolerating individual differences, confronting stereotypes and racial and gender biases, and so on. Similarly, "wellness" as an educational agenda in residence hall programming reflects this orientation toward the residence hall as classroom.

When viewing the residence hall as a classroom, residence halls are not simply services delivered to students in response to demand; they are the settings within which programs, activities, and staff are directed to educate or instruct students in ways that extend beyond the instruction that occurs as part of the formal curriculum. When the residential environment is an out-of-class classroom, residence hall programs are lessons or courses, the collective residential experience is a multifaceted array of courses with varied pedagogy (that is, a curriculum), the residence life staff are educators, and the resident is viewed as learner or student. A traditional educational perspective prevails. Therefore, student learning is a focal point of this perspective on the role of residence halls, and educational outcomes are centered in such content areas as life skills, communication, self-awareness, and personal and interpersonal development.

Assessment Strategies. The process of assessing any learning that students achieve in this residential classroom parallels the process of doing so in the traditional classroom. The first step naturally is to identify the specific skills to be acquired, content to be mastered, or lessons to be learned. Then the assessment focuses on the attainment of these learning objectives; it attempts to determine the degree to which any demonstrable learning is in fact attributable to the instructional program. Hanson (1988) provides an especially cogent discussion of the methodological problems inherent in assessing the "value added" by particular educational interventions. Moreover, as Yanikowski has suggested (cited in Terenzini, 1989, p. 650), the prevailing perspective should be "progress assessment" rather than "outcomes assessment." The types of learning generally pursued in the residential classroom seldom have any final completion or mastery as the goal, but rather are lifelong processes of, for example, developing cultural sensitivities, social and interpersonal competencies, tolerance of individual differences, awareness of self, physical fitness, and so on.

The types of assessment questions that are then pursued when the residence hall is considered a classroom include the range of student needs for various educational programming, the degree to which instructional programs are implemented in a manner consistent with their educational design, and the extent of student progress toward the stated educational objectives. Like traditional classroom assessments, the approach would include the testing of abilities, understandings, and baseline competencies, as well as the evaluation of the educational programs. Particular assessment instruments would vary by content area (for example, instruments addressing alcohol and drug awareness, wellness, or gender-role stereotypes) and are increasingly in use in student affairs. The focus of the assessment effort is on monitoring student progress toward certain learning objectives, providing feedback to the student as part of the assessment effort, and incorporating that assessment information in the refinement of the instructional program. In addition, the assessment effort should include evaluating the direct and indirect influences on student performance in traditional academic curricula when the residence hall is in fact a bona fide classroom, as with living-learning centers.

The Residence Hall as a Catalyst

Theories of student development have emerged as dominant conceptual underpinnings for understanding the importance of a wide range of student services in higher education and for defining the role of the student affairs profession in general and residence life in particular. There are many excellent reviews of the major schools of developmental theory (Knefelkamp, Widick, and Parker, 1978; Rodgers, 1980, 1989; Pascarella and Terenzini, 1991). From the inception of the various developmental perspectives, the importance of the college environment as a stimulus for developmental change has been asserted (Baird, 1988). Conceptual frameworks generally referred to as "interactionist" (Huebner, 1989; Kalsbeek, 1985; Walsh, 1973) have also focused attention on the importance of the interaction of the individual student with the college environment.

Though the various theories differ somewhat in how developmental change occurs, a common theme is that argued twenty-five years ago by Sanford (1962, 1967) that development occurs in response to some challenge to the individual's current developmental state. Subsequent scholarship (Blocher, 1974; Chickering and Reisser, 1993; Knefelkamp, Widick, and Parker, 1978; Perry, 1970; Pascarella and Terenzini, 1991) has suggested that the level of challenge that individuals can successfully accommodate is a function in part of the level of support in the environment, and that the *balance* in an environment between elements of challenge and support is the key to facilitating developmental change. The literature on developmental change in college students recognizes that the residence hall setting in particular is an especially potent and dynamic component of the college environment (Pascarella and Terenzini, 1991). Therefore, viewing residence halls as catalysts for developmental change focuses attention on the varying degrees of challenge and support inherent in the residential environment and on balancing sources of challenge with sources of support to achieve optimal developmental conditions (Kalsbeek, Rodgers, Marshall, and Nicholls, 1982; Schroeder, 1976, 1981; Rodgers, 1980, 1989).

By considering a developmental catalyst metaphor, the residence hall is more than a passive milieu in which residents are changing, maturing persons, embryos in various stages of natural human development. Regardless of the particular developmental theory considered when one embraces a catalyst metaphor, the collective residential experiences (the facilities, programs, staff, activities, policies) become the multifaceted stimuli necessary for that development, the richly variegated catalysts that either promote or hinder development by being the source of challenges and support for the resident student. Staff can be defined as *milieu managers,* constructing and structuring the residential environment in ways that foster development. A developmental psychology perspective prevails. Educational outcomes center not so much on content learning as on human development or growth (cognitive, moral, spiritual, emotional, psychosocial, or personality development).

Assessment Strategies. With the residence hall as catalyst, assessment focuses on the elements of the residential environment that likely affect developmental change, especially the sources of challenge and support inherent in that residential environment as well as the actual developmental outcomes affected and realized. The assessment effort therefore includes both *environmental* assessment and the assessment of *developmental* change or outcomes. Specific instruments are reviewed or cited in the many excellent summaries of developmental theory (Rodgers, 1989) and in the many studies cited by Pascarella and Terenzini (1991). While Hanson's (1988) discussion of the difficulty in assessing developmental outcomes attributable to particular stimuli in the residential setting is noteworthy, a growing literature provides residence educators with helpful guidelines for assessing the developmental outcomes associated with residence life (see Erwin, 1991; Pascarella and Terenzini, 1991).

The Residence Hall as a Climate

The idea of campus climate is hardly a new one (Baird, 1988, 1990). As Peterson and Spencer (1990) have pointed out, the extensive research in organizational climate has many implications for higher education and can be a useful construct in the assessment of higher education effectiveness and outcomes. Despite the breadth of the literature, the task of defining *climate* remains difficult. Peterson and Spencer (1990) argue the notion of climate is often used to describe a wide variety of abstract phenomena.

Nevertheless, Peterson and Spenser (1990) do suggest that the concept of climate is rooted in prevailing *perceptions* of the members or inhabitants of an environment. Interest in the climates of particular residential environments grew in the 1970s as a result of the work of Moos and his associates (Moos, 1976, 1979; Insel and Moos, 1974). In Moos's approach, a climate is also defined in terms of the prevailing perceptions of the individuals inhabiting a given residential environment. The so-called "social climate" of a residence hall is identified by having residents describe their subjective impressions of a particular living environment; by aggregating those impressions, one develops a profile of the consensual perceptions of the residential environment and thereby defines and describes the social *climate*.

When one focuses on the residence hall's social climate, the focus is on the prevailing temper or conditions of a residential setting as perceived by the inhabitants, particularly in terms of relationship and support opportunities, personal growth opportunities, and dynamics of systems maintenance and change in the residential environment. The residential experience then becomes the full range of environmental dynamics and cues that trigger the residents' perceptions of social climate. With the residence hall as a perceived social climate, the student is the means by which that climate is established and through which it can be described; it is in the collective subjective perceptions of the residents that the residence hall is a social climate. An environmental psychology perspective prevails. Educational outcomes in this metaphor can vary widely; this metaphor focuses more on the degree to which the climate is perceived by students to be supportive, neutral, or hostile to student learning objectives than on any specific learning outcomes.

Assessment Strategies. Thinking of the residence hall with a climate metaphor suggests a range of specific assessment strategies that have been and can be used in residence hall research. Overall, the assessment questions become threefold. First, what is the prevailing social climate of the residential environment(s)? Baird (1988, 1990) discusses a number of approaches to defining and assessing campus climate, some using instruments that have been in use for decades. These include the College Characteristics Index (CCI) (Pace and Stern, 1958), the College and University Environment Scales (CUES) (Pace, 1969), the College Student Questionnaire (CSQ) (Peterson, 1968), the Institutional Functioning Inventory (IFI) (Peterson, 1970), and the Institutional Goals Inventory (IGI) (Peterson and Uhl, 1977). Adopting Moos's approach to the assessment of the social climate of residence halls leads to the use of the University Residence Environment Scale (URES) (Moos, 1976, 1979), an instrument that enables the development of social climate profiles for different residence halls, different floors in a single residence hall, or even multiple suites of residents on a single floor (Schroeder, 1981; Kalsbeek, Rodgers, Marshall, and Nicholls, 1982). Perhaps more than most other metaphors, the notion of the residence hall as a climate leads to an established set of assessment instruments.

Second, the assessment of climate requires consideration of the impact of specific programmatic and policy initiatives on the social climate. This might include evaluating the impact on social climate of alternative roommate or floor assignment strategies, intramural activities, student governance, architectural arrangements, or personalization programs, for example (see Kalsbeek, Rodgers, Marshall, and Nicholls, 1982).

Third, the assessment agenda includes how the social climate relates to other educational or developmental outcomes. Models of college impact such as Tinto's (1975) and Astin's (1984) and some developmental perspectives (Chickering and Reisser, 1993) identify dynamics such as social climate (and the congruence of the prevailing climate with individual expectations and preferences) as determining factors in a wide range of student outcomes. Outcomes influenced by social climate can include academic performance, retention, and academic and social integration (in Tinto's models), involvement and student satisfaction (in Astin's approach), and advances in certain psychosocial dimensions such as developing autonomy and freeing interpersonal relationships (in Chickering and Reisser's approach).

The Residence Hall as a Culture

The burgeoning literature on organizational culture and its implications and applications for higher education has focused attention on campus culture, faculty culture, and student culture (Peterson and Spencer, 1990; Kuh, Schuh, Whitt, and Associates, 1991). This surge of interest suggests that the assessment of the student experience in residence halls may be effectively framed in terms of a student culture or subculture metaphor.

Peterson and Spencer (1990) acknowledge the difficulty in differentiating culture from climate, yet their efforts to do so are helpful. They suggest that the notion of culture focuses on deeply embedded and enduring patterns of behavior and the shared values, assumptions, beliefs, and ideologies that dominate a given environment; climate is more concerned with current perceptions and attitudes and is more likely to change and change quickly than is culture. As Morgan (1986, p. 128) notes, "Shared meaning, shared understanding, and shared sense making are all different ways of describing culture." Culture, as an approach to understanding the residential experience, evokes more deeply ingrained features of student groups than any of the prior metaphors. While it could be argued that a residential unit cannot have or be a culture because of the constant turnover of the resident population, a cultural perspective can perhaps frame an assessment effort in subtly different ways than other metaphors.

What is *student* culture? Kuh (1990) explores the notion of student culture at three levels: national, institutional, and subcultural. At the subcultural level, he suggests that student culture even on one campus is often far from homogeneous, with certain subgroups of students varying considerably in the aspirations, assumptions, attitudes, beliefs, expectations, and values that they share. This notion of student subculture, reflected in a literature that reached fruition over thirty years ago (Kuh, 1990; Baird, 1988; Ewell, 1988), may be the most applicable to residential environments. Such a subculture perspective focuses attention on three important dimensions (Kuh, 1990). For a student group to be a *subculture,* there first must be a value system shared by a group of students who have "persisting interaction" with each other. Second, the value system of the group must differ in some way from that of the broader or aggregate student culture. Third, the group of students must engage in some type of social control to ensure conformity to the values and norms of the group.

Viewed in this way, the residence hall is a setting that may be part of a student culture or a subculture, a setting in which persistent student interaction results in a collective set of enduring values and behavioral norms shared by the group. The student is the inhabitant of that culture and either fits or does not fit with the prevailing cultural norms; students who fit with that culture are the means by which the culture is perpetuated, promulgating cultural values through their actions and attitudes. The residential experience is the partial reflection of the prevailing culture; the kinds of activities, beliefs, and behaviors that comprise the residential experience are manifestations of cultural values and norms and the means by which that culture is perpetuated and by which it can be described. An anthropological perspective prevails. In a culture metaphor, the educational outcomes valued by the college may or may not be central to the prevailing norms or shared values of the group; in this framework, the student learning that matters is the learning that is perpetuated student to student through the enculturation process.

Assessment Strategies. Kuh (1990, p. 52) argues that assessing student culture is "essential for determining the effects of college and university life on students and the sources of variation related to higher education outcomes." He argues that this assessment must include an exploration of the reference groups to which students belong and the discovery of any similarities among groups of students by assessing a comprehensive set of student characteristics including abilities, aptitudes, attitudes, values, expectations, and aspirations. Assessments must also include explorations of behavioral expectations and values of student groups, the degree to which such expectations are shared throughout the groups, and an assessment of the degree of person-environment fit. Kuh's expansive work in the area of assessing college culture (Kuh, Schuh, Whitt, and Associates, 1991; Kuh, 1993) offers many clues and avenues for describing and assessing residence halls and the residential experience, approaches that can and should include both quantitative and qualitative methodologies. A culture metaphor encourages the consideration of ethnographic or anthropological approaches to assessment and is exemplified by such studies as Moffatt (1989) and Kalsbeek (1989b).

The Residence Hall as a Community

The notion of the residence hall as a community has been in the student services literature for some time (Ender, Kane, Mable, and Strohm, 1980; Mable, Terry, and Duvall, 1977; Crookston, 1974). Though *community* is often used casually to describe *any* residential unit or residence hall, the full implications of this metaphor for understanding residence halls are often overlooked. Several features of a community metaphor distinguish it from others such as climate and culture.

First, the notion of community necessarily involves a clear set of values and normative standards, while both the climate and the culture metaphors generally suggest a value-free approach. The notion of cultural relativity suggests that one assesses culture first by describing it in great detail and then comparing one with another, not by evaluating it by a normative or value-based standard. But the community metaphor is value laden. Not all climates or cultures meet the higher order criteria or the normative standards to be "community." While precise definitions of community are as evasive as definitions for culture and climate, community is perhaps more enveloped in a set of values about interpersonal relations and interdependence, civic responsibility, democratic participation, service, and justice. Cultures and climates can exist where these values are not interwoven in the social fabric; community cannot.

The second distinction is that in the community, individuals have social responsibility and social influence. Members actively *participate* in communities; they undertake tasks and activities that benefit all members and that benefit the community itself. As Crookston (1974) argues, in the democratic community the welfare and development of the community is as much a goal as the welfare and development of the individual, with members participating democratically in setting the collective direction of the group. Unlike culture or climate, a focus on community necessarily directs attention to issues of governance, citizenship, involvement, influence, participation, and service.

A third distinction is that community is integrally tied to place; the notion of community implies physical boundaries. Community brings to mind the concepts of public and private space and the responsibilities for and ownership of public places and public properties by community members. Community boundaries are established, understood, respected, even defended. A community metaphor focuses attention on the concept of *territoriality* — how students demarcate the boundaries of their private and their community space within the physical facilities of the residence hall, how they stake out and communicate ownership for community space, and how they personalize space (Schroeder, 1979, 1981).

With the residence hall as a community, the focus is on the student living group in a specific place, with a set of public and private spaces with understood boundaries. The student is not only a member of the group but an active participant in the life of the residential unit. The residential experience is characterized by opportunities for student involvement, influence, and investment in the development and improvement of the community and a clear set of values and normative expectations for active participation. Notions of territoriality and physical boundaries, student governance and civic responsibility, and voluntary inclusion are all central to the understanding of the residential community. A sociological-political perspective prevails. Educational outcomes focus on students learning these types of civic or community responsibilities and competencies, including leadership and service skills.

Assessment Strategies. Community is manifested in so many ways that a wide variety of assessment methods potentially can be employed, many of which have already been discussed in earlier sections. For example, much of Kuh's (1990, 1993) work on assessing student culture and Moos's (1976, 1979) work on social climate could apply equally as well to assessing levels of community. However, as noted above, a community metaphor focuses attention on certain types of values and behaviors that offer clues as to community health and community development in residence halls. Jackson and Serrot (1990) and Kalsbeek (1991) suggest a "kaleidoscopic" approach to community assessment in residence halls and outline a number of possible assessment projects to gauge relative levels of community development. For example, they suggest that residence hall staff use informal interactions with students to pose a variety of assessment questions about the nature and health of the community. They also suggest a number of unobtrusive measures for assessing community life and community values in the residence hall, including document analysis, observations, and some more obtrusive measures such as norm violations techniques and traditional sociological assessments of community relationships. In addition, their work and that of Schroeder (1976, 1979, 1981) suggests some innovative approaches to assessing the territorial boundaries of residential communities and how the thresholds between private and public spaces in the residence hall shape student behavior, activities, and experiences.

Assessment and the Power of Metaphor

A useful literature is emerging in the assessment area that could provide an organizational framework for a chapter on assessing the educational role of the residential experience. For example, one could organize this discussion by outlining the generic *steps* in the assessment process: organizing the effort, specifying objectives, determining appropriate methodologies and instrumentation, implementing the assessment project, analyzing data, preparing and presenting results, and using information for program development. Erwin (1991) is an example of such an approach. Alternatively, one could discuss the major *issues* to be considered in assessing the residential experience, including definitional issues, implementation issues, methodological and measurement issues, and so on (Terenzini, 1989).

But the key questions focus on the multiple ways one understands the residential experience and its role in the educational enterprise in the first place, fundamental ways of understanding that determine all subsequent questions about what to assess and how. A premise of this chapter is that varied ways of understanding the residential experience perhaps can be explored by considering, juxtaposing, and comparing alternative metaphors for the residence hall that prescribe what are viable assessment strategies. Table 12.1 shows one attempt using the metaphors explored in this chapter, outlining how different metaphors frame the educational nature of residence halls, define in various ways the role of the student, and suggest various approaches to the assessment of the residential environment.

For the hypothetical outcomes assessment committee, the heuristic value of exploring alternative metaphors is in stimulating consideration of assessment strategies that might not otherwise be considered. If one understands the residence experience primarily as a range of consumable services for students, as the chief business officer apparently does, the assessment strategies that come to mind or that are considered legitimate might not include ethnographic inquiry into the shared meanings of a student subculture or measuring psychosocial developmental outcomes associated with the residence experience. Likewise, if one assumes that the residence hall environment is best understood using concepts of perceived social climate, as the dean of students apparently does, assessment strategies probably would not focus as explicitly on the physical boundaries of community space, on the sources of challenge and support that characterize the living environment, or on student needs for and satisfaction with specific services or facilities. Considering alternative metaphors for the residential experience can trigger new ideas about assessment strategies and can broaden the range of approaches to the assessment task. In addition, for the committee to evaluate any proposed assessment strategy from this

Table 12.1. Six Metaphors for the Assessment of the Residential Experience.

Role of Residence Hall	Role of Student	Focus of Educational Assessment	Relevant Assessment Methods
Consumable	Consumer, tenant	Student behavior, use of services, consumer behavior, student satisfaction, response to needs/demands	Consumer research, needs assessment, market research, satisfaction surveys, business methodologies
Classroom	Learner, student	Learning outcomes, progress toward content mastery, baseline competencies and levels of knowledge of awareness	Traditional testing for content mastery, program evaluation, education/testing and measurement methodologies
Catalyst	Developing human	Student development/growth, environmental stimuli (challenge and support)	Developmental instrumentation, environmental assessments, developmental psychological methodologies
Climate	Perceiver	Student perceptions of the social climate, relationships of climate to other educational outcomes, person-environment fit	Survey research, standardized instrumentation, environmental psychological methods
Culture	Inhabitant	Shared meanings, values, norms; student characteristics	Ethnographic, culture audit, qualitative methods, participant observations, anthropological methods
Community	Participant	Involvement, territorial boundaries, community health, governance, civic participation	Document analysis, survey research, case study methods, observations/interviews, norm violations, sociological/political methodologies

perspective effectively takes the discussion of "which approach is better?" far deeper than issues of cost or logistics or methodological rigor and focuses first on the fit of the assessment strategy with the preferred way of understanding or defining the residential experience.

There are four cautions to keep in mind as one considers the relationship of metaphors to assessment. First, metaphors are not mutually exclusive in the assessment strategies they suggest. Some assessment strategies or methodologies can fit as easily in either a climate or culture metaphor, for example; likewise, assessing the health of a residential community certainly can and should include assessing student satisfaction with basic consumable services. When one considers alternative metaphors, any number of assessment techniques can perhaps come to mind, some of which naturally overlap. The value of exploring metaphor is to stimulate alternative insights, not draw impermeable definitional or methodological boundaries.

Second, most assessment techniques do reflect specific metaphors or assumptions about the nature of the residential experience. For example, employing Moos's (1979) URES instrument in effect dictates that a climate metaphor is the frame of reference driving the assessment. Since the instrument is designed to assess perceived social climate, its use means one has embraced, consciously or not, a climate metaphor for the residential experience, its impact and its outcomes. All assessment methodologies are necessarily grounded in a set of assumptions about the nature of the residential experience, assumptions that can be explored and articulated through metaphor.

Third, many educators can and do simultaneously entertain more than one metaphorical perspective on residence halls. For example, most residence hall staff consider services and programs to be essential consumables while they simultaneously perceive the goal of the residence life program to include educational or developmental programs in pursuit of specific learning objectives. These metaphors generally are not monlithic and immutable paradigms. Nevertheless, many educators certainly do have preferences for one metaphor over others, preferences for specific perspectives on the educational role of residence halls. Such inclinations naturally result in their preference for certain assessment methods and a greater likelihood of their finding certain assessment data more usable (Kalsbeek, 1993a).

Fourth, as suggested in the dialogue among the hypothetical outcomes assessment committee members, different groups within the educational community are likely to entertain different metaphors of the residential experience. The metaphors students use to describe their own experience vary widely from those noted here that may characterize common perspectives of student affairs professionals (Kalsbeek, 1988, 1993a). Faculty, alumni, and parents are likely to embrace different metaphors than administrators. Metaphors for the educational experience that frame the perspectives of legislative bodies, accrediting agencies, and various governing boards will probably be quite different from those of students, faculty, or staff. Understanding the various metaphors for the educational role of residence halls that shape the perspectives of different groups can be instructive — not only as an intellectual exercise in comparing different frames of reference, but pragmatically in managing the logistics of assessment. The assessment process typically evolves in a politically charged environment, with numerous stakeholders having deeply vested interests in both the process and the product of any assessment of educational outcomes, organizational productivity, or educational "value added." Considering the prevailing metaphors of various stakeholders assists those designing the assessment in maneuvering through the political quagmire; knowing how decision makers define the problem at hand is critical to ensuring that the information resulting from an assessment in fact will be informative and usable (Kalsbeek, 1993a).

Conclusion

This particular book is not the first to call for the American higher education community to recognize and affirm the vital educational role of residence halls. But now colleges and universities increasingly are expected to define and assess a broader array of their educational outcomes and to determine and evaluate many factors affecting those outcomes. At many institutions, that assessment process creates unprecedented opportunities for discussing the residential experience as a critical component of the educational enterprise. Therein lies both promise and peril.

The promise is that outcomes assessment is a potent means by which residence educators can promote the educational role of the residential program. Through assessment, information about how the residential environment actually contributes to outcomes valued by the institution can help advocate for a tighter integration of the residential program with the institution's educational mission. Achieving student development outcomes through information management is a theme that has been discussed for the past decade (Kalsbeek, 1984, 1989a) and has stimulated the creation of numerous student affairs research offices (Beeler, Benedict, and Hyman, 1994); the assessment and quality improvement movements add impetus to this particular approach to student affairs administration in higher education. All of this can encourage the realization of the educational potential of college residence halls.

The counterbalancing peril is that assessment is also the impetus for institutions to focus critical attention on the nature and quality and impact of the residential program. The outcomes assessment committee will at some point focus on the legitimacy of calling dorm staff "residence educators" and on the capacity of "student development specialists" to demonstrate through disciplined assessment the extent of their espoused contribution to educational outcomes. On some campuses, the response to this challenge will determine the allocation of increasingly scarce resources. Residence educators who are not prepared for exploring and assessing the educational impact of their programs are vulnerable.

On most campuses, the process of assessing the educational role of residence halls will elicit a number of differing perspectives from various campus groups, just as it did in the hypothetical outcomes assessment committee. This chapter encourages us to consider alternative metaphorical constructs that can and do frame our definition of the role of residence halls and the residential experience in the overall educational process and to do so as one approach to broadening and enriching the discussion of what and how to assess the educational outcomes of the residential experience. The faculty chair of the committee asks, "Does anyone know where to start?" Perhaps exploring the prevailing metaphors for the residential experience is a useful beginning.

References

Astin, A. "Student Involvement: A Developmental Theory for Higher Education." *Journal of College Student Personnel,* 1984, *25,* 297–308.

Baird, L. L. "The College Environment Revisited: A Review of Research and Theory." In J. C. Smart (ed.), *Higher Education: Handbook of Theory and Research.* Vol. 4. New York: Agathon Press, 1988.

Baird, L. L. "Campus Climate: Using Surveys for Policy-Making and Understanding." In W. G. Tierney (ed.), *Assessing Academic Climates and Cultures.* New Directions for Institutional Research, no. 68. San Francisco: Jossey-Bass, 1990.

Baldwin, R. G., and Thelin, J. R. "Thanks for the Memories: The Fusion of Quantitative and Qualitative Research on College Students and the College Experience." In J. C. Smart (ed.), *Higher Education: Handbook of Theory and Research.* Vol. 6. New York: Agathon Press, 1990.

Beeler, K. J., Benedict, L., and Hyman, R. *Successful Student Outcomes Assessment: Six Institutional Case Studies Including the Role of Student Affairs.* Washington, D.C.: National Association of Student Personnel Administrators, 1994.

Blimling, G. S. "Residence Halls in Today's Compartmentalized University." In G. S. Blimling and J. H. Schuh (eds.), *Increasing the Educational Role of Residence Halls.* New Directions for Student Services, no. 13. San Francisco: Jossey-Bass, 1981.

Blocher, D. H. "Toward an Ecology of Student Development." *Personnel and Guidance Journal,* 1974, *52,* 360–365.

Chickering, A. W., and Reisser, L. *Education and Identity.* (2nd ed.) San Francisco: Jossey-Bass, 1993.

Crookston, B. "A Design for an Intentional Democratic Community." In D. DeCoster and P. Mable (eds.), *Student Development and Education in College Residence Halls*. Washington, D.C.: American College Personnel Association, 1974.

DeCoster, D. A., and Mable, P. "Residence Education: Purpose and Process." In D. A. DeCoster and P. Mable (eds.), *Student Development and Education in College Residence Halls*. Washington, D.C.: American College Personnel Association, 1974.

Ender, K., Kane, N., Mable, P., and Strohm, M. *Creating Community in Residence Design and Delivery*. Cincinnati, Ohio: American College Personnel Association, 1980.

Erwin, T. D.*Assessing Student Learning and Development: A Guide to the Principles, Goals, and Methods of Determining College Outcomes*. San Francisco: Jossey-Bass, 1991.

Ewell, P. T. "Outcomes, Assessment and Academic Improvement: In Search of Usable Knowledge." In J. C. Smart (ed.), *Higher Education: Handbook of Theory and Research*. Vol. 4. New York: Agathon Press, 1988.

Hanson, G. R. "Critical Issues in the Assessment of Value Added in Education." In T. W. Banta (ed.), *Implementing Outcomes Assessment: Promise and Perils*. New Directions for Institutional Research, no. 59. San Francisco: Jossey-Bass, 1988.

Huebner, L. "Interaction of Student and Campus." In U. Delworth, G. R. Hanson, and Associates, *Student Services: A Handbook for the Profession*. (2nd ed.) San Francisco: Jossey-Bass, 1989.

Hutchings, P. *Behind Outcomes: Contexts and Questions for Assessment*. Washington, D.C.: American Association for Higher Education, 1989.

Insel, P. M., and Moos, R. H. "Psychological Environments: Expanding the Scope of Human Ecology." *American Psychologist,* 1974, *29*(3), 179–186.

Jackson, G. S., and Serrot, S. E. "A Kaleidoscopic Approach to Assessing Residential Communities Through Case Studies." Unpublished manuscript, Saint Louis University, 1990.

Kalsbeek, D. H. "Student Development Through Information Management." Paper presented at the Saint Louis Forum on Student Development in the 1980s, St. Louis, Mo., May 1984.

Kalsbeek, D. H. "Environmental Assessment: A Review of Related Conceptual and Methodological Approaches." In C. C. Schroeder, S. Jackson, and D. Kalsbeek (eds.), *Student Development Through Environmental Management: New Perspectives for Residence Educators.* St. Louis, Mo.: Division of Student Development, Saint Louis University, 1985.

Kalsbeek, D. H. "The Use of Metaphor in Understanding Student Life." Unpublished research paper, Saint Louis University, 1988.

Kalsbeek, D. H. "Managing Data and Information Resources." In U. Delworth, G. R. Hanson, and Associates, *Student Services: A Handbook for the Profession.* (2nd ed.) San Francisco: Jossey-Bass, 1989a.

Kalsbeek, D. H. "Rhetoric and Reality: Using Qualitative Methods to Assess Campus Life." Paper presented at the American Association of Higher Education Assessment Forum, Atlanta, Ga., June 1989b.

Kalsbeek, D. H. "Assessing Community Development in Residence Halls." Paper presented at the Community Development Strategies Workshop, St. Louis, Mo., July 1991.

Kalsbeek, D. H. "Assessing the Student Experience: The Power of Alternative Metaphors." Paper presented at American Association of Higher Education Assessment Forum, Chicago, March 1993a.

Kalsbeek, D. H. "Exploring Information as a User Construct." Unpublished doctoral dissertation, Department of Public Policy Studies, Saint Louis University, 1993b.

Kalsbeek, D. H., Rodgers, R., Marshall, D., and Nicholls, G. "Balancing Challenge and Support: A Study of Degrees of Similarity in Suitemate Personality Type and Perceived Differences in Challenge and Support in a Residence Hall Environment." *Journal of College Student Personnel,* 1982, *23,* 434–442.

Knefelkamp, L., Widick, C., and Parker, C. A. (eds.). *Applying New Developmental Findings.* New Directions for Student Services, no. 4. San Francisco: Jossey-Bass, 1978.

Kuh, G. D. "Assessing Student Culture." In W. G. Tierney (ed.), *Assessing Academic Climates and Cultures.* New Directions for Institutional Research, no. 68. San Francisco: Jossey-Bass, 1990.

Kuh, G. D. *Cultural Perspectives in Student Affairs Work.* Washington, D.C.: American College Personnel Association, 1993.

Kuh, G. D., Schuh, J. H., Whitt, E. J., and Associates. *Involving Colleges: Successful Approaches to Fostering Student Learning and Development Outside the Classroom.* San Francisco: Jossey-Bass, 1991.

Lakoff, G., and Johnson, M. *Metaphors We Live By.* Chicago: University of Chicago Press, 1980.

Mable, P., Terry, M., and Duvall, W. J. "A Model of Student Development Through Community Responsibility." *Journal of College Student Personnel,* 1977, *18*(1), 50–56.

Moffatt, M. *Coming of Age in New Jersey: College and American Culture.* New Brunswick, N.J.: Rutgers University Press, 1989.

Moos, R. H. *The Human Context: Environmental Determinants of Behavior.* New York: Wiley-Interscience, 1976.

Moos, R. H. *Evaluating Educational Environments: Procedures, Measures, Findings, and Policy Implications.* San Francisco: Jossey-Bass, 1979.

Morgan, G. *Images of Organizations.* Newbury Park, Calif.: Sage, 1986.

Pace, C. R. *College and University Environment Scales: Technical Manual.* Princeton, N.J.: Educational Testing Service, 1969.

Pace, C. R., and Stern, G. G. "An Approach to the Measurement of Psychological Characteristics of College Environments." *Journal of Educational Psychology,* 1958, *49*, 269–277.

Pascarella, E. T., and Terenzini, P. T. *How College Affects Students: Findings and Insights from Twenty Years of Research.* San Francisco: Jossey-Bass, 1991.

Perry, W. G., Jr. *Forms of Intellectual and Ethical Development in the College Years.* Troy, Mo.: Holt, Rinehart & Winston, 1970.

Peterson, M., and Spencer, M. "Understanding Academic Culture and Climate." In W. G. Tierney (ed.), *Assessing Academic Climates and Cultures.* New Directions for Institutional Research, no. 68. San Francisco: Jossey-Bass, 1990.

Peterson, R. E. *College Student Questionnaire: Technical Manual.* Princeton, N.J.: Educational Testing Service, 1968.

Peterson, R. E. *Institutional Functioning Inventory: Technical Manual.* Princeton, N.J.: Educational Testing Service, 1970.

Peterson, R. E., and Uhl, N. P. *Formulating College and University Goals: A Guide for Using the IGI.* Princeton, N.J.: Educational Testing Service, 1977.

Phillips, B., and Schuh, J. "Residence Life." In G. D. Kuh (ed.), *Evaluation in Student Affairs.* Cincinnati, Ohio: American College Personnel Association, 1979.

Rodgers, R. "Theories Underlying Student Development." In D. B. Creamer (ed.), *Student Development in Higher Education: Theories, Practices, and Future Directions.* Cincinnati, Ohio: American College Personnel Association, 1980.

Rodgers, R. "Student Development." In U. Delworth, G. R. Hanson, and Associates, *Student Services: A Handbook for the Profession.* (2nd ed.) San Francisco: Jossey-Bass, 1989.

Rossman, J. E., and El-Khawas, E. "Thinking About Assessment: Perspectives for Presidents and Chief Academic Officers." Washington, D.C.: American Council on Education and American Association for Higher Education, 1987.

Sanford, N. *Where Colleges Fail: A Study of the Student as a Person.* San Francisco: Jossey-Bass, 1967.

Sanford, N. (ed.). *The American College.* New York: Wiley, 1962.

Schroeder, C. C. "Strategies for Structuring Residential Environments." *Journal of College Student Personnel,* 1976, *17,* 386–390.

Schroeder, C. C. "Territoriality: Conceptual and Methodological Issues for Residence Educators." *Journal of College and University Student Housing,* 1979, *8,* 9–15.

Schroeder, C. C. "Student Development Through Environmental Management." In G. S. Blimling and J. H. Schuh (eds.), *Increasing the Educational Role of Residence Halls.* New Directions for Student Services, no. 13. San Francisco: Jossey-Bass, 1981.

Schuh, J. "Assessment and Redesign in Residence Halls." In L. A. Huebner (ed.), *Redesigning Campus Environments.* New Directions for Student Services, no. 8. San Francisco: Jossey-Bass, 1979.

Silverman, R. J. "The Potential of Metaphor for Student Personnel Work." *Journal of College Student Personnel,* 1981, *22,* 60–64.

Terenzini, P. T. "Assessment with Open Eyes: Pitfalls in Studying Student Outcomes." *Journal of Higher Education,* 1989, *60*(6), 644–664.

Tinto, V. "Dropout from Higher Education: A Theoretical Synthesis of Recent Research." *Review of Educational Research,* 1975, *45,* 89–125.

Walsh, W. B. *Theories of Person-Environment Interaction: Implications for the College Student.* Iowa City, Iowa: American College Testing Program, 1973.

Thirteen

Realizing the Educational Potential of Residence Halls: A Mandate for Action

Charles C. Schroeder
Phyllis Mable

The principal aim of this book is to provide a greater understanding of the educational role of residence halls in higher education. Previous chapters have described innovative approaches to increasing the educational effectiveness of residential settings and have highlighted a variety of challenges that must be addressed to ensure success. In reviewing those chapters, we have identified five transcendent themes that provide implications and recommendations for realizing the educational potential of residence halls. We make these themes explicit in this chapter under the following headings: Challenge Prevailing Assumptions; Focus on Student Learning; Expect Broad-Based Student Participation and Involvement; Create Collaborative Partnerships; and Make Residential Education More Intentional. We then offer fifteen suggestions for implementing a residence hall curriculum based on the themes.

Challenge Prevailing Assumptions

Recently, one of the authors was being introduced at a banquet honoring alumni of one of the colleges at his university. As the presenter briefly reviewed his bio, she mentioned that he was coauthoring a book titled *Realizing the Educational Potential of Residence Halls*. She paused for a moment and then commented, "Most of us in the room never thought of residence halls as educational . . . " That comment brought spontaneous laughter from the audience. In retrospect, we should not be surprised by the audience's reaction. As described in Chapter Twelve, there are widely varying perspectives on the role of residence halls, and we should seek to understand how different constituents view those purposes. Do faculty, for example, believe residence halls are powerful educational settings that intentionally support the academic mission of the institution, or do they view them as social settings that distract students from serious intellectual pursuits? Can students articulate the educational value added to their lives as a result of residential experiences? For business officers, are residence halls simply collections of nocturnal storage bins that generate revenue for the institution? How do presidents, governing boards, and the general public view residence halls — do they see them as inherently educational? Finally, how are they regarded by student affairs educators and residence life staff?

Answers to the preceding questions depend primarily on one's assumptions and frame of reference. The powerful role that assumptions play in defining reality is illustrated by the following story (Parker, 1982; compare Turnbull, 1962):

A noted British anthropologist, Colin Turnbull, spent almost 20 years studying a tribe of pygmies that lived in a totally isolated rain forest in South Africa. The rain forest was so dense that over time members of the tribe had become functionally nearsighted — they simply had no need to see long distances. After weeks of coaxing, Turnbull persuaded the old chief to return with him to England. Since the chief had never left the rain forest, this was a most formidable challenge. The chief eventually consented, and he and Turnbull spent weeks hacking their way through the thick vegetation. On the

nineteenth day, they finally stepped out of the rain
forest onto a plain or savanna. Off in the distance,
perhaps 200–300 yards, were some water buffaloes.
Turnbull asked the chief to identify the objects. The
chief, without hesitation, said they were bees. As
they walked closer and closer to the herd, Turnbull
again asked the chief to identify the creatures. After some deliberation, the chief stated they were buffaloes. Turnbull said, "But chief, I thought you said
they were bees." The chief responded, "They were
bees, but magic has changed them into buffaloes."

This story illustrates phenomenological absolutism — the assumption that the world is as we see it. Although we often subscribe
to the notion that seeing is believing, in reality, believing is seeing. Our fundamental assumptions and beliefs ensure that our
established truths and traditional practices provide security, stability, and continuity — as the rain forest did for the chief. And,
like the chief, many staff find it disquieting to journey beyond
familiar boundaries to explore realities in other rain forests. Even
when change is viewed as desirable, we often long for the safety
of the known. Thus, we create systems to maintain balance and
continuity and, in such a process, custom tends to become a
tyrant. The tyranny of custom prevents us from challenging
prevailing assumptions, and, like the processionary caterpillars
described in Chapter Six, staff continue using the same routine
behavior, even when changing circumstances require radically
new responses.

　　As emphasized in Chapter One, the basic assumptions
of this book are that residence halls should be powerful and purposeful educational settings and that residence hall staff are, first
and foremost, educators. Although these are espoused values
for most residential life programs, they are not necessarily values
in practice. Many housing programs continue to be characterized by a student services orientation with facility management
as the priority. As "auxiliary enterprises," these departments
function like stand-alone business units that rely on auxiliary
revenue to cover all expenses. Although housing programs must

provide certain basic elements to ensure a context for educational success (see Chapter Three), a student services orientation, with a principal emphasis on facility management, must be viewed as a means to a much greater end—fostering student learning and personal development.

Promoting student learning and development must be a priority even for housing staff who view themselves as facility managers. With the decline of traditional-age college students, many residence hall systems are experiencing low occupancy rates, which threaten their ability to meet bond payments. In such instances, curators and boards of trustees are increasingly eager to explore the option of "outsourcing" or privatizing these facilities. Furthermore, since residence halls cannot offer students accommodations and amenities comparable to those provided by off-campus apartments, they can only compete with these alternatives through adding educational value to students' lives. To increase the educational value of residential experiences, many housing staff will need to journey beyond the predictable, the comfortable, and the familiar boundaries of their rain forest to explore some new and somewhat uncharted territory—territory usually regarded as under the control of more powerful tribes: faculty and academic administrators. We must be willing to challenge our prevailing assumptions about our roles and purpose and focus our energy on the primary goal of higher education, promoting student learning.

Focus on Student Learning

The multitude of reports generated in recent years on the status of higher education clearly indicate that student learning must be the primary focus of colleges and universities. This imperative is driven by a range of social, economic, and political forces that are transforming our society and our institutions. As state governments struggle to do more with less, governors are asking, "What are we getting for our investment in higher education—are students learning anything?" Academic administrators and faculty can point to credit hours generated, content mastery in the disciplines, and progress in achieving academic outcomes. But what can we in student affairs point to—what contributions are we making to fostering student learning in our residence halls?

Residence hall staff are often perceived—perhaps rightly so—as focusing on trivialities and marginalia, and we will continue to be so perceived unless we join the rest of the higher education community and focus on student learning! This is certainly not a new or radical notion, because the philosophical foundation of the student affairs profession—the *Student Personnel Point of View*—considers students as learners (American Council on Education, 1937). If we are to realize the educational potential of residence halls, we must return to our roots, to our espoused values, to our deeply held convictions about students and we must commit anew to focusing our efforts on student learning. As the central theme of higher education, student learning provides common ground on which academic affairs and student affairs can speak with a unified voice. By focusing on student learning, residence hall staff can engage faculty colleagues and extend the conversation beyond the often-narrow emphasis on the core curriculum to include the importance of core experiences; from exclusively teaching-centered and staff-centered environments to student-learning-centered environments; from what is customarily academic to what is uniquely educational. By focusing on student learning, residential hall programs can become interwoven with the fabric of the academy, bringing integration and coherence to a traditionally fragmented, compartmentalized, and often random approach to achieving important educational outcomes.

From an institutional perspective, one of the greatest challenges associated with facilitating student learning is to create a new definition of "the classroom." Although it is well established that students learn as much, if not more, from cocurricular experiences than from formal academic ones (Pascarella and Terenzini, 1991), most faculty and student affairs staff view the acquisition of knowledge and the development of various intellectual skills as occurring solely in the traditional classroom. In this setting, faculty usually communicate knowledge to students through a lecture format—often described as "teaching by telling" (Cross, 1986). One study estimates, for example, that teachers in the average classroom spend about 80 percent of their time lecturing to students, who are attending to what is being said only half of the time (Pollio, 1984). Although many faculty and staff prospered under the traditional lecture system, there is increasing evidence that this approach may not work for the majority of today's students, most of whom exhibit learning styles quite different from those of contemporary faculty (Cross, 1986; Schroeder, 1993). As recommended in Chapters Four and Nine, new pedagogical approaches are needed to respond to students' diverse learning characteristics. By extending the definition of the classroom beyond bounded, physical space with a definitive temporal element to include learning environments and learning communities within residence halls, institutions can significantly increase the probability of achieving a broad range of learning objectives.

As described in Chapters Four and Eight, residence halls can become nontraditional classrooms by providing students with a variety of active modes of learning. This form of learning bridges the traditional gap between knowing and doing through encouraging students to become more actively engaged in the subject matter of their disciplines. Active modes of learning are experiences and activities that encourage collaboration and cooperation, such as the team-centered approaches highlighted in Chapter Four. Residence halls can be learning communities where students focus on problem-centered learning, case method, and peer feedback approaches, all of which help them work together to seek mutual understanding while developing specific interpersonal and cognitive skills. By providing active modes of learning, residence hall staff can be integrating agents, bringing relevance and coherence to the undergraduate experience. Indeed, active learning can integrate classroom and cocurriculum experiences into a total learning environment.

The design of purposeful and powerful learning environments is perhaps the greatest opportunity facing residence life staff today. A great deal is known about environmental conditions that foster student learning and personal development (Moos, 1976; Huebner and Lawson, 1990; Pascarella and Terenzini, 1991; Chickering and Reisser, 1993). As evidenced by the literature, students develop in different ways, and both learning and development need to be nurtured by an environment that accommodates this diversity. The following parable illustrates this point:

> A farmer was sowing grain in his field. As he scattered the seed across the ground, some fell beside a hardened path and the birds came and ate it. And some fell on rocky soil where there was little depth of earth; the plants sprang up quickly enough in the shallow soil; but the hot sun soon scorched them and they withered and died for they had so little root. Other seeds fell among thorns and the thorns choked out the tender blades. But some fell on good soil, and produced a crop that was 30, 60, and even 100 times as much as he planted. If you have ears listen [Matthew 13:4–9, Living Bible].

We can learn a number of lessons from this parable. First, the seeds that fell in areas where the soil was rocky and shallow eventually wilted and died. This occurred because the environment was much too rigid — it lacked appropriate nutrients and the security usually afforded seeds in deep furrows. Next, the seeds that fell among thorns had a similar fate. Their growth was constricted because of the constant struggle to compete with the more powerful thorns for the limited resources. Finally, the seeds that fell on good soil eventually prospered because the deep, rich soil provided optimum conditions for growth — appropriate amounts of nutrients, security, and stimulation — all balanced in accordance with the unique requirements of the seeds.

How many students are like the seeds that fell beside the hardened path, or on the rocky soil, or among the thorns — how many are overwhelmed by the challenges they encounter in and outside their classrooms? Unprepared to handle college-level work, many students become frustrated by the lack of environmental support to help them succeed and, as a result, they drop out. Kelly (1990) reports that over a twenty-year period, academic skills and performance have significantly declined. One explanation is that students spend less time on academic tasks. According to the congresssionally mandated National Assessment of Educational Progress Report, many students read no more than ten pages a day, spend about one hour on homework, write fewer than one paper every three weeks in class, and avoid rigorous science and math classes (Kelly, 1990). Similar concerns about student performance were described in the report *An American Imperative: Higher Expectations for Higher Education* (Wingspread Group on Higher Education, 1993). To succeed in college, these students need intrusive academic assistance and supportive, educationally focused residential environments — settings that affirm diversity in academic preparation and learning styles.

When we think about the learning characteristics of contemporary students, we are reminded that effective education is a lot like gardening. Successful gardeners not only know a great deal about different kinds of seeds, they also know that certain seeds need various facilitative conditions at particular times in their development. Gardeners attempt to provide a balance between these various conditions to promote growth and healthy development. By designing environments that provide a range of learning options, residence hall staff, like knowledgeable gardeners, can create multiple paths to the achievement of specific outcomes. The successful attainment of such outcomes, however, is dependent on the degree of student participation and involvement in the educational process.

Expect Broad-Based Student Participation and Involvement

In his most recent book, *What Matters in College? Four Critical Years Revisited* (1992), Astin stressed the importance of involvement by stating that the more time and energy students devote to educationally purposeful activities, the more they benefit. The findings from several institutions that have attempted to track students' use of time reveal, though, that students who carry fifteen-hour loads devote just ten hours a week to out-of-class study but twenty hours to part-time work and another twenty to television viewing (T. Marchese, personal communication, October 1993).

Because learning as an outcome is highly dependent on student motivation, effort, and time on task, staff must create high expectations for student performance and encourage broad-based student participation and involvement in a variety of educationally purposeful activities. Too often, students are quite willing to adopt a passive role, allowing staff to do things to them or for them. Such a transaction exemplifies a dependent, parent-child relationship instead of a more appropriate independent, adult-adult relationship.

Encouraging broad-based student involvement must start with a new definition of the student-institution relationship. Prior to the 1960s, the relationship was governed by the in loco parentis doctrine. Institutions of higher learning would exert considerable control over student conduct because they acted "in place of parent," assuming parental authority for most aspects of students' social and academic experiences. Although the post–in loco parentis period provides students with many freedoms unknown to their predecessors, on many campuses students still are not regarded as adults, and their involvement is not viewed as central to the educational enterprise.

Stamatakos (1991) has suggested a new model of the student-institution relationship, one that focuses on student learning. In this model, the student is viewed as a transactive learner and staff relate to the student as a friend and mentor who encourages active involvement in a variety of educational activities and experiences. The central role of staff is to help students engage in self-managed learning with a life-centered focus. In this model, valued student behaviors are awareness, ingenuity, self-reliance, and transactional competence. The following core assumptions are central to this perspective:

1. *All students matter.* All students in the residence halls are viewed as important and essential, and staff take them and their learning seriously.
2. *All students are capable.* All students are seen as having poten-

tial, and encouraging their active involvement is a primary means of realizing that potential. Furthermore, creating high expectations is an absolute prerequisite for student performance (Angelo and Cross, 1993).

3. *All students are viewed as wanting to be successful.* It is a rare student, indeed, who enters a college or university with the explicit goal of not succeeding. Students' ability to succeed, however, can be limited by certain policies, practices, and staff attitudes.

In Chapter Ten, Komives challenged residence hall staff to create a new paradigm for student involvement, one that focuses on empowerment and grassroots, bottom-up student participation. This challenge can only be addressed if staff are willing to create authentic partnerships with students. In such partnerships, students are treated as respected colleagues, as equals. They are expected and encouraged to substantially influence the quality of their educational experiences in their residence halls. To employ this new approach will require a dramatic shift from the traditional hierarchical, controlling, and power models characteristic of many housing programs, particularly those at large institutions. The new model must not only emphasize empowerment but must be inclusive and encourage broad-based participation.

As emphasized in Chapters Two and Eight, most of the impact of residence halls is transmitted by peer influences. Although this has been a dominant theme in the literature for well over fifty years, student affairs professionals, in general, and residence hall staff, in particular, have not recognized and utilized the powerful impact of peers on student learning. As Levine points out in Chapter Five, the principal educators of students are students, not faculty or administrators. This assertion challenges residential life staff to focus on the centrality of students in the educational process, to encourage them to influence their learning and development in a more intentional fashion. When staff collaborate with students in the design of learning environments and learning communities, students assume more responsibility for both the quantity and quality of their learning. The creation of such environments, however, must involve more than student affairs staff and students working together—there must be collaborative partnerships established with faculty and academic administrators if the full educational potential of residence halls is to be achieved.

Create Collaborative Partnerships

During the past thirty years, college and university enrollments have quadrupled. As institutions have become more complex, we have attempted to address complexity with specialization, and in the process our organizations have become increasingly fragmented and compartmentalized. Today many campuses are characterized, not by a sense of community, but rather by a constellation of independent principalities and fiefdoms, each disconnected from the others and from any common institutional purpose or transcendent value. Not only does this description fit many large student affairs divisions, it also points to the traditional and persistent gap that has existed between academic affairs and student affairs for decades. As Blake (1979, p. 280) says, "People in student affairs, knowing that education is, after all, the mission of their institution, justify their activities as educational. Yet the more they do this, the less often they convince their faculty colleagues. A persistent gap seems to exist between the two groups of people on campus who work most closely with students." There are many consequences associated with this gap; the most profound concerns limiting the institution's ability to promote student learning.

A number of chapters in this book—in particular, Chapters Four, Seven, and Eleven—stress the importance of creating collaborative partnerships between student affairs educators and faculty and academic administrators. On most campuses, collaboration between academic affairs and student affairs is certainly more the exception than the rule. One might ask, "What prevents collaboration between the two groups on campus most directly involved with students?" Although responses to this question vary by institution, a number of major factors inhibit collaboration. First, there appears to be a consistent lack of understanding and appreciation for the unique and distinctive roles of student affairs and academic affairs in higher education. Blake (1979) has suggested some fundamental cultural differences between the two groups in terms of their educational preparation, values, and purposes. For example, for decades we have separated the formal curriculum from the informal cocurriculum. As a result, many student affairs staff view teaching and learning to be the primary responsibility of the faculty. From this perspective, the role of student affairs is ancillary, supplementary, or complementary to the academic mission of the institution. Another factor that substantially limits collaboration is the rigid and encapsulated organizational roles characteristic of both student affairs and academic affairs. Staff in student affairs have kept their educational efforts focused almost exclusively within their organizational boundaries, rather than reaching out and assuming a broader, institutional-boundary-spanning perspective essential for collaboration (Garland, 1985). Finally, Astin (as reported by Richmond, 1986, p. 94) states that the dichotomy between academic and student affairs will never go away until we "see ourselves in student affairs as educators and . . . view what we do as part of the educational process."

As previously stated, student learning is the central focus of higher education, and it provides the common ground on which academic affairs and student affairs can speak with a unified voice. It provides a basis on which collaborative partnerships can be forged between these two important constituencies. Throughout this book, the authors have described collaborative efforts—efforts that include the creation of living-learning centers, academic interest houses, residential colleges, and learning communities. Unfortunately, these initiatives represent only a small portion of educational program choices available to students in most campus housing systems. As institutions continue to be challenged by such things as steady-state funding, the decline in the number of traditional-age college students, increasingly intense competition between institutions to enroll these students, public demand for quality and accountability, increasingly diverse student populations, and widening gaps between ideal academic standards and actual student learning, the need for collaborative partnerships between academic and student affairs becomes more than a desirable option—it becomes an imperative! As many institutions examine prevailing paradigms about teaching and learning, some are experimenting with alternative perspectives. When faculty are encouraged to work with student affairs staff in designing learning communities around academic disciplines, faculty become invested in the process. They also become aware of different pedagogical processes that foster greater student motivation and time on task. Furthermore, as faculty and staff experiment with alternative perspectives, they can design residence halls as learning laboratories, settings where students, faculty, and staff are brought together in a form of intellectual communion.

A critical element in fostering collaborative partnerships is intentionality: clearly defining mutually agreed-on educational outcomes, allocating appropriate resources, and utilizing a variety of new pedagogical approaches, including sophisticated technological tools, to ensure success.

Make Residential Education More Intentional

Although the literature on the impact of college clearly indicates that residence halls do, indeed, foster student learning and development, it is relatively unclear as to how much of this impact is the result of specific programs, policies, or staff roles (Pascarella and Terenzini, 1991). As Levine suggested in Chapter Five, many of the educational outcomes of residence life seem to occur in a serendipitous fashion—that is, they occur more by default than by design. This statement may come as quite a surprise to many residence hall staff who invest considerable time and energy in the design and delivery of various educational programs. But, as Stamatakos (1984) argues, few of these programs appear to have been carefully planned for content and developmental impact, and few have proved to be effective, other than superficially.

If residential education is to become more intentional, and hence more effective, staff should consider doing the following.
    1. *Residence hall staff must develop a philosophy of student learn-*

ing consistent with the academic mission of their institution. Historically, the student affairs profession has shifted its emphasis from controlling students, to serving students, to the current emphasis on fostering students' development. Although most student affairs professionals embrace the student development perspective, it has been extremely difficult to translate the concept into operational behavior accompanied by measurable results. Part of the difficulty is the result of using the concept in interchangeable ways—as a philosophy, theory, process, and outcome.

Student learning, as opposed to student development, is a much richer and well-respected focus within higher education. By developing a philosophy of student learning, residence hall staff can use student development theory and process models as a means to facilitate student learning. Furthermore, by creating a philosophy of student learning, residence hall staff will more closely align themselves with the academic missions of their institution, thereby increasing the probability of developing collaborative partnerships with faculty and academic administrators.

2. *Residential life programs and policies should be informed by a growing body of knowledge about how students learn and by systematic assessment initiatives.* As outlined in Chapter Two, considerable information is available about how students learn and develop. All too often, however, residence life programs and policies are created without the benefit of this knowledge. Hence, keys to program and policy development include utilizing this existing knowledge as well as creating systematic assessments that focus on students' residential experiences and what these experiences contribute to learning. By developing a systematic assessment program, residence hall staff can explore the effectiveness of their programs and services from multiple perspectives, including questions related to how and why students change intellectually as a result of their residential experiences.

3. *Staff should develop a clear and coherent statement of their educational purpose.* A philosophy of student learning enlightened by an ongoing, systematic assessment effort should help staff develop a clear and coherent statement of educational purpose. As part of this statement, staff should define appropriate and measurable outcomes. What should students be learning as part

of their residential experiences? How is this learning to occur? What specific programs, policies, and staff roles will facilitate student learning?

Without a clear and coherent statement of educational purpose, residence life staff will continue to function in a vacuum, with their efforts characterized as unsystematic and random. Clear and coherent statements of educational purpose are probably the single most important factor in directing staff and student efforts toward educationally purposeful activities.

4. *Learning communities should be created through collaborative partnerships with students, academic administrators, faculty, and others.* Many chapters in this book have emphasized the importance of developing collaborative partnerhips. Such partnerships require student affairs educators to leave the comfort, security, and predictability of their bounded organizational space and build linkages with other members of the campus community, in particular, faculty and academic administrators. To continue to keep our focus *within* our organizational boundaries strips our efforts of most of their impact. Collaboration is imperative if we are to be players in the student learning arena. Indeed, our impact on student learning will be in direct proportion to the degree to which we build partnerships and linkages with important internal and external constituencies. Finally, we must encourage and reward faculty members who help make residential life more intentional and effective.

5. *The educational role of residence halls should be consistently communicated to important institutional constituencies — students, parents, faculty, staff, alumni, legislators, and so on.* Because most student affairs educators focus their energy within their organizational boundaries, the contributions they make to student learning are often somewhat invisible. As a result, faculty become increasingly amused by our claims of being "educators." By demonstrating, through a variety of assessment approaches, the contributions we make to student learning, we can more effectively demonstrate our educational role within our institutions.

Creating more intentional and effective residence hall environments is a challenging endeavor, one that will require a careful examination of prevailing assumptions, a review of current organizational roles and responsibilities, and the examination of the traditional student-institutional relationship. The degree to which the educational potential of residence halls is realized, however, is the degree to which residence halls become intentional, purposeful, and effective learning environments, settings that are designed in keeping with a residence hall curriculum.

Implementing the Residence Hall Curriculum

Implementing the residence hall curriculum is a function of academic and student affairs leadership. Setting the direction identifies the path for movement; aligning faculty, staff, and students together places them in a position to create and accomplish the tasks; and encouraging the development of strong informal relationships focuses effort on using residence hall learning communities in ways that relate to courses, particularly general education. The chapters in this book inspire vision and direction; they also point to the strategies for a residence hall curriculum.

As many institutions continue to be confronted by higher expectations and demands for effective undergraduate education, a well-developed residence hall curriculum can assist in meeting this challenge. Members of the Wingspread Group on Higher Education (1993, p. 14) challenge educators to put student learning first: "Putting learning at the heart of the academic enterprise will mean overhauling the conceptual, procedural, curricular, and other architecture on most campuses." The residence hall curriculum can begin to make a difference as strategies are adopted in accord with what has been described in various chapters of this book. In particular, we recommend that educators in student affairs and academic affairs consider the following suggestions:

1. Determine what knowledge, skills, and attitudes the institution wants residence hall communities to contribute to student learning and personal development. As suggested in Chapter Four, create a compelling and motivating vision along with strategies for setting high standards for students' performance, involvement, and responsibility.

2. Involve the institution's student affairs leaders and the housing director, along with the president and academic leaders, in conversations about innovative ways residence halls can meet students' educational needs and interests — ways that can be exciting and challenging, like creating living-learning centers (Chapter Seven), learning communities (Chapter Eight), and residential colleges (Chapter Eleven).

3. With the involvement of academic deans, recruit faculty who want to design and implement a residence hall curriculum focusing on the applications of classroom learning to how students live their lives. Select faculty members who are excited about the possibilities and potential of active learning.

4. Develop ways to integrate the institution's general education architecture program with residence hall learning communities, so that students are expected and encouraged to be involved with real-world challenges and experiences as responsible learners. Create interdisciplinary cluster courses such as "Sociology of Gender Roles" and "Social and Political Philosophy" and co-enroll students from the same residence hall floors. Students in coed halls, for example, could utilize their residential experience as a social science laboratory to explore various themes in "Sociology of Gender Roles."

5. As recommended in Chapter Eight, implement a first-year-experience program, staffed by both academic and student affairs educators, and create intellectual and interpersonal environments for student involvement, learning, and academic and social success.

6. Utilize a residence hall curriculum to challenge and support students to apply their formal classroom learnings to their experiences, involvements, and activities, especially with regard to how they want to live their lives: What values guide their lives? What are their goals for shaping personal and professional aspects of their lives? How do they want to connect with society, friends, and peers in purposeful ways? To help address these issues, involve students from the same residence halls in credited, service learning activities that are integrated with their academic courses.

7. To enhance the academic and social success of residence hall students, recruit upper-division students to serve as

peer educators. These highly trained students would be members of "student success teams" that also include professional staff from Academic Advising, Career Planning and Placement, and the Learning Skills Center. Peer educators would serve as mentors, providing assistance in academic and career planning, study skills enhancement, tutoring, and other support services to students on their floors. In exchange for these services, peer educators would receive Residential Leadership Grants (room-and-board stipends).

8. Nurture the commitment to embrace and celebrate diversity, thus honoring differences, seeking community, and respecting individuals regardless of gender, race, or creed (see Chapter Nine). Establish internships for outstanding students who can create educational programs on diversity and teach them to residence hall students.

9. As illustrated in Chapter Six, teach staff and faculty who work with the residence hall curriculum the concepts and practices of community building, collaborative and team-centered learning, structured experiences, and holistic approaches to learning. Stress the importance of the development of students' character as well as their intellect.

10. Emphasize civic leadership education by designating one weekend per semester for a leadership retreat. The goal of the retreat would be to create an effective student government in each residence hall. Students *and* staff would focus on the empowering paradigms described in Chapter Ten. The elements of these paradigms could be the benchmarks for assessing the development of effective civic leadership in each hall.

11. Incorporate new technologies, such as Internet, interactive video satellite broadcast networks, virtual reality, CD-ROM, and personal computer–based multimedia instruction, as learning tools to make learning more accessible, challenging, and engaging.

12. Adopt certain basic and fundamental strategies. Establish the day before classes as a "residence hall day for community building." Develop a residence hall weekend symposium each year where academic and social activities emerge from the residence halls, and create learning themes each year for shaping, guiding, and influencing particular educational outcomes.

13.   As recommended in Chapter Five, improve the environment of the residence halls by redesigning semipublic and public spaces in support of student learning. Create attractive, engaging spaces for exhibits, libraries, current events, computing and multimedia laboratories, book and movie reviews, fitness centers, travel features, and so on.

14.   Describe for prospective students and their families the value of residence hall learning communities and the central role of student involvement in the learning process.

15.   Sustain and nurture the implementation of the residence hall curriculum by rewarding the contributions of student affairs and academic leaders, professional and student staff, and students. Formally celebrate outstanding achievements and consistently communicate successes to various institutional constituencies.

The preceding are but a few suggestions for implementing a residence hall curriculum. The principal, integrating construct in each of these recommendations is that the only way to bring "education" and "student learning" back into the residence halls is to craft a curriculum for the residence halls that is similar in intent and purpose to the classroom curriculum.

Conclusion

This chapter, along with previous ones, has described a variety of approaches for making residence halls meaningful and effective educational settings that promote student learning and personal development. To develop innovative approaches such as these, educators must demonstrate three forms of leadership—conceptual, educational, and administrative.

Conceptual leadership reflects a broad vision of the educational potential of residence halls. It means periodic departures from the comfort, security, and predictability of one's "rain forest" to challenge prevailing assumptions and beliefs. Conceptual leadership focuses on fundamental questions of purpose, continuously seeking to relate the educational mission of residence halls to the mission of the institution. Conceptual leadership envisions the "big picture," understanding how residence halls, as particular educational settings, can directly contribute to the achievement of broad undergraduate educational outcomes.

Educational leadership provides the plan of action and strategies for realizing the educational potential of residence halls. This form of leadership refers to the knowledge and skills needed to design environmental and programmatic efforts within residence halls that meet specific educational objectives. Educational leadership involves using theories and models to design learning communities, residential colleges, living-learning centers, and other programs that foster student learning.

The third form of leadership — administrative leadership — refers to the organizational development and change efforts that may be needed to achieve the educational objectives of the residence hall system. It focuses on how to implement organizational change. Administrative leadership facilitates the development of collaborative partnerships between various institutional stakeholders — students, faculty, academic administrators, student affairs educators, and others — and it creates an ethos of collective responsibility among these institutional agents, promoting learning and personal development.

This chapter commenced with reference to an alumnus who, while introducing one of the authors at an alumni banquet, commented, "Most of us in the room never thought of residence halls as educational . . . " Such an observation is all too common, not only among alumni, but among faculty, parents, trustees, administrators, and students as well. If perceptions such as these are to change, and change dramatically, educators in both academic affairs and student affairs must extend effective conceptual, educational, and administrative leadership to the residence hall environment as a critical locale for promoting student learning. If educators accept this responsibility, perhaps the next time one of the authors is introduced at an alumni banquet, the speaker will comment, "The most important part of my college experience was what I learned through my residence hall." And perhaps next time, instead of spontaneous laughter from the audience, there will be spontaneous applause.

References

American Council on Education. *The Student Personnel Point of View.* American Council on Education Studies, Series 1. Washington, D.C.: American Council on Education, 1937.

Angelo, T. A., and Cross, K. P. *Classroom Assessment Techniques: A Handbook for College Teachers.* (2nd ed.) San Francisco: Jossey-Bass, 1993.

Astin, A. W. *What Matters in College? Four Critical Years Revisited.* San Francisco: Jossey-Bass, 1992.

Blake, E. S. "Classroom and Context: An Educational Dialectic." *Academe,* 1979, *65,* 280–292.

Chickering, A. W., and Reisser, L. *Education and Identity.* (2nd ed.) San Francisco: Jossey-Bass, 1993.

Cross, K. P. "Taking Teaching Seriously." Paper presented at the annual meeting of the American Association for Higher Education, Washington, D.C., Mar. 1986.

Garland, P. H. *Serving More Than Students: A Critical Need for College Student Personnel Services.* Washington, D.C.: Association for the Study of Higher Education, 1985.

Huebner, L. A., and Lawson, J. M. "Understanding and Assessing College Environments." In D. Creamer (ed.), *College Student Development: Theory and Practice for the 1990s.* Alexandria, Va.: American College Personnel Association, 1990.

Kelly, D. "Report: U.S. Students Not Improving." *Lansing* [Michigan] *State Journal,* Oct. 8, 1990, p. 5-B.

The Living Bible. Wheaton, Ill.: Tyndale House, 1971.

Moos, R. H. *The Human Context: Environmental Determinants of Behavior.* New York: Wiley-Interscience, 1976.

Parker, W. C. "Black Culture: Implications for Educational Change." Address delivered for Black History Week, Saint Louis University, Feb. 1982.

Pascarella, E. T., and Terenzini, P. T. *How College Affects Students: Findings and Insights from Twenty Years of Research.* San Francisco: Jossey-Bass, 1991.

Pollio, H. R. "What Students Think About and Do in College Lecture Classes." *Teaching-Learning Issues* (University of Tennessee Learning Research Center), No. 53, Spring 1984, 54–68.

Richmond, J. "The Importance of Student Involvement: A Dialogue with Alexander Astin." *Journal of Counseling and Development,* 1986, *65,* 92–95.

Schroeder, C. C. "New Students—New Learning Styles." *Change,* 1993, *25*(4), 21–27.

Stamatakos, L. C. "College Residence Halls: In Search of Educational Leadership." *Journal of College and University Student Housing,* 1984, *14*(1), 10–17.

Stamatakos, L. C. "The Great Expectations of Student Affairs and Lessons from Reality: A Contextual Examination." Paper presented at the Virginia Association of Student Personnel Administrators/Virginia Association of College and University Housing Officers fall conference, Wintergreen Resort, Va., Oct. 1991.

Turnbull, C. *The Forest People.* New York: Simon & Schuster, 1962.

Wingspread Group on Higher Education. *An American Imperative: Higher Expectations for Higher Education.* Racine, Wis.: Johnson Foundation, 1993.

Name Index

Subject Index

329